Dickens on Screen

Television and film, not libraries or scholarship, have made Charles Dickens the most important unread novelist in English. It is not merely that millions of people feel comfortable deploying the word "Dickensian" to describe their own and others' lives, but also that many more people who have never read Dickens know what Dickensian means. They know about Dickens because they have access to over a century of adaptations for the big and small screen. Because Dickens has proven to be the most easily adapted of major novelists, he has become, somewhat ironically, one of the foremost novelists in the English canon. This is ironic because it was just this capacity to entertain that once confined him to the margins of the "great tradition" in fiction. *Dickens on Screen* is an invaluable resource for students and scholars alike. It provides an exhaustive filmography and further reading, and is well illustrated.

JOHN GLAVIN is Professor of English, and Director of the John Carroll Scholars Program Georgetown University in Washington DC. He is the author of *After Dickens: Reading, Adaptation and Performance* (Cambridge 1999).

Dickens on Screen

Edited by
John Glavin

CAMBRIDGE
UNIVERSITY PRESS

PUBLISHED BY THE PRESS SYNDICATE OF THE UNIVERSITY OF CAMBRIDGE
The Pitt Building, Trumpington Street, Cambridge, United Kingdom

CAMBRIDGE UNIVERSITY PRESS
The Edinburgh Building, Cambridge, CB2 2RU, UK
40 West 20th Street, New York, NY 10011–4211, USA
477 Williamstown Road, Port Melbourne, VIC 3207, Australia
Ruiz de Alarcón 13, 28014 Madrid, Spain
Dock House, The Waterfront, Cape Town 8001, South Africa

http://www.cambridge.org

First published 2003

Printed in the United Kingdom at the University Press, Cambridge

Typeface Plantin 10/12 pt.   *System* LATEX 2$_\varepsilon$ [TB]

A catalogue record for this book is available from the British Library

ISBN 0 521 80652 6 hardback
ISBN 0 521 00124 2 paperback

1396 4336

Contents

v

Illustrations

Contributors

REGINA BARRECA, Professor of English and Feminist Theory at the University of Connecticut, is the author of *They Used To Call Me Snow White But I Drifted*; *Perfect Husbands (And Other Fairy Tales)*; *Sweet Revenge*; *Untamed and Unabashed*, and *Too Much Of a Good Thing Is Wonderful*. She has recently edited *A Sit-Down With The Sopranos* and *Don't Tell Mama: The Penguin Anthology of Italian American Writing*.

MURRAY BAUMGARTEN, Professor of English and Comparative Literature at the University of California, Santa Cruz, is the founding director of The Dickens Project, a multi-campus research consortium on nineteenth-century literature and culture. He has published extensively on Dickens and on Victorian culture, and is the editor-in-chief of the Strouse Edition of the works of Thomas Carlyle.

GREGORY BELLOW is a psychiatric social worker with an enduring interest in literature. His current concerns center on expanding contemporary, non-Freudian applications of psychoanalytic theory to concepts such as narrative that bridge the humanities and the clinical consulting room.

JOHN BOWEN is Professor in the Department of English, Keele University, and the author of *Other Dickens: Pickwick to Chuzzlewit*. He is a member of the editorial board of the *Journal of Victorian Culture*, and has edited Dickens's *Barnaby Rudge* for Penguin.

MURIEL BROTSKY is a psychotherapist in private practice in San Francisco. She serves on the Board of the California Institute of Clinical Social Work.

KAMILLA ELLIOTT, Assistant Professor of English at the University of California, Berkeley, teaches Victorian literature and the interdisciplinary study of literature and film. Her book, *Rethinking the Novel/Film Debate*, is forthcoming from Cambridge University Press.

JANE JORDAN, a Training and Supervising Analyst, is a faculty member and the coordinator of the Institute of Contemporary Psychoanalysis North (California). She maintains a private practice in San Francisco and Santa Cruz.

JOHN JORDAN is Professor of English and Director of The Dickens Project at the University of California, Santa Cruz. He has written widely on Dickens and on Victorian culture, and recently edited *The Cambridge Companion to Charles Dickens*.

GERHARD JOSEPH, Professor of English at Lehman College and at the Graduate Center of the City University of New York, teaches Victorian literature and literary theory. He has published a wide variety of essays on literary and cultural subjects; two books, *Tennysonian Love: The Strange Diagonal* and *Tennyson and the Text: The Weaver's Shuttle*, and is working currently on the dialectic of interest and disinterestedness in post-Renaissance thought.

PAMELA KATZ is a screenwriter and novelist specializing in historical subjects. Her recent work includes a novel and two-part television series based on the life of Lotte Lenya, as well as two projects with the renowned film director, Margarethe von Trotta: a theatrical film, *Rosenstrasse*, about the only successful resistance to Hitler during World War II; and *F—ing For the Fatherland*, a film about the East German secret police (Stasi) and their use of seduction during the Cold War.

KATHLEEN C. LONSDALE recently received her Ph.D. in English literature from the University of Southern California. While working as a lecturer and braving the academic job market, she has published several reviews as well as articles on feminist theory and Jack the Ripper. She is currently at work on a book-length study of anatomical and figurative dismemberment in Victorian culture, including the novels of Charles Dickens.

MIRIAM MARGOLYES OBE is an award-winning actress, renowned for her versatility on stage, screen, and radio. Her one-woman show, *Dickens' Women*, has toured the world following awards in Edinburgh and London.

MARTIN F. NORDEN, Professor of Communication at the University of Massachusetts-Amherst, has published widely on movies and disability. He presented a slightly different version of his chapter in this collection at the 2002 North East Popular Culture Association (NEPCA) conference in New London, New Hampshire.

ROBERT M. POLHEMUS, Joseph S. Atha Professor in Humanities and Chair of the Department of English at Stanford University, is the author of *Erotic Faith: Being in Love from Jane Austen to D. H. Lawerence*; *Comic Faith: The Great Tradition from Austen to Joyce*; *The Changing World of Anthony Trollope*, and an author and co-editor of *Critical Reconstruction: The Relationship of Fiction and Life*. He is currently working on a book entitled *Lot's Daughters*, about father–daughter, older man–younger woman, parent–child relationships in fiction, art and culture.

MARGUERITE RIPPY, Assistant Professor of Literature at Marymount University (Virginia), has published articles on performance studies and contributed to *Spectacular Shakespeare: Critical Theory and Popular Cinema* and *Classic Hollywood, Classic Whiteness*. She is currently working on a book-length study of Orson Welles and his radio series, "First Person Singular."

JOHN ROMANO, the author of *Dickens and Reality*, is an Emmy-nominated screenwriter-producer who, for his sins, has worked on over a dozen television series. He co-wrote the movie, *The Third Miracle*, and has recently adapted Philip Roth's Pulitzer Prize-winning novel, *American Pastoral*, for Paramount Pictures.

JEFFREY SCONCE, Associate Professor of Radio/TV/Film at Northwestern University, is the author of *Haunted Media: Electronic Presence from Telegraphy to Television*. His current research centers on the politics of irony in recent American film and television.

ESTELLE SHANE is a Founding Member, Past President, and Training and Supervising Analyst at the Institute of Contemporary Psychoanalysis (California). She is on the faculty of the Department of Psychiatry at the University of California, Los Angeles, and is co-author of *Intimate Attachments: Toward a New Self Psychology*.

GARRETT STEWART is James O. Freedman Professor of Letters at the University of Iowa. He is the author of *Dickens and the Trials of the Imagination* among other books on Victorian fiction, and most recently of *Between Film and Screen: Modernism's Photo Synthesis*.

ALESSANDRO VESCOVI is a Researcher in the Department of English of the Universita degli Studi di Milano. He has written *Dal focolare allo scrittoio*, a study of the Victorian and modernist short story, and co-edited a volume of essays on *Dickens, The Craft of Fiction*. Since 1999 he has been the editor of *Carlo Dickens*, a website in Italy devoted to Dickens studies.

KATE CARNELL WATT, lecturer in English at the University of California, Riverside, is completing a dissertation on the tensions informing representations of poor children, corruptive parents, and middle-class intervention in Victorian literature. She has presented papers at numerous conferences, including MLA, PMLA, and the Dickens Universe.

STEVE WURTZLER, Assistant Professor in the English department of Georgetown University, is currently working on a book-length study of sound technologies in the 1920s and 30s. His historical work on film, mass media, and US culture has been published in the journal *Film History* and in the anthologies *Sound Theory/Sound Practice*; *Keyframes: Popular Cinema and Cultural Studies*, and *Communities of the Air: Radio Century, Radio Culture*.

Acknowledgments

I am deeply grateful to each of my contributors, those who wrote chapters and those who allowed themselves to be interviewed for chapters. Without their courtesy, generosity, and knowledge there could have been no *Dickens on Screen*.

And even with their sterling qualities *Dickens on Screen* would have remained a mere notion were it not for the generous, patient, and constant assistance I received from Donna Even-Kesef, Andrew Jacobs, Zoe Kalendek, and Karen Lautman of the Georgetown English department; from Nicholas Scheetz and Jodie Roussel in the Special Collections branch of the Georgetown University Library, and from my unflappable and resourceful research assistant, John Frank Weaver.

I am also indebted to Rachel De Wachter of Cambridge University Press, who has guided the book through production. Indeed, this book is not only a Cambridge product but a Cambridge idea. It originated there with Linda Bree. It was carefully reshaped by her over a long and tricky period of redesign. Its final content and form are almost entirely due not only to her unmatched editorial skills, but to her wisdom, and to her wit.

Finally, and as always, I am happy to proclaim my profound reliance on my wife Margaret O'Keeffe Glavin, who continues to make everything that is good in my life possible.

Introduction

John Glavin

A great deal that follows in this book is likely to seem not just strange but *very* strange to a reader who thinks that adaptation is supposed to copy an original reliably, transferring it to a new medium intact, and with respect. In this, the standard view, a good adaptation is good precisely because it gets a better source *right*. And here, just to be even-handed, is a strong argument for just that view, put with her usual eloquence and force by the novelist Fay Weldon, replying to my request for a preface.

Dear John,

Thank you for asking me to write your preface – I am flattered – but my problem is though good on Austen I am bad on Dickens. (I don't know why this antithesis occurs so naturally – she was born in 1775 and he in 1812, separated by nearly four decades: but I suppose in our heads Dickens and Austen both are just vaguely way back around then.) They made me read Mr. Pickwick at school, and I simply could not laugh. The book was illustrated – line drawings of corpulent men with pot bellies in tight waistcoats, which seemed not just outlandish but revolting. (This was in New Zealand: the old men I knew were skinny, gnarled pioneers.) I do admire that energy, that rolling prose, that Rushdie-ish freedom with language, at least when it's read aloud, but I simply cannot bear to read it myself. Thackeray I love: that smart, male, sophisticated man-about-town overview. Dickens's heart bled without stringency all over the place – though I do get on with his Household Narrative, the sheer accepting penny dreadfulness to which our own newspapers are fast returning. Nor do I think for a moment that Dickensian London was as he described it – Victor Hugo, born 1802, if we're on to comparisons, an equal gusher about the lives of the poor, got Paris more subtly, and at least had some reforming political zeal to add to the relish.

If life copies art – and it does (look how much worse the pea-soupers got after Monet with his eye cataract started painting the Thames, as Oscar Wilde pointed out) – I suppose it's going too far to blame Dickens for our descent from Georgian elegance, free-thinking and aspiration into messy Victorian sentimentality, but I am inclined to. I bet he had awful taste in furniture. Hans Christian Andersen (born 1805, there we go again) came from Copenhagen to stay and was such a difficult and neurotic house guest Mrs. Dickens longed for him to go away, and he never would, but at least he had the gift of parable. Search her husband's work for subtext and search for ever. Dickens turned London into a theme park long before they were invented. Perhaps he had the gift of self-referential prophecy? You see how I am desperately looking for good things to say about this prolix writer?

As for watching Dickens on screen, I never do, not since being frightened out of my wits by Maggs in *David Copperfield* (was it?) when barely grown. I never watch adaptations on TV because of all that murky smog and grotesquerie, everyone over-acting and full of self-congratulation from the PR department to the producers to the set designers to the cast. I like coolness, elegance, control. Mind you, I only ever watch my own adaptations on screen, and no one, wisely, has even asked me to do Dickens, so I am not a reliable witness, just piqued at not having been the one asked to do it. Not that I would, even if asked – all that text. I turned *Jane Eyre* (Charlotte Brontë, born 1814) into a stage play once and that nearly killed me.

Why was Thackeray (born 1811) so much more sparse? I think because he was a lazier man than Dickens: he started the monthly instalments of *Vanity Fair* only a couple of days before he was due to deliver them, and sent desperate notes to his friends to come round to dinner and brief him about life in India. He was discursive, the better to get his word-count in, but still in a hurry with deadlines looming. Whereas Dickens was ceaselessly busy and active, and hard-working. Jane Austen was lazy too – only six novels in twenty years of writing – perhaps that's why she's so curt and precise and economical. She just wanted to get it over with and go shopping. She might have speeded up if she'd lived longer, poor thing.

Walter Scott, Austen's contemporary (born 1773) is another writer I have a problem with: when a student I worked nights in a coffee shop to pay a friend to read them for me and explain them. His critical essays, on the other hand, and oddly enough, I relished. Dickens died at fifty-eight, Jane Austen at forty-one, Brontë at thirty-nine, Scott at sixty-one and Thackeray at fifty-two. Victor Hugo got to eighty-three and had a state funeral. I don't know why I tell you this except one begins to take it personally.

I never knew I thought all this until now. To dislike Dickens so actively is not a proper thing to admit in public. I don't think I am the right person for this job. Nor do I wish to belittle another writer in print, though he is dead. We must stick together, whatever our degree of decomposition, or how much down to bleached bone. Anything else I would be delighted to write for you. How are you getting on? When you're in London, please do drop by.
Best wishes
Fay

And here is my *resistant* response to her reply.

Dear Fay,

Thank you for providing so witty an anti-preface to what I hope its readers will find an equally unexpected, though scarcely so witty, book. I couldn't be more delighted. But I must say I believe you do yourself a serious injustice when you say you are "bad on Dickens." Nothing could be less true. You get him absolutely right. You say that you "do not think for a moment that Dickensian London was as he described it." You say "Dickens turned London into a theme park, long before they were invented." You say, perhaps to be fair, you suggest, "he had the gift of self-referential prophecy." Right on all three counts. What can you mean, then, by claiming you are bad on Dickens?

Of course, Dickens is "self-referential." His London is his invention, his triumphant invention, not a copy of a embedded, total reality but a thematic farrago designed to surprise and move an audience to pleasure and concern. What he called in a refreshingly pre-theoretical way: the romantic side of familiar things. The people who think of Dickens as a kind of verbal photogravure couldn't be more wrong. Dickens made up London, just as he made up life, because he couldn't bear the way it tended to be lived. *Your* Dickens then is right on the money. And so is your preface because it anticipates the recurring thesis of many if not most of the chapters that follow: that the best way to respond to Dickens's fiction is not with *mimesis*, but through and as *montage*.

I am deploying those terms here as they are contrasted by the Australian critic, Jonathan White – not New Zealand, I know, but close enough, I hope – to get at the difference between an older model of art, enunciated classically by Erich Auerbach, and a new model, supremely realized by film, and magisterially described by Sergei Eisenstein. For Auerbach, copy is all: "the serious realism of modern times cannot represent man otherwise than as embedded in a total reality, political, social, and economic, which is concrete and constantly evolving." But for Eisenstein, mimesis pales before "the new concept" made possible by montage: "two film pieces of any kind, placed together, inevitably combine into a new concept, a new quality, arising out of that juxtaposition." And of course, as many of the chapters that follow point out (Bowen, Elliott, Stewart), it was the work of Dickens that Eisenstein, and other film pioneers, pointed to as the great predecessor and paradigm for what they thought the cinema was now able to achieve.

And so dear Fay, you see I knew I was right to ask you to do this. I couldn't ask for a more apt entry to the chapters that follow.

And now that the book is done, I am getting on very well, thank you very much for asking.

And of course when I am next in London I certainly intend to drop by, and I trust you will do the same the next time you are in DC.

Best wishes

John

Even after reading Fay Weldon's anti-preface and my response, you will, I trust, find much that follows surprising, and perhaps even scandalous. Particularly if, attached to the primacy of mimesis, you think a book on Dickens and screen ought to be (a) mostly about adaptations of Dickens's novels and (b) about how closely those adaptations copy those novels. This book, it should now be obvious, wears its Dickens with a difference. It assumes that:

> *because*: film adaptation disrupts, rather than copies, fiction;
>
> *and because*: by the end of the twentieth century, film had become the ground of fiction, all fiction, including fiction produced before the twentieth century;
>
> *it follows that:* the Dickens film now shapes Dickens's fiction;
>
> *and it follows as well that*: while film as montage may be deeply reflective of Dickens, most *Dickens* films aren't.

Which means that most of the chapters that follow celebrate discrepancies between the fictions and the films, and several don't treat what is recognizably a Dickens adaptation at all. To understand why, let me briefly strip out each of these propositions, one at a time.

Film adaptation disrupts, rather than copies, fiction. Alberto Farrasino describes writers and filmmakers as fellow travelers sharing the same boat but regularly trying to shove each other overboard. He is talking here about scriptwriters in the film industry jostling to hold their place against directors and producers. But the novelist and those who adapt a novel into film aren't even in the same boat. Film is not fiction by other means. People who care about film know that. And people who care about fiction should know it. Film has its own patterns and its own rhythms. They are primary and omnipotent. They depend on a medium which makes meaning only as it passes you by. You can't pause the film to reread several frames as you reread a passage. (I'm talking about film here, not video: film as it is intended to be screened.) You can't put the film down to ponder, as you do a book. You watch a film in a set period of duration, ninety minutes, generally, or two hours, rarely more. Even a brief novel is read over several days with intervals of lots of other activities in between. And when we watch a film, things are shown to us in place of words. But when we read a book, words are offered us in infinite displacement for the possibility of things. Film, then, is not fiction's copy but another, and by no means a parallel, universe. To make a good film, or indeed any sort of film, must mean inevitably to refuse, to disrupt, to subvert, the makings of fiction. We can even suggest a kind of counter-scale and claim that the more closely a film adaptation approaches its fictional predecessor the less it interests us as film.

Not only are film and fiction, then, by no means the same sort of thing, but *by the end of the twentieth century, film had become the ground of fiction, all fiction, including fiction produced before the twentieth century.* How can this be so? Here's the late critic and director Kenneth Tynan, as "smart, male and sophisticated" a "man-about-town" as even Fay Weldon's high standards could demand. In his diary entry for 19 October 1975, he observed that the "most powerful influence on the arts in the west is – the cinema. Novels, plays *and films* are filled with references to, quotations from, parodies of – old movies. They dominate the cultural subconscious." He isn't saying here what is obvious: that newer films rewrite older films. That *Gosford Park* is, at its best, but a shorn replica of Renoir's transcendent *The Rules of the Game*, or that Cameron Crowe's *Almost Famous* is almost but not quite *The Apartment* of his idol Billy Wilder. Nor is he merely claiming that novels and plays today tend to be built like films; indeed, most are written in order to become, or in the hope of becoming, films. Which came first, the *pulp* or the *fiction*? Tynan's making an even larger and perhaps more scandalous claim: that the way we think now is shaped – not by films (we watch far more television) – but by *film*, as the prime way of organizing and evaluating experience. As he presciently put it: "we have a civilization entirely molded by cinematic values and behavior patterns."

He doesn't specify those *values* and *patterns*. But if I had to (and at this point my hunch is I have to), I'd summarize them as follows. All life is Manichean. It has two sides, only two sides, and only one of those sides is right at any time. It is composed of and by affect. Sound thought should therefore always subordinate itself to strong feeling. Abstraction is irreal, because the real can always be seen, and must be felt. Lives thus invariably take the shape of efficient and affecting stories, in which nothing ambiguous or ambivalent should be tolerated. Anything that does not fit the tight arc of an unfolding narrative is extraneous, and therefore meaningless. Life moves, life changes, life goes somewhere. It always offers at least a second chance. The past is back in the day, amusing as nostalgia, but fundamentally irrelevant. A trap when it makes claims. All problems can be solved. All persons have agency. And while it is nice to be good, and good to be smart, it is best to be beautiful.

Insofar as you recognize this as the fundamental set of values and patterns of the world in which you operate (whether or not you share them) you can see how Tynan can claim that film shapes and evaluates the rest of our lives, even when we are looking at a pre-cinematic past. It's not the look of the past that we get from film. We have other sources for that. It's the script of the past that we get from film, the rules by which it is to be read.

Which leads us to this book's key thesis: that *the Dickens film now shapes Dickens's fiction*. Of course, Dickens's books *came* first (in time). They just don't come first (in meaning) any more. Baldly stated: all but specialists in Victorian fiction know Dickens's fiction primarily on and through the screen. I don't mean that most people are more likely to have seen *Great Expectations* than to have read it, though that is of course true. I mean, much more significantly and subversively, that if they do get around to reading *Great Expectations*, they will, and can, only see it as film, screened through what, following Tynan, I've outlined as the values and patterns of cinema. Remember: I am not talking about people who work in English departments, though I certainly hope that I am talking, *inter alia*, to them. For everybody outside of English departments, including most of the people who produce the adaptations, Dickens's fictions don't generate Dickens films. Just the reverse: it's those adaptations, for the big screen and the small, that generate whatever possibilities remain for reading the fiction.

Of course, it is also true, as several of the chapters that follow argue, that Dickens – or at the very least an idea named Dickens – has in significant ways shaped film itself, not only the films that adapt his stories and novels, but the fundamental ways in which film characteristically arranges narrative and psychological pattern. Nevertheless, while *film as montage may be deeply reflective of Dickens, most Dickens films aren't.* Kenneth Tynan again seems to help us to get this just right. On 20 July 1972 his diary records that he was "certain that the full potential of the cinema will not be achieved until it concentrates on the development of *full-length cartoons.*" He goes on to explain that "What the cinema ought to be doing (and to have done) is to present colored *images* of reality (or fantasy) designed by *artists.* At present – by using the camera merely to photograph *reality* [that is, to *copy* à la Auerbach] – it is confining itself to a function that is part newsreel and part photographed theatre. In pure cinema there would be no real actors and no real background" – just as, as Fay Weldon suggests, there are no *real* persons or places in Dickens. Tynan concludes: "Only thus will cinema achieve its historic mission of rising above and eventually replacing the novel." But there, of course, he falters. He should have said something like: Only thus will cinema achieve its historic mission of eventually matching Dickens's achievement. But in the meantime most (though thankfully not all) Dickens films are forced into the real-persons-in-real-places format that dominates feature-film syntax, but which has almost nothing to do with Dickens's pioneering imagining of high-colored, high-contrast montage.

The chapters that follow argue these ideas in much fuller, and certainly more persuasive, detail, from a wide variety of decentered and (happily) not entirely harmonious points of view. They are divided into four quite different parts. In the first section, a roundtable discussion among film critics, literary critics, and psychotherapists, led by the Victorian scholar Gerhard Joseph, heralds the book's wide-ranging exploration of connections between film, fiction, and culture, particularly the culture of Freudian and post-Freudian psychotherapy. This is followed by a second section in which literary critics, experts on Dickens's fiction, explore connections between the novels and film. But even here difference asserts itself, with para-Dickensian texts as unexpected as Alessandro Vescovi's discussion of Italian filmmaker Sergio Rubini's *La stazione,* Murray Baumgarten's comparison of two *Christmas Carol*s from the American comedian Bill Murray, or Robert M. Polhemus's reading of Dickens and Woody Allen as twin makers of screen dreams and *Stardust Memories.* Each of these emerges as much (or as little) a Dickensian film as the more expected versions of *David Copperfield* analyzed by John Bowen or of *Great Expectations* explored by both Regina Barreca and John O. Jordan, though Jordan also does his Dickens with a difference. His *Great Expectations* is primarily the *untold* Australian variant.

In the third section individuals who have contributed to the Dickens film project, a screenwriter, John Romano, a director, Alfonso Cuaron (interviewed by Pam Katz), and an actor, Miriam Margolyes, describe the peculiar challenge and delight of co-creating with Dickens. In the fourth section, a group of experts in film criticism and film history situate what we can call the Dickens film project within the larger history of film through the twentieth century. These studies range from crucial revisions of the canonical connection between early film and Dickens's fiction by Kamilla Elliott and Garrett Stewart, to Steve J. Wurtzler's historical study of Dickens as a device of pedagogy, to Jeffrey Sconce's contrast of reverent and deeply irreverent adaptations for television, to important Dickens films that were never made (by Orson Welles, restored by Marguerite Rippy), or made from fiction Dickens never wrote (Tiny Tim on screen, rescaled by Martin Norden).

The book concludes with a selective filmography by Kate Watt and Kathleen Lonsdale to help the reader move from the pages of this book to the shelves of her or his video store.

Together these chapters make it clear how far *Dickens on Screen* ranges beyond the hundreds of filmed versions of Dickens's fiction. *Dickens on Screen* can never be a comprehensive account of its subject. There's been simply too much screened Dickens for that. But even a base camp to that towering archive has to include not only efforts to put Dickens on the screen but also equally important attempts to screen what merely claims to be Dickens; or what could not have been screened without Dickens; or what screens Dickens from what Dickens wrote, or meant; or what culture or power use in the name of Dickens to follow their own, and arguably un-Dickensian, ends; or what screens us, in the name of Dickens, from what we need to, or cannot bear to, see. Like the great man himself, screened Dickens is inexhaustible in the fecundity, the variety, the sheer inventedness of its infinitely expanding range of acknowledged and covert performance.

And now just three final warnings before I release you to the book itself. One: the book makes no distinction between film and television adaptations. Big screen, little screen, it's all, as Robert M. Polhemus says, screen dreaming. Two: the book tacitly assumes what may prove more rebarbative than any individual argument: that, although Dickens's novels are indisputably British, the *Dickens film* must be, largely, an American topic, since film is, largely, an American topic. And three: despite our attempt at wide-ranging coverage, there's still missing, sadly, what Tynan rightly called for – a discussion of what I with others regard as the greatest, and certainly the most Dickensian, of the Dickens films, the many and brilliant Dickens cartoons. But perhaps it's just as well to end by pointing you to a guide for your own further research, argument and pleasure.

REFERENCES

You can't have a footnote to what is essentially a pair of letters, can you? But for clarity's sake let me add that I read the Tynan diaries in the 7 and 14 August 2000 issues of *The New Yorker*. And Jonathan White's juxtaposition of Auerbach and Eisenstein appears in chapter 6, "Mimesis or Montage? Reflections on the Languages of Literature and Cinema," of his *Italy: The Enduring Culture* (London: Continuum, 2000), 227–56. You'll find the Farrasino quote on page 1 of Millicent Marcus's *Filmmaking By the Book: Italian Cinema and Literary Adaptation* (Baltimore: Johns Hopkins University Press, 1993).

Part I

1 Dickens, psychoanalysis, and film: a roundtable

Gerhard Joseph

The Dickens novel, modern psychology, and film line up from past to present, with the Dickens novel of the mid-nineteenth century followed by the invention of psychoanalysis at century's end, followed in the twentieth century by the evolution of film and film theory. If (*pace* David Hume) we buy into a unidirectional thesis of past cause to present effect, we might then affirm that the earlier discourse may in some measure have affected the later. That is to say something like: the family structure within a Dickens novel is one of the primary determinants of modern psychological, or at any rate psychoanalytical, theory. (We remember that Freud named his famous Dora after David Copperfield's child bride.) And in turn, the Dickens novel and the psychological tradition initiated by Freud contributed in some combination or other to the technical, narrative and psychic structures of film, as Kamilla Elliott's and Garrett Stewart's chapters on Sergei Eisenstein and D. W. Griffith show.

Conversely, influence may be said to flow from present to past. The past is arguably always in some measure a back-formation of the present moment, a function of the present reader or viewer's "horizon of expectations," what Freud would call a "screen memory" writ large of something irrecoverable in full historical actuality. Thus, the way we nowadays read Dickens is crucially informed by classical psychoanalytic theory, Freudian, Jungian, Eriksonian, Lacanian, Kleinian, or Kohutian, to name a small sample. As to the back-formation of Dickens by film, can we ever again read *A Christmas Carol* without remembering Alastair Sim's wide-eyed comic terror, or re-encounter Sikes murdering Nancy without envisioning David Lean's projection of her brutal end, the horrified dog frantically yowling and scratching at the closed door?

Or we can ignore thinking of historical connections running in either direction, and think instead of synchronic, theoretical links that have nothing to do with temporal sequence or influence. We can, that is, try to calibrate the conceptual analogues, the similarities and differences among the three areas, Dickens, psychoanalysis, and film, with respect to such matters as how stories of lives begin and end, how narrative continuities and ruptures alternate, how the coder and the decoder – author/reader, analysand/analyst, auteur/audience – transfer with and affect one another.

To follow up these suggestions we brought together in January 2001 a group of literary scholars, experts in film, and psychoanalysts and psychotherapists, sharing only a common enthusiasm for Dickens, on the page and on the screen. The work of the literary critics, Rob Polhemus and Murray Baumgarten, and the film experts, John Romano and Kamilla Elliott, is also represented elsewhere in this collection. The representatives from psychology and psychoanalysis, Estelle Shane, Muriel Brotsky, Jane Jordan, and Greg Bellow, are all practicing analysts and/or therapists. We provided a common starting point for our discussion by viewing together one of the indelible moments in the entire spectrum of Dickens adaptations, the murder of Nancy in David Lean's masterwork *Oliver Twist* (1948).

Kamilla Elliott: Ninety percent of the things written on film today in academia, unless they're historical, are written by feminists responding to Lacan's idea of the mirror stage, combining that with Freud's theory of voyeurism and castration anxiety. This began in the late 1970s when Laura Mulvey wrote an article on the male gaze in cinema. Basically her argument was that –

Greg Bellow: When you say that, I –

Kamilla Elliott: Want to cringe?

Greg Bellow: No, I want to say that I can't quite even half understand what you are saying.

Kamilla Elliott: OK. Let me introduce my question differently. It's for the psychoanalysts and psychotherapists in the group. We have shifted from a Victorian morality of Good and Evil, sometimes associated with class, sometimes not. And obviously psychoanalytic theory has also changed from a Freudian idea that what is bad is what is damaging or destructive for an individual, or for society. How then does this trajectory – from Dickens through film and psychoanalysis, from a world of good guys and bad guys – seem to strike you when you look at this scene from David Lean's *Oliver Twist*?

Estelle Shane: Lean's film is told in a much more complex way than just a simple opposition of good vs. bad or good vs. damaging. You see a complex configuration of "She's bad, I'll kill her" moving to "Maybe she's not bad. Maybe I've been lied to. Maybe I've killed the wrong person." And this is accompanied by a cluster of connections, configured with the dog's howl. You're not sure where it comes from, the dog, the man, this *conscience howl*. There is guilt, whether it's his conscience howling or it's the evil he's done coming back to him. It's brilliant. I love that scene.

John Romano: About the conscience: it's prepared for by both Lean and Dickens very carefully in the conversation with Fagin. Fagin is a philosopher. He's always laying out the principle of self-interest. And he takes Bill through a litany very carefully. "What would you do if I did it [betrayed the gang]? What would you do if Dodger did it... And so forth. Therefore, if Nancy did it, you must kill her." Sikes sees the inexorable logic and he goes out, and he does it. And he himself does not understand why, if his ideas commit him to this act, there is something else in him that objects. So, this scene, it's almost like a discovery of conscience. Except that I find this Bill Sikes, Robert Newton, wooden compared to Oliver Reed, the Sikes in Carol Reed's musical version (1968), who always carries, from the beginning, this anxiety.

Gerhard Joseph: When Fagin, just before Bill goes out to do the killing, says "Don't be too violent, Bill," does he really mean don't be too violent? Or –

John Romano: He says "Don't be violent beyond safety." So as violent as necessary. Fagin's ever the Benthamite, really, always saying "Do just as much as will get us there, but don't go beyond that, that would be foolish."

Estelle Shane: This is the harnessing of the superego and the id by the ego, because – to go back to Kamilla's question – it's really the ego that is the instrument of evil here. He says "If this is true then that, but do it in a way that doesn't get us into trouble." That's not id, that's ego.

Greg Bellow: It's a conscious decision, a rational decision.

Kamilla Elliott: So ego isn't the good guy all the time?

Greg Bellow: Not at all!

Kamilla Elliott: It's not just a mediator between superego and id?

Muriel Brotsky: It's a compromise formation.

Greg Bellow: The ego, to use John's term, is the utilitarian, the pragmatist.

John Romano: Whereas Dickens represents the English objection to Cartesian rationalism. The same in Hume. There's something in us that makes us, that will innately object to having to kill. Why would someone kill? Even if logic takes you there, Dickens is saying to the rationalist tradition among the utilitarians, that even in a Sikes, there is a part of us that cries out against this. That's where we look for the answer to Kamilla's question. Dickens is not just interested in giving us evil, he wants to say what makes a person evil, the way that David must be made the hero of his life, *by events*. That's not complete in the early novels, but there's a striving toward it even then, and Lean fills it out.

Estelle Shane: It's this complexity, latent in the Dickens text, that Lean points out, makes explicit in the film.

Greg Bellow: Does Sikes seem to have pangs of conscience in the book?

John Romano: "The eyes, the eyes."

Others: Yes.

Muriel Brotsky: In the book I felt that he was experiencing this sense of loss. Does that come out at all in the film?

Greg Bellow: Is it conscience or is it something more selfish like "What am I going to do without her?"

Gerhard Joseph: What about the focus on the bed? All that the bed means, with Nancy that's also lost.

Kamilla Elliott: And the flowers that she put in the pot. It's like the trace of her presence.

Gerhard Joseph: And the shot that moves from her hand to her dressing table. I think there's a humanization. What's great about the scene is that Lean doesn't emphasize it, but I think those shots do something to make us feel the loss and to show us that Sikes also feels it.

Estelle Shane: And the emptiness that comes from that extended silence with the lushness of natural imagery.

Muriel Brotsky: The sunrise. The whole deal. Yes, I agree.

Murray Baumgarten: One of the things the episode does so well is something that I like in Dickens a lot, and that's part of his vision of the city, what he called the attraction of repulsion. You look at that scene and you're repulsed, but you're also fascinated – you're deeply attracted. And Sikes has the same experience in looking at the dead body. At least in my memory both of the rest of the film but also of the book, there is an echo of the crucifixion issue, the attraction of repulsion, looking at the crucified body. So we have a kind of fundamental moment.

Kamilla Elliott: Which reminds me of something I also want to bring up. There's a whole sense in which Lean psychologizes through – not just things like the dog howling – but through all sorts of externals. So he shows you that shadow of the curtain, the family touch that Nancy's put into the house. And so one of my questions about this idea of Dickens, film, and psychoanalysis has to do with what happens between the book and the film.

For the most part I'd say that film cuts language and in the process it reduces the complexity of the psychological patterns in the books it adapts. But what happens with Lean is this consistent externalizing of things that aren't made explicit or revealed in the book. A great example comes from his *Great Expectations* (1946) where the boy Pip (Anthony Wager) is running terrified across the moors, being chased, but we see he's actually being chased by his own shadow. And also in the clip we just watched, right before Bill kills Nancy, Lean does something with the lighting that creates a facial psychology that doesn't have to do with the actor's expression nearly as much as it has to do with the movement of the lighting. And there's no language. So, again a question for psychoanalysts: narrative apart, this kind of externalizing of the unrepresented and the unspoken, does it reveal ways in which film suggests you may not actually need language to encounter the psyche?

Estelle Shane: Right. It's the nonverbal, the paraverbal, that we have become so interested in nowadays.

Kamilla Elliott: But Freud and Lacan are absolutely insistent: the bottom line is language. Lacan says the unconscious is structured like a language. Freud claims you interpret the dreams, get those visuals into words, then you've got it. So are you saying there is now a new movement?

Estelle Shane: Definitely: nonverbal, paraverbal, non-linear.

Kamilla Elliott: Oh good! I'm so excited!

Estelle Shane: Now change is conceptualized as nonverbal. There is a whole school –

Kamilla Elliott: Psychoanalytic? A new branch?

Estelle Shane: Well, yes. Daniel Stern and the Boston Change Group. They began to publish in the late 1970s. They focus on what they call the "now moments," the moments of meaning which have nothing to do with verbal interaction. But they have everything to do with what they call procedural knowing or implicit knowing, where it's not put into words at all, and it never needs to be. Stern's idea is: interpretation is nice, but it's irrelevant when it comes to change, because change occurs in that nonverbal moment. That's arguable. Lots of people don't agree, but –

Gerhard Joseph: But that's the brilliance of this scene. It doesn't expound with sounds, it does everything not only in but with silence. There's no music. There's nothing. It's not too long, but it's very powerful.

Rob Polhemus: The relationship between picture, vision, and image is a very complex one and it shifts from novel to novel and from film to film as well as from specific novel to specific film. But, in general, this idea of externalized psychology is I think, what, tends to draw people to Dickens. And that's one of the reasons why people who are interested in vision, in pictures, find these books so rich and so suggestive. If we talk about that dog in *Oliver Twist*, the external psychology there, you could write volumes on the complexity of that image. If you take

Miss Havisham in *Great Expectations*, Dickens's or Lean's. What is a neurotic who lives in the past like? She's like those ruins, those surroundings. And somehow this not only strikes us, it convinces us.

Greg Bellow: But this business that Estelle is talking about, that we associate with Stern and the Boston Change Group, isn't just about the external elements telling us the story. It's really more concerned with a shift which emphasizes the relationship as curative as opposed to interpretive. With this emphasis on the paraverbal and the non-linear, you get away from the literal, from the word, from some sign standing for something else, and you get more interested in relationship and the transactions that go on between the patient and the therapist. It's the relationship that explains the cure, as opposed to what you learn verbally, or what you say verbally, or what emerges from the unconscious into consciousness through language. And so therapy gets away from the idea that all you need to do is get the thing worded right. "Aha! That's why I hate my mother," and having said it you're a changed person.

Estelle Shane: Which means that repression is kind of out and association is in. Things aren't kept *down*, they're just kept *out*. They can be conscious, or non-conscious, or unconscious, but coherence comes not just from naming, or seeing, but from bringing all of that stuff that's been outed not just into awareness or consciousness, but into the larger notion of "Who I am." *I am all of these things as well as these things that I want to focus on*.

Greg Bellow: Which also connects to the issue of the split between affect and idea. You can be aware of these things as items in a narrative but you're not aware of the emotional implications of them. And so you can go along in a kind of a robot-like or zombie-like existence, which is admittedly an extreme way to describe it. Knowing but not changing. Now the emphasis is bringing about a closer connection between what the self knows about itself and what it feels as a result of that knowing. You can live a great alienation from your feelings and still have awareness of what are the sources of these difficulties.

Gerhard Joseph: Which brings us right back to what Sikes feels when he kills Nancy.

Kamilla Elliott: And to Nancy herself.

Greg Bellow: Exactly. It's why for Dickens Nancy has redeeming features and Fagin does not. Throughout the novel, Dickens keeps saying that she has something of the woman in her, that sentimentality. She's touched by Oliver's looks, etc., and she saves his life at the cost of her own. And those are very redeeming qualities without a doubt, because she integrates her feelings with her life even at the cost of her life. But

Bill brings us back to the whole issue of disassociation. In order for Bill to kill Nancy, he's got, at least temporarily, to forget how important she is to him. He's got to eradicate the power of the relationship, in order to destroy her. And that's what people mean by disassociation, from a psychoanalytical point of view. The moment has to escape that emotional connection in order to do that sort of evil. Even though you know it you can't feel it. And then after she dies he says "Holy cow, what did I do?"

John Romano: And that's what Lean manages to register so perfectly through that long silent sequence, through the nonverbal choice and editing of his images.

Estelle Shane: But it's crucial that you realize that this kind of disassociation is not something you do deliberately. Disassociation is not something you can control. It is something that happens to you.

Greg Bellow: But we've also agreed that Bill was under the sway of Fagin's logic in the earlier scene. So there is some element of rational deliberation here.

John Romano: He's like those paid state executioners one reads about. They're pro-death penalty but their question is: "Why do I feel so guilty?" But they do, and their logic can't provide an answer.

Estelle Shane: What happens in this scene is this: what Bill does, what the ego does, invokes a certain side of him, and he has no control over that. It just happens to him. And when he sees the dead body and all of the paraphernalia Lean so beautifully depicts for us, he can't help it, the other part, the part that has an emotional tie to Nancy, comes to the fore. It's not that he says, "Let me sit and think and remember" or "I can now give up this other side."

Greg Bellow: It's not the return of the repressed, either.

Estelle Shane: No, it's not the return of the repressed. You can see how out of control he is because he couldn't stop where Fagin said to stop. If it were just "She put us at risk and I will get rid of her," he would have been able to stop without the brutality of the killing.

John Romano: And there is something about the way in which editing works in film – and we have to remember that David Lean was the premier film editor in the UK for a whole decade before he became a director – there is something about editing that makes this process of disassociation even more striking when we watch the scene than when we read it.

Kamilla Elliott: Because editing is based on disassociation. It relies on splicing together connections between things that are actually not connected. I shoot some film. And then I shoot some more film. And then in the editing process I take a bit from the first piece and snip it together with a bit from the second. So editing associates but it also keeps pointing toward disassociation.

John Romano: And when it's presenting an experience of disassociation, as it is here, then the technique really comes into its own.

Rob Polhemus: As opposed to coherent prose narrative, which is always, syntactically and in other ways, making an ordered, coherent whole out of things.

Murray Baumgarten: Which is why, as Garrett Stewart argues, Dickens is always working against the cohering tendency in language, in favor of the ellipses. Which is what makes him – what? Proto-cinematic?

Jane Jordan: But I want to get back to Fagin. We keep on referring to him but we haven't really discussed him yet. Why does Lean depict Fagin with the huge nose prosthesis? Why is he depicted in a way that mobilizes such an anti-Semitic caricature?

Kamilla Elliott: This film was not allowed to be released for three years in the United States because of what they considered to be anti-Semitism. In the US we still see the cut version. There are other scenes where Fagin is even more clearly racialized. And the defense that Lean and Alec Guinness, who played Fagin, used was that they were copying George Cruikshank's original illustrations. Of course, if you go to Cruikshank's illustrations, you encounter a whole physiognomical tradition where the middle class including Monks are all depicted with these wonderful Grecian aquiline noses, and the lower classes, even lovable good people or mixed people like Nancy, all have that kind of lower physiognomy. This tradition of racial representation, with its class-based notions of nobility and morality, gets changed in the twentieth century, particularly after World War II. And this is further complicated in Hollywood with a significant number of Jewish filmmakers. But it was comfortably released in England without any question.

Gerhard Joseph: And of course the musical version, *Oliver!*, gives us a pretty attractive Fagin.

John Romano: Although it's well known that Sir Carol Reed stole shot for shot from Lean's version for the narrative portions of the musical. The storyboards are the same. If it were a world in which you could copyright shot selections and storyboards, this would be actionable, because in so many places he used exactly the same decision: we will shoot the scene by tracking Oliver this way, then we'll get the girl, then we'll cut broad.

But with Fagin, we have to realize there are at least hints of likeability in the Dickens. Dickens is giving us a charmer, but it's still an anti-Semitic portrait, for which he apologizes with the creation of Mr. Riah in *Our Mutual Friend*.

Kamilla Elliott: And Guinness's Fagin is also comical, a little bit. He makes Oliver laugh quite a bit in the scene. So you've got the seeds of Ron Moody in the musical.

Murray Baumgarten: But what's very interesting, both in the novel and in Lean's version of it, is that in the scene of Nancy's murder there is none of this guilt, or punishment, or sadness that Sikes imagines when he's "killing" Fagin. Fagin is clearly outside. As the Jew he's outside that Dickensian world of the attraction of repulsion. He's off the page, the positive evil other. Fagin should have been the one Sikes killed; instead, Fagin, the evil Jew, makes Sikes kill Nancy. And that seems to me a dreadful moment in terms of the history of this film and it seems to me a dreadful moment for western culture in its mythological articulation of the Jew as outside of the human realm of disassociation, repression, feeling.

John Romano: I certainly agree, what a disgraceful moment this is for all of us, but I also think that as viewers we get to choose. Jane referred to his nose. Whenever you look at the character on film, you are looking at his nose. That is, the anti-Semitic figure representation is always present to you in film. But when you are reading a book, you get to choose among the many aspects that we are speaking to. But there is a sense that Fagin's Jewishness is ever present in the film in a way it is not in the novel.

Murray Baumgarten: Well it is in the later editions, where he is called "The Jewish Devil." Not in the first edition.

John Romano: But Dickens's point is that Fagin has taken himself out of the human equation by asking Sikes to think according to a calculus of benefit and loss, the Benthamite calculus. So in a way the death of Fagin is not guilt-causing because he asked to be seen that way. Nancy is saying "Ah Bill, Bill, see me in our interpersonal way." That's what leads to the later attack of conscience.

But here we are also close to observing something very important about Dickens in films. My experience of adapting novels for the movies, and of comparing others' adaptations to the originals, suggests that what film always does is call the novelist's bluff. You called him a Jew, you've made him a Jew, you could have made him anything, but you made him a Jew. Which means that every time you see him, he will have this nose. Film says to the novel: Are you really willing to stand by the ever-present consequences, because I have no other way of shooting him? He's always who he is. A novelist can screen out other valences according to a context.

A wonderful example is in the version of *Women in Love* that was made by Ken Russell, where you are asked to remember the German lover when he was a young skier in a sweatshirt instead of a soldier. If you are shooting it you don't get to see him as a skier, you can only see him as a soldier. But the novel can take you to the hilltops by saying "I was a boy in these hills," while the filmmaker is saying "I'm sorry, you put him in a uniform, sir. Whenever I show him he must be a soldier." So that kind of literalization means that, no matter how creatively inventive you are, novels get asked to show their cards. Of course films can screw it up too.

Gerhard Joseph: Except that this is the perfect example of the way in which that doesn't happen. In Ron Moody's Fagin you get a totally different interpretation from Alec Guinness's, so that Lean didn't have to go to the extreme that he did in the portrayal of Fagin as a Jew. In doing it, by totally racializing the face, the choice is made. So it's Lean's choice, not Dickens's.

John Romano: Well, Ron Moody is arguably less unpleasant, but his characterization is no less Jewish, to my mind. He does the song about the money. He uses Yiddish comedy. He uses Yiddish theater, which Ron Moody came out of.

Gerhard Joseph: But he does it through language, whereas your argument has to do with the visual.

John Romano: You're right. It's a visual argument.

Kamilla Elliott: And often in film, too, anybody who is a performer, who's entertaining, is inevitably going to be better received by the audience. Even in Lean's film, where Guinness can be funny and make people laugh. And by the time you get to the musical, the audience is valuing performances not so much for their morality or even for their ethnic status but because you value people you see on screen for how they entertain you. It's different from ethics and morality, from good guys and bad guys. And it's probably more marked in musicals.

Greg Bellow: What do you mean by entertain?

Kamilla Elliott: Singing, making jokes, making you laugh, engaging your attention in a way that in a book might not leap out at you any more than some deep and psychological introspection or some kind of description would. But in a performance medium, a theatrical film, the more entertaining character is the more engaging. That's why Pip in *Great Expectations* becomes this kind of lifeless, dull character surrounded by a pack of lively ones, because you lose that wonderful narrative voice.

Rob Polhemus: But it's also the casting. John Mills, who is so good so often, he's just terrible as Pip. Estella as Jean Simmons is perfect, but then she turns into Valerie Hobson, who is just dopey. On the screen we have responses that are not to Dickens's characters but to the actors playing those roles and that can produce a very different impact than the text does.

Jane Jordan: But isn't anyone else haunted by the scene at the end of this movie, where the crowd swoons, and there's a sense of mob violence, particularly at the point where they say they've got Fagin? Murray, can you speak to this? It goes back to the latent anti-Semitism, only it's not so latent.

Murray Baumgarten: No, it seems to be very explicit there and very directly visualized for us, the whole response of the mob. Sikes ends up hanging himself, so the mob doesn't get him. But they get Fagin as the just punishment of the monster, if you will, who's the cause of all of this.

Greg Bellow: That speaks to the whole issue of group fantasia, to mob psychology.

Murray Baumgarten: But that violence is not seen as a bad thing at the end of the movie. It's like a football game: we're cheering the victors.

Muriel Brotsky: The contagion of the virus.

Rob Polhemus: But we need to separate out all the different things we are talking about here. We're talking about *Oliver Twist* in the Victorian era. Then we're talking about *Oliver Twist* at the end of World War II. And in addition this big subject of adaptation, and the relations between film and novels. And in this film by Lean there are many different and maybe even contradictory elements going into it, anti-Semitism, the mob, violence, all of these things which have been settled out for us since 1946 but were still jumbled in the wake of the war.

Gerhard Joseph: Exactly, because even with the anti-Semitism in Fagin, there is also, of course, in those early scenes, where the orphans are in the hall, a kind of concentration-camp effect. And that has to be intentional. Talk about a contradiction. The concentration camp being depicted in its gruesomeness and the anti-Semitic portrayal of Fagin: how do you get those two things into the same film?

John Romano: Let me add to that. I think we have to register deeply the anti-Semitism of Dickens's creation of Fagin. I agree with everything that's been said about that. But if one is trying to gauge the flow of our sympathies at the end of this movie, there's a real difference in how we feel about Sikes coming off that roof and how we feel about the cornered Fagin, victim of the mob. And I think that's a turn that we really have to mark. When you call Fagin the cause of Sikes's evil, I don't think that's a very good description of our sense of Sikes. Fagin may be the cause of the Artful Dodger's corruption. But we are looking at a certain very psychologically thick portrait of adult evil in Sikes. In Fagin we're seeing someone victimized by their own game: evil, a Jew, many things to say. But I don't think our sympathy is with the mob as it turns on Fagin. It's about saving Oliver, and it's about killing the bad guy. And the bad guy of this moment isn't Fagin. It's Sikes.

Estelle Shane: You know I saw Fagin as very appealing at the beginning. I did. I thought he was a rescuer of those kids, like a Pied Piper. He sends these guys out to pick pockets, but what would have happened to Oliver had he not been saved by Fagin? Fagin took care of him, fed him at the beginning, in order to make him a useful member of his gang. I suppose that's the utilitarian aspect of it, but still – I liked him.

Kamilla Elliott: Until he shoves the poker in Oliver's face.

Estelle Shane: Well that wasn't nice.

Greg Bellow: They're what you would call non-violent criminals, Fagin's gang, other than Bill, what you would call non-violent criminals in today's metaphors.

Kamilla Elliott: Even philosophical non-violent criminals.

Estelle Shane: Yes.

John Romano: In a sense, you know, it's a shame that the Lean movies are so good as movies, both *Great Expectations* and *Oliver Twist*. They are better films than, let's say it, Cukor's *David Copperfield*. As a result, a certain interpretation of Dickens got the best film outing, an interpretation Lean shared with 1940s literary critics like Edmund Wilson and Lionel Trilling and (someone a little later) Steven Marcus – very Germanic, angst-ridden, Freudian. Posit a Frank Capra, posit a genius of David Lean's order with a more humanistic, more J. S. Mill view of the world, which in many respects we might agree is closer to Dickens's own, you would have an equally great movie with a different color, because we are really getting the dark valley, the film noir, the Freudian driven, Edmund Wilson Dickens in Lean, where anxiety is cooler than resolution.

Rob Polhemus: And when Lean goes into and tries to do the Capra stuff, when he does the dances and so forth in *Great Expectations*, it's terrible, it's just terrible.

Gerhard Joseph: Well, of course, Capra's *It's A Wonderful Life* is a version of Dickens, isn't it, an adaptation of *A Christmas Carol*?

John Romano: Right. And that's what makes you wish Capra had actually done an adaptation of one of the novels.

Gerhard Joseph: My point is that *It's A Wonderful Life* is a version of Dickens, as much an adaptation of a Dickens story as any of the *Oliver*s or *Copperfield*s.

John Romano: Yes, that's right. But you also have to remember that it's only for the convenience of discussion that we talk about Lean's *Oliver* or Carol Reed's. Lean's film is different from Reed's because – to give just one reason – of Arnold Bax's great score, for which, of course, there is no equivalent in Dickens's novel. A great filmmaker welcomes in the parts of the other filmmakers that are not parts of himself or parts of Dickens, and folds them all in together.

Greg Bellow: But W. C. Fields is exactly the way you expect Micawber to look and behave.

Gerhard Joseph: But isn't that because Fields based his earlier performance persona on Micawber, so that when he did finally come to play Micawber he was, in a sense, playing "himself"?

Greg Bellow: Except that Fields includes in Micawber things that Fields could do – he was an acrobat and a juggler – that aren't in Dickens.

Rob Polhemus: But now they have become so identified with Micawber that if we see a new performance from an actor who doesn't use Fields's stuff we'd think the performance wasn't accurate.

Greg Bellow: And we don't want Micawber ever to change. Is that, in part, what makes Dickens Dickens, this experience of repetition? Is that what we want from him, a guarantee against change?

Murray Baumgarten: Another way to put that question would be to ask whether reading a Dickens novel parallels the therapeutic experience. Do the ways in which Dickens impacts the reader parallel the analytic "work"? Is the moral discourse of Victorian society what we can now see and use as a therapeutic discourse?

Kamilla Elliott: We can see that question clearly with the ending to Lean's *Oliver*. There's a sequence that leads up to that ending, with Monks and Bill, where there's a lot of different people spying on other people, and it's particularly layered. It seems to me a place where all of it: psychoanalysis; uncovering secrets; watching to find out, to know; the narrative coming out, in film and in the novel – all of it happens, but happens here in a specifically kind of filmic way. You start out with Nancy watching Monks and Fagin, and Dodger is watching her and keeping an eye on her. And then they get some women singing and all the eyes go to the performing women, which is a sort of commune. Nancy's able to spy but then she is being spied on. The Dodger gets paid to watch her. We're paying to watch the film. But at the end, this mob comes and breaks down the barrier between the masses, the audience, and the characters who were doing the secret, bad deeds. And this again is what Murray called the attraction of repulsion. We're allowed to have this sort of catharsis because we watched and we were kind of implicit in the bad deeds, and now we can join the punishing mob.

Greg Bellow: One of the interesting things about both Dickens and psychotherapy has to do with the need for secrecy. In both the film and the novel the gang is secret, and it has to stay secret to survive, and one of the things that Nancy did is that she betrayed the gang's secret, she publicized them. She opened them up to the view of respectable society because they made the mistake of trying to corrupt a respectable child. Had they just stuck to their own kind they would be in business to this day, because they were below the threshold of capital law. And so there is this whole idea of how looking at things and learning about them can get you into a whole lot of trouble.

Rob Polhemus: And a whole lot of pleasure.

Kamilla Elliott: It's like those scenes where Sikes pulls down the "man wanted" posters. Which have to remind a film audience of film posters. In film, there's this tension between wanting to tell that someone did a crime and hiding them so that we stay the audience, until –

Greg Bellow: Until, finally, everyone knows. By the time the mob gets there at the end everybody knows everything there is to tell.

Estelle Shane: But not everybody tells.

Gerhard Joseph: Or wants to.

Rob Polhemus: Or should.

Look at the two endings for *Great Expectations*. Which is the preferred ending? The "healthy" one: Pip's obsessions are removed and he is no longer interested in Estella. But "no," Bulwer-Lytton tells him, "you can't print that, Charles." So Dickens writes the other ending. Everything stays the same including the obsession with Estella. Does the fact that everyone prefers the second ending – and that's the one that gets filmed –

Kamilla Elliott: I've now seen five different versions of *Great Expectations* and they all end differently.

Rob Polhemus: But they also use the with-Estella ending, right, not the without-Estella.

Kamilla Elliott: Yes.

Rob Polhemus: Which seems to mean that we actually prefer repetition to change.

Gerhard Joseph: And with all the reading I have done, I have to ask myself: has it changed anything, has it made a difference? And if so, what kind of a difference has it made? Reading is a deeply vicarious experience, not just reading but moviegoing too, a way of not dealing with your experience, but giving yourself over to fantasies. Books, films, aren't they ways of evading living? You pay more attention to the pain on the page or the screen than to the pain in your life.

Muriel Brotsky: But you have to distinguish reading – books or films – when you are young from reading as a adult. For adults, yes, it is a way of trying to remove yourself. But for young people, it can have a very different outcome.

John Romano: Well Dickens certainly tries not to be guilty of providing a leisure activity that would not change his readers.

Jane Jordan: There's a joke about how many therapists it takes to change a lightbulb. Only one, but the lightbulb has to be willing to change. One can read a book or view a film, and be transformed, or not be transformed. Films, novels, or therapy, it all depends on the readiness to take in the new experience.

John Romano: Yet I know that when I sit down to read a book, any book, I do it with a different frame of mind than the one I assume when I go out to see a film. And I think that contributes toward a different readiness for mutability.

Kamilla Elliott: When you read, the cognitive process moves from the symbol on the page to the perceptual world you create in the mind. In film, you are looking at all these extremely vivid perceptual stimuli, and you are reading meaning into them. Reading is the inverse process to viewing.

But with Dickens it becomes much more complicated because of the long history of adaptation of Dickens to the screen, virtually as long as the history of film itself. When we come to a Dickens text we are likely to come with the concrete images already predetermined. It's what we were saying a while back about W. C. Fields and Micawber. We may not have seen this particular novel adapted, but we have seen lots of Dickens and we know what Dickens, what Victorian, looks and feels like.

Murray Baumgarten: But there's also the other issue you raised earlier: entertainment. We take books more seriously than films because we treat film as entertainment. And maybe that ties film to therapy in a different way. I have friends who have told me, quite seriously, that the reason they started psychoanalysis was for entertainment.

Kamilla Elliott: To be entertained, or to entertain others?

Murray Baumgarten: How much should we see moviegoing, and at least some reading, and therapy as forms of entertainment?

Estelle Shane: Our patients today are very different from Freud's. Now they speak of a kind of emptiness, a sense that life is not complete or meaningful. The neurotic symptoms that confronted Freud are not what we see. Emptiness, I'm sure, is the reason you read a book, or go out to see a film, or go to an analyst.

Greg Bellow: To get your life to become more entertaining.

Gerhard Joseph: To make my experience something that interests me.

John Romano: And therefore gives me pleasure.

Murray Baumgarten: So is that why we should continue to teach Dickens to undergraduates, because Dickens is the first place they get to see the seriousness of Freud?

John Romano: And therefore the seriousness of pleasure.

Part II

2   David Copperfield's home movies

John Bowen

David Copperfield is perhaps the most important exploration in Dickens's work of a character's conscious recollection of the past. It is also a deeply cinematic novel. This essay explores how *David Copperfield* narrates scenes of memory and retrospection in quasi-filmic ways, and how these ways are implicated in questions of male sexual identity, which it explores through various kinds of fetishism, voyeurism, sadism, and sexual transgression. *David Copperfield* tells the story of the production through narration of a particular kind of subject: male, bourgeois, heterosexual, monogamous. That process is, I want to argue, deeply cinematic. However, when we compare the novel with its most important film adaptation, we find a complexly disjunctive relationship between the modes of narration of the two media and their respective representations of masculinity and male desire.

It is striking how often in *David Copperfield* memory is presented not just as having a visual dimension (which would be unsurprising) but as constitutively visual and indeed cinematic. Remembering is seeing, many times in this book: "What else do I remember?", asks David, "Let me see" (1983: 11). The second chapter of the novel, in which David's memories begin, is entitled "I observe" and, particularly in its opening pages, is concerned with what he sees: "the first objects that assume a distinct presence before me, as I look far back, into the blank of my infancy, are my mother ... and Peggotty" (10). Memory is vision before it is anything else, a silent film running in the older David's head, short reels, fragments of home movies, without scratching or fading. It is not simply in these early scenes, though, that David's memory and memories seem so cinematic. Indeed, one of the most powerful and distinctive effects in Dickens's fiction occurs at moments when a character is able to witness, with hallucinatory clarity, a scene from his or her past, and yet is unable to participate in it or change anything. Scrooge, for example, is taken by the figure of Christmas Present to scenes from his childhood and young manhood to witness the breaking off of his engagement, his dead sister, and his time at Fezziwig's. At such times, his position is very akin to that of a modern cinema spectator, existing as s/he does in "a hermetically sealed world which unwinds magically, indifferent to the presence of the audience" (Mulvey 1989: 17). *A Christmas Carol* uses a frankly super-natural mode of writing; *David Copperfield*, much more closely bound to realist conventions (there are no spirits here), both takes and transforms this mode of presentation. Here, it is the property not of an external su-pernatural agency but of an essentially subjective capacity, a cinema of the mind, by which the subject replays scenes of *his* subjective formation and past. (I shall argue later that it is an essentially masculine structure, at least in this novel.)

Here, for example, is David recounting the moment that he last saw his mother alive:

I was in the carrier's cart when I heard her calling to me. I looked out, and she stood at the garden-gate alone, holding her baby up in her arms for me to see. It was cold, still weather; and not a hair of her head or a fold of her dress, was stirred, as she looked intently at me, holding up her child.

So I lost her. So I saw her afterwards, in my sleep at school – a silent presence near my bed – looking at me with the same intent face – holding up her baby in her arms. (97)

Sound – the sound of his mother's voice – yields to vision, and to an imperturbable stasis, as not a hair of Clara Copperfield's head or a fold of her dress moves, as if she is already dead. David's mother, for the last time, is standing and, in a phrase repeated and repeated, "holding up . . . holding up . . . holding up" herself, her baby, and time itself, which mem-ory in vision here arrests, in a brief moment that seems to last for ever.

The play of gazes in this scene – David's at his mother, his mother's at him, and the doubled look in which David "saw her . . . looking at me" in his sleep – echoes an earlier passage in the book, in which David, speaking of his dead mother, asks himself:

Can I say of her face – altered as I have reason to remember it, perished as I know it is – that it is gone, when here it comes before me at this instant, as distinct as any face that I may choose to look on in a crowded street? Can I say of her innocent and girlish beauty, that it faded, and was no more, when its breath falls on my cheek now, as it fell that night? Can I say she ever changed, when my remembrance brings her back to life, thus only; and, truer to its loving youth than I have been, or man ever is, still holds fast what it cherished then? (20)

Vision, memory, loss, and mourning meet in the face of the mother. She is "girlish"; he is in his "loving youth." David's mother is his mother, but also his contemporary, whom he mourns and brings back to life in memory, in a vision of her face close to hallucination; at the same time, he brings back his own former self, truer to its loving youth. It is not a sound, a taste, a touch, or a smell that he remembers, but the sight of her face, a single close-up, as it were, burned on his memory, whose uncanny presence, both more and less than real, disturbs David's sense of the distance between the past and present, the living and dead. In the reiterated rhetorical questions "Can I say?... Can I say ?... Can I say?", there is doubt about what one can say for sure, even about the simplest and most certain things – my mother is dead. What creates this doubt is the extraordinary and disruptive power of memory, visual memory for the most part, but at times capable of the sensory and tactile: "its breath falls on my cheek."

The most important chapters of the book in creating these complex passages between the constitution of memory and identity on the one hand and what one can call the cinematic or quasi-cinematic on the other are the three Retrospects. They divide the novel, not into volumes, but into a threefold movement of consciousness, which culminates respectively in the end of David's schooldays and his adolescent crushes on Miss Shepherd and Miss Larkins, his wedding to Dora, and his married life with Agnes. These chapters punctuate the book and, as their titles tell us, look backwards. Each is concerned with a qualitative change in David's life, which is marked by the foregrounding of questions of sexual desire and sexual difference. The first is narrated by David "hovering above those days, in a half-sleeping and half-waking dream" (217) into which one or another figure "breaks upon me" (218) as they broke upon Scrooge, or the modern cinemagoer. What David watches in this chapter is essentially a comic film, in which scene dissolves into scene: "The shade of a young butcher rises... A blank... And what comes next!... Some brighter visions arise before me..." (219–21). The second Retrospect, David's and Dora's wedding and the novel's erotic climax, begins: "Once again, let me pause upon a memorable period my life. Let me stand aside, to see the phantoms of those days go by me, accompanying the shadow of myself, in dim procession" (511). There then follows a montage: "of... the pew-opener arranging us, like a drill-serjeant, before the altar-rails... Of the clergyman and clerk appearing; of a few boatmen and some other people strolling in; of an ancient mariner behind me, strongly flavouring the church with rum; of the service beginning..." (516). Here is our wedding video, says David, who narrates these scenes from the position of their silent witness: I am a camera. The final Retrospect is similarly distinctive in its narration: "And now my written story ends. I look back, once more – for the last time – before I close these leaves. I see myself with Agnes, journeying along the road of life. I see our children and our friends around us... What faces are most distinct to me in the fleeting crowd?" (714). His written story both ends and continues, as David looks back in a writing that simultaneously liberates itself into a different narrative space and subordinates itself to vision, and the vision of faces in particular.

Even more striking than the cinematic qualities of the Retrospects is how intimately they are bound up with figures of women – Clara Copperfield, Miss Shepherd, Miss Larkins, Dora Spenlow, Agnes Wickfield – and of male desire for them. This is not surprising, however, for, as Laura Mulvey has argued, there are close links between spectatorship and the construction of masculine identity in narrative. Mulvey's influential account of male desire and, in particular, male pleasure in looking argues that the fear of castration "activates the fetishistic aspects of voyeuristic pleasure" and in consequence "inflects scopophilic pleasure towards misogyny" (xi–xii). There are difficulties with this as a general account of visual pleasure, as it underestimates the variety and complexity of subject positions and identifications available to the spectator of narrative film and other media. Nevertheless, in David's narration there are clear affinities between the ways in which he represents the objects of his desire to himself and Mulvey's account of voyeurism and fetishism in the male gaze. Indeed, it is striking how often the relationships between the narrating David and the women characters in the book resemble the structures of fantasy that Mulvey describes, of "woman, plus phallic substitute . . . woman minus phallus, punished and humiliated, often by woman plus phallus . . . [and] woman as phallus" (7). The novel is deeply concerned with sadistic male desire, both within and outside erotic relationships, as we see in the pursuit of Agnes by Uriah Heep, the violence of Betsey Trotwood's husband, Steerforth's wounding of Rosa Dartle, and Murdstone's and Creakle's pleasure in beating. In Murdstone's cruelty to Clara Copperfield and his second wife, the fall into prostitution of Martha Endell, the possible adultery of Annie Strong, the seduction of Emily and Rosa Dartle's sadistic pursuit of her, the novel constantly returns to violent and transgressive sexual relationships, to which David's relationship is at crucial points an essentially voyeuristic one. John Carey describes sexuality in *David Copperfield* as "driven underground to emerge in perverted and distorted forms." (Carey 1973: 154). But "driven underground" is hardly the right metaphor. In the novel perversity is flagrant and all-pervasive.

There is, furthermore, a good deal of fetishization of women in the novel. Betsey Trotwood wears "masculine" clothing, including collar and cuffs, and tries to discourage her maids from marrying. Jane Murdstone has "very heavy eyebrows, nearly meeting over a large nose, as if, being disabled by the wrongs of her sex from wearing whiskers, she had carried them to that account" (37), and ornaments herself with "little steel rivets and fetters" (38). Both Agnes and Rosa at times possess phallic attributes.

These fetishized representations of women are accompanied by, and perhaps predicated on, male anxiety, in particular David's doubts about his masculinity and potency. The recipient of his adolescent crushes, Miss Larkins, crushingly, calls him a "bold boy" (22), and Steerforth "Daisy" (237). His aunt wants him to be a girl and often compares him to his imaginary sister. He is embarrassed by being asked to step down off the box of the coach and by a maid bringing him shaving water. Littimer makes him feel very young, as does Miss Mowcher who suggests that she build up a fake pair of whiskers for him. His rival for Dora has a pair of Red Whiskers, after which he is named. In the first chapter, almost the first page, of the book, David loses a part of himself that he does not need at the time, but may later. Not a phallus but a caul, which he sees again when it is auctioned off when he is ten years old (at about the time that he too is disposed of, cut-price, to Murdstone and Grinby's bottle warehouse) and without which he is powerless to save Emily, Ham, and Steerforth from their fates.

It is hard not to link the recurrent feeling of masculine inadequacy to the deep sense of loss that pervades the book. David loses his father, his mother, Emily, Steerforth, his unborn child, Dora and, for a long time, believes that he has lost Agnes. The sense of powerlessness is both gathered within and exceeded by his "vague unhappy loss or want of something" (411), that deep ontological absence or void that simultaneously shapes and deranges his story and his life.

There are two particularly striking examples of David's representation of women, both of which center on the vision of a female face in close-up and which are strongly inflected by these erotic and fetishistic drives and their underpinning sense of loss. Both culminate in scenes of humiliation or punishment of a young woman and are narrated in deeply voyeuristic ways. The first is his recounting of Annie Strong's story. As a boy, David silently witnesses a scene between the young Annie and her elderly husband: she is wearing a white dress and has lost the cherry-coloured ribbon in her bosom, which seems to have been taken by her ne'er-do-well cousin, Jack Maldon. David silently watches a silent play of gazes between husband and wife:

she was looking up at him. But, with such face as I never saw. It was so beautiful in its form, it was so ashy pale, it was so fixed in its abstraction, it was so full of a wild, sleep-walking, dreamy horror of I don't know what. The eyes were wide open, and her brown hair fell in two rich clusters on her shoulders, and on her white dress, disordered by the want of the lost ribbon. Distinctly as I recollect her look, I cannot say of what it was expressive. I cannot even say of what it is expressive to me now, rising again before my older judgement. Penitence, humiliation, shame, pride, love, and trustfulness – I see them all; and in them all, I see that horror of I don't know what. (200–1)

It is a remarkable passage, both akin to and the reverse of the memory of his "innocent and girlish" young mother. A woman's face rises before him, then – in his youth – and now; he looks into its wide open eyes which in their "wild, sleep-walking, dreamy horror" seem to speak, incomprehensibly, directly to his unconscious. The image comes back, recharged with erotic meaning, at the end of David's schooldays, at the very moment that he becomes "a young man at his own disposal" (223), when the sight of her face "began to return upon me with a meaning it had never had" (230) in a newly sexualized *Nachträglichkeit*. It is akin to a primal scene or David's own domestic Medusa's head: a face, disordered hair, and dress, and the sign in a missing ribbon of the possibility of female sexual transgression, are for David a traumatic loss of innocence, simultaneously beautiful and horrific. "It was", he writes, "as if the tranquil sanctuary of my boyhood had been sacked before my face, and its peace and honor given to the winds" (231). Annie, the innocent woman, who, we later learn, was earlier unable to speak of or name her own sexual horror, has then to live through much of the novel humiliated and suspected, until David and his aunt, Mr Dick and ourselves finally witness her kneeling once more at the feet of her "husband and father" (536) publicly to implore his forgiveness. In David's silent movie, it is the price the woman pays for being an object of desire.

The most powerful of the scenes which deal with female sexuality and which causes the most intensely voyeuristic humiliation of a sexual woman is the confrontation in chapter 50, "Mr Peggotty's Dream Comes True", between Emily and Rosa Dartle. When David first meets Rosa, he is fascinated and repelled by the facial scar given to her by Steerforth when she was a child, and simultaneously sexually attracted to and fearful of her. Much of this is expressed in a strange play of gazes in his bedroom that night. Seeing Rosa's picture on the wall "looking eagerly at me" (243), David notices that there is no scar on the portrait, but then, he tells us, "*I* made it; and there it was, coming and going: now confined to the upper lip... and now showing the whole extent of the wound inflicted by the hammer, as I had seen it when she was passionate" (243). Looking at her picture, which then gazes, simultaneously wounded and unwounded, back at him, David tells us that he "undressed quickly... and went to bed. But... I could not forget that she was still there looking" (243). Undressed, in the dark, David remembers the image of a woman who seems to be gazing at him, as his dead mother did when he was a child at school. It is, though, a darker, more disturbing gaze. Rosa's "wasting fire", David tells us earlier, "found a vent in her gaunt eyes" (238). Her wound, which Steerforth made, the painter removed, and David makes and unmakes anew, disturbs him. As her reiterated questions come to haunt and possess his dreams, his capacity to recognize the real, to know and to mean, is lost. Waking in the night he finds himself "uneasily asking all sorts of people . . . whether it really was or not – without knowing what I meant" (243). Rosa, the most persistently eroticized, fetishized and perverse figure in the novel, has a profoundly disturbing, not to say castrating, effect, on David's psyche. It is, however, another woman who will pay.

Later in the novel, before she is herself condemned to a ceaseless, punitive repetition of the loss of Steerforth, David watches Rosa punish another woman to whom he has been sexually attracted, in a poor lodging-house that is only a step away from a brothel. In what is akin to a sado-masochistic scene between the two women, Rosa is hyperbolically cruel – "I would have this girl whipped to death" (587), she says at one point – as she confronts the abject Emily. David, as elsewhere in the book's peripeteias and revelations, is a silent and passive witness. Here he is also a voyeur as, from "a garret . . . little better than a cupboard" (584). In the company of Martha Endell, the former prostitute, he overhears and watches in the fragmented, compulsive, melodramatic interplay of these two women, the signs of his own desire, moving in and out of his and our vision, fetishized and phallic, punished and castrated.

So far I have discussed what we can call quasi-cinematic forms of narration within Dickens's text, and the ways in which they are linked to certain modes of fetishism and voyeurism in the structures of male desire. I turn now from the quasi to the cinematic itself. The novel, unsurprisingly, has been a popular one among moviemakers. Graham Petrie notes that it was filmed some half-dozen times before the advent of sound (Petrie 2001: 7). However, its most important screen version is clearly George Cukor's 1935 adaptation for MGM. David Thomson calls it a "magnificent . . . landmark in literary adaptation because of its fidelity to the spirit and the look of Dickens" (Thomson 1994: 162).

Cukor's adaptation has a complex relation to both the erotic and the cinematic qualities of the novel. In general, the film attempts to streamline and "normalize" the sexuality of the book, downplaying or omitting its overtly perverse, sadistic, transgressive, and fetishistic aspects. Rosa Dartle, Annie Strong, and Martha Endell do not appear. Jane Murdstone does not return as Dora's companion, and Betsey Trotwood does not have a violent husband. Instead of the multiplicity of perverse erotic relations of the book, the film is dominated by two familiar stories: the romance and courtship of David and Dora, followed by her death and his marriage to Agnes; and the seduction of Emily by Steerforth. More importantly, and unlike the recent BBC television adaptation, the film does not have a retrospective narrative voice. Cukor's is a *David Copperfield* without autobiographical framing and without retrospect. David's home movies here become everybody's.

Despite, or perhaps because of, this fundamental change in the nature of the narration, there are striking continuities between the presentation of male desire in the novel and the film. We can see this in two scenes which begin David's adult life and lie at the centre of the film. Both are explicitly concerned with erotic looking. After David leaves school, he visits the theater. Here he meets Steerforth, and sees, for the first time, Dora Spenlow with her two aunts in the adjoining box. The novel's more elaborate sequence of events – David's meeting Steerforth by chance, his work at Spenlow and Jorkins, his introduction to Dora, their secret courtship, and Jane Murdstone's betrayal of it – are here compressed into a single, quasi-allegorical scene of romance. London is theater here. And all we see of London is theater, in a theatrical scene in which men desire and observe women. Unlike the novel, in which David and Steerforth meet after a performance of *Julius Caesar*, David and Steerforth here meet by design at a performance of a ballet entitled *The Enchanted Bird*. The ballet narrates a story in which the female dancers are transformed into birds, the central figure of whom, as she is about to be shot by a male archer, escapes and flies away. (For a more detailed reading of the theater scenes, see Stephens 2001: 235–41).

Technically, it is a brilliantly compacted scene, with a complex play of differently gendered, differently partial, differently powerful gazes. David's "dreamy" gaze at the dancers gives way to his adoring gaze at Dora, from which she averts her gaze. We then learn of the partial view of the stage from Dora and her aunt's box, and the better one from Steerforth and David's box. Steerforth then causes Dora's aunt to lose her opera glasses, in order to lend her his. This, in turn, becomes the cue for his invitation to join them in their box. We are constantly incited to see parallels between the events offstage and the erect, fetishized, and silent dancers, whose broken shadows fall across and behind the specta- tors' faces and bodies. Dora's dress and fan echo their costumes. At the climax of the counterpointed scenes, as the prima ballerina anticipating her fate rises in the air, Dora rises too, as she agrees, finally, to David's request to call. Male desire is complexly differentiated in the movie's presentation. It appears in the destructive, phallic form of the archer, in David's romantic "innocence," and in Steerforth's seductive guile. But in each case it centers on the figure of a fetishized and silent, or near-silent, woman. Neither on stage nor off does she survive for long.

The immediately following scene, set in Yarmouth on the night of the engagement of Ham and Emily, both inverts and reinforces its prede- cessor's space of vision and desire. It too is a scene of erotic meeting, impelled by and culminating in a performance. Here, by contrast, the performer is male, powerful and bourgeois; the spectator silent, female and working-class; the desire illicit and transgressive. Before they enter the Peggottys' home, Steerforth has promised David that he will be "anything you please – comic or sentimental, or whatever the scene suggests." He is a performer throughout, but most explicitly so at the moment of seduction of Emily. Celebrating her betrothal to Ham, he sings, as she silently gazes up at him, "Catch hold of my hand, my fair pretty maid, and I will make you my bride." Emily, the female spectator of male seductive power, yields to Steerforth's hollow performative, to be later abandoned and betrayed. It is Steerforth who betrays her, of course, but so too does the movie, which silences her voice and desire even more radically than does the novel. In the entire course of her story's telling, she is never once permitted to speak.

According to the pioneering theorist of montage, Sergei Eisenstein, Dickens's work provided not merely essential parts of the grammar of film, but also important parts of its subject-matter and content. Like the cinema of Griffith, Dickens's fiction unites for Eisenstein two apparently contradictory qualities: modernity of expression and "the traditional, the patriarchal, the provincial" in subject-matter (in Eisenstein 1949: 198). Yet, as we can see in both the novel and film of *David Copperfield*, Dickens's legacy is a complex and often troubling one, propelled as it is by a deeply voyeuristic and at times sadistic dynamic of male desire. The novel has an extraordinary, perhaps unprecedented, ability to evoke the visual dimensions of consciousness and memory, as it tells its essentially comic story of David's overcoming of the pain and violence of his early life to attain domestic and patriarchal bliss with Agnes. It does so, however, in ways that often silence and fetishize the women conjured up in his memory. It is, in short, David's home movies that we are watching, whose structures of fantasy and voyeurism permeate both David's narration and Dickens's legacy to cinema. Joss Marsh has recently described Dickens as the "father of fathers" of modern cinema (Marsh 2001: 221). That may indeed be the problem.

REFERENCES

Carey, John. 1973. *The Violent Effigy: A Study of Dickens's Imagination*. London: Faber and Faber.
Dickens, Charles. 1983. *David Copperfield*. Ed. Nina Burgis. Oxford: World's Classics. All references in the text are to this edition.
Eisenstein, Sergei. 1949. "Dickens, Griffith, and the Film Today." *Film Form: Essays in Film Theory*. Ed. and trans. Jay Leyda. New York: Harcourt, Brace & World, Inc. 195–255.

Marsh, Joss. 2001. "Dickens and Film." *Cambridge Companion to Charles Dickens.* Ed. John Jordan. Cambridge University Press. 204–23.

Mulvey, Laura. 1989. *Visual and Other Pleasures.* London: Macmillan.

Petrie, Graham. 2001. "Silent Film Adaptations of Dickens. Part I: From the Beginning to 1911." *The Dickensian* 97: 7–21.

Stephens, John Russell. 2001. "David Copperfield and *The Stranger*: a 'Doctors' Commons sort of play'?" *The Dickensian* 97: 215–41.

Thomson, David. 1994. *A Biographical Dictionary of Film.* London: André Deutsch.

3   David Lean's *Great Expectations*

Regina Barreca

In his 1946 *Great Expectations* David Lean didn't film Dickens's novel. He remade the novel into David Lean's film. Lean completely reversed the thrust of Dickens's story. In the novel the power of the manipulative (step-)godmother is displaced by the benevolent godfather. Throughout the narrative, the male–male bonds of Magwitch–Pip, Herbert–Pip, Joe–Pip, and even Orlick–Pip structure the protagonist's moral and social development, and completely determine the book's final third. But with Lean the most interesting relationship is not among men but between women, Estella and Miss Havisham. And the final third of the film seems to evaporate into inconsequence in contrast to the power of the childhood sequences the women dominate. In contrast to the haunting and haunted child Pip (Anthony Wager), the adult Pip (John Mills) feels like a nonentity. Notoriously, the Lean ending is banal and unconvincing, a wet spot the viewer wants to avoid rolling onto once the best parts of the film are over. His now infamous "hand-in-hand toward the sunset" finish effectively swipes from beneath Dickens's novel its entire moral, ethical, and aesthetic foundation. It is the young Estella and her "aunt" who capture our imagination, and who provide the images that remain most firmly in our minds, long after the actual viewing ends.

Lean's portrayal of Miss Havisham is so replete with both conventional and subversive images of women, it is as if he took into account the complete catalogue of possible readings of the character and then created from them a character powerfully unlike any other. We have it on good authority – critics too many to mention – that Miss Havisham is one or all of the following: a caricature of Melanie Klein's bad mother; a demonically powerful untapped well of feminine sexuality; a representation of the crumbling, rotting, degenerate caste system in England just after (or, if Lean's film is under discussion, just before) the half-century mark; Medea in a wedding gown; the evil almost-mother, the distinctly non-maternal guardian of every child's fairy tale and nightmare. That "impostor of a woman," as Estella calls Miss Havisham, apparently carts around a good deal of our socioeconomic, psychological, cultural, and emotional baggage.

I want to argue that Miss Havisham is perhaps not so much an "impostor" as a female impersonator. Clearly, Lean feels drawn powerfully enough to the Havisham–Estella pairing to draw it indelibly. But he also needs ultimately to destroy it, because he envies and fears it too deeply to permit its continuation. He seems to have felt that Miss Havishams and Estellas are like Lady Macbeths or Ophelias, the more bitter the better, contorting both women into wholly bizarre shapes, making them even odder than Dickens's original conception.

In Lean's film we associate Miss Havisham, played with dignity and cunning by Martita Hunt, with candles, an unseen fire, an empty hearth, and her vanity table. The frame's image places her near candle flames, with her face lit by a fire before her which we do not see. The effect of this close juxtaposition of images is to make Miss Havisham seem already damned in some genteel hell, full of cobwebs and old ribbons, or already on her funeral bier lit dimly by candles which offer no warmth. In the scene where Miss Havisham is prompting Pip to love Estella, only to be interrupted by the arrival of Jaggers, she is framed against a bare, black, cold hearth, which acts as a kind of visual correlative to her heartless, cold, and bitter words.

Miss Havisham trains Estella how to embrace and wield power in a world of men. She is both the star and the director of the film within the film. Miss Havisham and Estella, then, are not fiends but sirens. And as sirens they must ultimately be refused by the hero when he has grown into his authentic male power, and then destroyed (Miss Havisham) or captured (Estella).

Only in the scene where Miss Havisham confronts and seems to repent her evil, with her hand over her heart asking Pip "What have I done?", is she pictured beside a roaring, smoking fire. But the effect here is really hellish; the piece of coal dislodged when Pip slams the door shut on her seems to roll as if animated by its own rage to set her dress on fire. Dickens uses the word "consumed" several times to describe Miss Havisham's obsession; her ultimate consumption by fire seems to indicate an outward movement of the anger and rage she has internalized for so long; it is as if, confronting her own power, she is consumed by it. The fire is only the outward and obvious manifestation. The key to that destruction comes in Lean's change of the coal. The coal does not leap on its own from the fire. It falls out because Pip slams the door. Lean thus makes Pip responsible for burning up Miss Havisham, and having destroyed her he can then go on to release Estella from her house and story.

Miss Havisham is also framed next to mirrors in a number of scenes, making visual the way the spinster wishes to multiply her image through Estella. Repeatedly, we see the young Estella behind bars, boxed in by windows, behind enormous gates. She is like a bird in a cage, imprisoned by her adoptive parent, who cannot go beyond the gate that separates Satis House from the rest of the world.

Even during the second part of the film when we hear Estella (now played rather demurely by Valerie Hobson) explaining to Pip Miss Havisham's plans for her as an adult, we see Pip and Estella sitting over tea: behind them are what look to be a series of bars – presumably just a leaded window – but the effect is to echo the gates of Satis House, the bars on the windows of that mansion, and to emphasize that although Estella is "out" in the world, the real activity of life takes place apart from her. In this scene, there is great bustle and motion taking place in the London portrayed behind that leaded glass, but Pip and Estella are stationary; Estella cannot move; she cannot join in the ordinary movements of daily routine. She is capable of a great deal of activity but no real action. True she can dance and skate, but surely that is to attract suitors, to make her look all the more desirable. She can also shoot an arrow and hit a bull's-eye. It is during the brief shot of Estella engaged in archery that Pip first comes to realize Estella has suitors. Estella has hit her bull's-eye; Pip is wounded by jealousy. Miss Havisham has constructed Estella precisely to inflict such a wound and this is the reason Pip must destroy Miss Havisham. The resilient, powerful, and dangerous Estella represents everything that Pip/Lean needs to subvert.

But to return to her childhood and her relationship with her guardian: the first interaction that we see taking place between Estella and Miss Havisham is the elder woman's placing of a jeweled necklace around the child's throat. In usurping the masculine privilege of providing loot as bribe for feminine compliance, Miss Havisham makes us uneasy in ways difficult to chronicle – except by Lean's careful depiction of the scene. Dickens mentions in the book that Miss Havisham "tries the effect of the jewels against Estella's pretty brown hair" but the gesture, when seen under Lean's direction, seems far more insidious and its implications far more wide-reaching. Estella is being collared, a jeweled noose being put around her neck. The jewels held by Miss Havisham are not suggestive of possible compensations for Estella's deformed and shallow life but proof of it. Miss Havisham withdraws the necklace when she commands Estella to play with Pip. The necklace then comes to represent the bait, the reward Estella will retrieve for destroying Pip's self-esteem and peace of mind, which she does with alacrity. Every time Jean Simmons says the word "boy" she sounds as if she is spitting some foul name at poor Pip.

In the film, Pip follows Estella in nearly every shot; she leads the way. She is the artificial light of the cloistered, nightmare environment created by Miss Havisham. Pip leaves the natural world behind to follow Estella and her candle. We see at several points Pip entering Satis House, with the "real world" behind a gate – like a frame within a frame – to the far left of the shot, and then the dark hallways which lead to the labyrinthine staircases. When Estella leaves the shot, the light goes with her. She is the go-between in these scenes, conveying Pip from the real world to a world created by obsession and madness, to a world which looks, in fact, ghostly.

Some adaptations of Dickens's novels try to satisfy an audience by reducing the number of complicated psychological overtones, but Lean's screenplay seems to enrich them. Lean was certainly conscious of the power of the hothouse or tomb-like atmosphere of the rooms in Satis House. The boy Pip seems dwarfed by the rooms and by the women. Simmons's Estella is noticeably taller and more mature than Wager's Pip. But they seem less imposing when he returns as an adult. John Mills, the adult Pip, is less easily intimidated than his younger counterpart. But the adult Pip, who has been smuggled, not accepted, into the upper class, is also less compelling than the uncertain child he once was. Money and height have made him less persuasive. Lean is best when he is giving us the terrified child's perspective on the incomprehensible world. This is in part, as film critics have noticed, by eye-level shots that express young Pip's fear of the adult world, creating a sustained series of images that emphasize the boy's sense of powerlessness.

In fact, it was Lean's original plan to build two completely different sets for Satis House on different scales. The original screenplay (now housed at the UCLA Theatre Arts library) states, when Pip returns to Satis House from London for the first time, "The set is smaller than when last seen in Pip's childhood." (They did not actually build the two sets, by the way, but achieved the effects through use of camera angle, lighting, and other methods less extravagant.) The two sets are the two halves of Lean's story. In the first half females dwarf males. In the second males recapture the scale. These effects allow for the psychological experience particular to film whereby the audience's and character's perspectives are conflated so that we see what the character feels.

We see this clearly in the scene where Pip watches as Estella sits and knits, reminding us of Madame Defarge. The prose which supplies us with visual images that permit entrance to a depth of character are not delineated by expository detail. Film can be, in the case of this adaptation, true to that quality of description offered by Dickens. The very act of knitting becomes, in Lean's film, a trope for the possibility of feminine cruelty. Knitting is anything but cozily domestic. What you have is a woman with weapons who can strike at any time; the acceptably feminine is a cover to outwit the dim and masculine.

So we associate Estella with locks, gates, windows, all sorts of barriers, as well as with those artifacts also associated with Miss Havisham, such as candles, white garments, jewelry. Pip, Herbert, Joe, and even Magwitch are outdoors: running along the marshes, walking the streets of the city, rowing on the Thames. Miss Havisham is seen indoors exclusively, Estella almost exclusively, except for the scenes I mentioned. Yes, Biddy is an exception here as she is everywhere else, and we have glimpses of her outdoors. It bears mentioning, however, that Lean shows her outdoors only while tethered to domestic tasks, such as hanging washing on a line.

For the most part, then, women have nothing to do with nature and everything to do with artifice, with the creation of another, parallel, hothouse nature. Miss Havisham seems to derive her power from swaddling her own pain, from feeding off the dark feelings in her own heart, wrapping herself in a web of misery the way that the spider crawling on her bridal cake and missal covers them with its own cloying gauze. Lean's film emphasizes her enclosed and trapped feeling as well as the sense that whatever Miss Havisham creates, she creates out of her own bile and waste.

The most glaring change from novel to film is, of course, Lean's alteration of the ending. We know that Dickens himself had enough trouble attempting to decide on a suitable ending for the book. His ambivalence about the ending has been well remarked. He originally wrote an ending which had a middle-aged, slightly shabby, and unmarried Pip encounter the middle-aged, divorced, and slightly battered Estella on the London streets, both of them now solitary, dispirited, disillusioned. He then allowed his fellow novelist Bulwer-Lytton to persuade him to exchange that ending for another, in which a still youthful Pip encounters a still beautiful Estella in the grounds of what had been Satis House. They leave the ruined garden together in a passage that deliberately echoes the ending of *Paradise Lost*, Pip telling us that he sees "no shadow of a future parting." Rather than using either of Dickens's endings, Lean inserted his own. The result feels as if someone has switched the channel, so to speak, from *Great Expectations* to *Wuthering Heights* or Danielle Steele. Suddenly we have Pip saying "You are part of my existence, part of myself...we belong to each other, let's start again," etc., instead of hearing "I saw no shadow of another parting from her." Not only is Estella unmarried, but she has been jilted (like Miss Havisham), unwilling to acknowledge the passage of time (like Miss Havisham), locking herself up in Satis House to avoid the world (like Miss Havisham).

Twentieth-century film audiences were even more conservative and demanding than nineteenth-century novel readers. Lean produces a final scene with both a happy ending, and interestingly, a virgin bride. In the novel, we recall, Estella had married and subsequently separated from her husband, the slimy Bentley Drummle. In the film, she comes to Pip broken-hearted but with everything else intact. Apparently a reading public nearly ninety years earlier than the late-1940s film audience was tolerant enough to accept Estella as Pip's future wife despite the fact that she had been married, divorced, and widowed.

In Lean's film, Estella has returned to be with Miss Havisham, who she claims is still a forceful presence in the house. It is interesting to note that Estella's back is to the camera for the entire first part of the scene. The film then cuts to a long shot. The total effect of all this is to eradicate the individuality of Estella and make it easier to see her as Miss Havisham. In rescuing her, Pip gives Estella back a chance at her own identity, the film implies, and we see Estella's face when she is in Pip's arms. Paradoxically, this scene perhaps offers the most significant piece of evidence suggesting that Pip is promiscuous in his attempt to be all things to all people. We sense that Pip, as both adult and child, is constantly performing a personality to win over his presumed audience. Pip becomes a hero in this ending scene, finally and truly in Lean's screenplay, rescuing Estella from her conditioning by ripping down the curtains and allowing the light to enter the dismal chamber, to rousing music, crying: "I have come back to let in the sunlight!"

Estella breaks away from the most important relationship of her life, ultimately choosing Pip over Miss Havisham. Natural replaces unnatural as light replaces darkness, but the transformation must also make Estella into an ordinary young woman romping about with an ordinary young man instead of setting her up as another Snow Queen or mistress of destiny. Then, very much echoing images of children running away from big bad houses, Estella and Pip flee through the gate into the quotidian world where time has meaning, back into a world of mortality (when clocks tick, time passes), daily routines, and no particularly great expectations.

Such is the ambiguity of even the most happy of endings.

4   *Great Expectations* on Australian television

John O. Jordan

I begin with two quotations. The first is from the opening paragraph of an essay by postcolonial theorist, Homi Bhabha. Bhabha writes:

There is a scene in the cultural writings of English colonialism which repeats so insistently after the early nineteenth century – and, through that repetition, so triumphantly *inaugurates* a literature of empire – that I am bound to repeat it once more. It is the scenario, played out in the wild and wordless wastes of colonial India, Africa, the Caribbean, of the sudden, fortuitous discovery of the English book. It is, like all myths of origin, memorable for its balance between epiphany and enunciation. The discovery of the book is, at once, a moment of originality and authority. It is, as well, a process of displacement that, paradoxically, makes the presence of the book wondrous to the extent to which it is repeated, translated, misread, displaced. It is with the emblem of the English book – "signs taken for wonders" – as an insignia of colonial authority and a signifier of colonial desire and discipline that I want to begin this chapter. (Bhabha 1993: 102)

Bhabha proceeds to give several examples illustrating the scenario of the "English book." The most famous of these is the passage from Conrad's *Heart of Darkness* in which the narrator, Marlow, discovers an English manual of seamanship in the middle of the jungle and takes moral support from its evidence of reason and ordered civility, so different from the waking nightmare that he experiences in the African interior.

My second quotation is an anecdote that, apart from its value as a curious instance of nineteenth-century reading practices, could easily be added to the list of examples that Bhabha cites in his essay. It comes from a nineteenth-century memoir written by an Englishman, James Demarr, who, for nearly twelve months during 1841–2, worked at a remote cattle station in the outback of southeastern Australia along the Devil's River. One of the hardships Demarr records from this period is the absence of reading material. Occasionally, he reports, a several-month-old newspaper would arrive at the station and be eagerly devoured, but, to his dismay, there were no books. He then goes on to explain how this situation dramatically changed for the better.

But at last one of the men rode in from the head station, and, with a joyful countenance, handed to me Charles Dickens's "Nicholas Nickleby," all the more welcome because I had never read it.

Now we were happy; and that night I commenced reading it to my companions, who were delighted . . .

The book, as a matter of course, was always read at night, and the hut was full of attentive listeners. The nights were cold and frosty, but we always had a glorious log fire, and our only light to read by, was the usual one, a piece of twisted rag stuck into a pint tin full of melted fat. It would have delighted the heart of a philanthropist to have seen how these fellows enjoyed the reading of this book . . . To them it was a real life history, and their sympathies were all with the honest and good characters in the story. Two of the listeners came from a station seven miles distant, but as all could not leave their stations, I agreed to read it a second time in order that those who were by necessity prevented from hearing it the first time, might experience the same enjoyment.

. . . So strong an impression did the incidents in this book make upon the minds of those who heard it read, that before I left, calves and puppies, and tame pet birds, were named after the characters in "Nicholas Nickleby." (Demarr 1893: 119–20)

Clearly, here is another instance of the inaugural power of the English colonial book, complete with its comic version of the naming of the animals in the garden of Eden.

On the basis of these two quotations and without attempting to offer any further evidence by way of support, I wish to propose two related hypotheses that will frame the rest of my remarks. First, insofar as there is any single English writer who embodies, with respect to Australia, the cultural authority and originary enunciative power that Bhabha describes in his essay – and who provokes the accompanying ambivalent colonial response – that writer is Charles Dickens. Second, insofar as there is any single text that can be said to function, for Australia, in the way that the "English book" does in Bhabha's prototypical scenario, that text is *Great Expectations*.

The shadow of Dickens falls heavily across Australian literary and cultural production of the past two centuries. Traces of Dickens can be found in many Australian texts, from Marcus Clark's nineteenth-century classic, *His Natural Life*, to Carmel Bird's postmodern gothic romance, *The Bluebird Café*. The impact of *Great Expectations* in particular can be traced most directly in three relatively recent Australian works: Michael Noonan's 1982 sequel, entitled *Magwitch*; the six-hour Australian Broadcasting Corporation television series, entitled *Great Expectations: The Untold Story* (1987); and Peter Carey's prize-winning novel, *Jack Maggs* (1998). Although the versions of *Great Expectations* by Noonan and Carey are of considerable interest, in the remainder of this essay I shall focus on *Great Expectations: The Untold Story*.

Written and directed by Tim Burstall, one of the country's leading producer-directors and an important figure in the Australian film industry since the 1970s, *Great Expectations: The Untold Story* is at once an adaptation of Dickens's novel and an imaginative expansion of it. As its subtitle indicates, it undertakes to recover the "untold" portions of the novel – essentially, the story of Magwitch's years in New South Wales. In this effort, it resembles Noonan's *Magwitch*, although it takes a very different approach to its subject. Unlike *Magwitch*, it is not a sequel, but a full-scale retelling that moves back and forth between the narrative of Pip's growing-up and events that occur simultaneously to Magwitch in the colony.

Burstall's script retains the basic armature of Dickens's story, from Pip's childhood encounter with the escaped convict on the marshes to Magwitch's return and recapture by the authorities. However, the film's inclusion of new material requires a considerable reapportioning of narrative time and space. Of its six hours' total running time, roughly one hour derives directly from Dickens's text. And while the scenes based on the novel stick fairly closely to their source, Burstall does not hesitate to change some elements in the story when it suits his larger purpose. In its willingness to take liberties with the "English book," the film differs once again from Noonan's *Magwitch*, which remains much more closely tied to its Dickensian source.

Burstall's larger purpose in revising *Great Expectations* is nothing less than an attempt to dramatize the founding of the nation. In this ambitious project, it participates not only in a long tradition of fictional, cinematic, and historical accounts of Australian nationhood but also in a specific context leading up to and culminating in the Australian Bicentenary celebrations of 1988. Appearing in the same year as the publication of *The Fatal Shore*, Robert Hughes's bestselling history of the convict settlement of Australia, and one year before the reenactment of the arrival of the First Fleet in Sydney harbor, with its attendant media fanfare, *Great Expectations: The Untold Story* belongs to a moment of heightened national self-consciousness in which the figure of the transported convict and the place of convictism generally in the life of the nation became newly available for imaginative and discursive investigation.

In its attempt to rewrite *Great Expectations* as a narrative of Australian nationhood, the film takes Magwitch as its central focus. Accordingly, it begins, not with the famous graveyard encounter on the marshes, but with the scenes of Magwitch's arrest, trial, and sentencing that precede his imprisonment on and subsequent escape from the prison "hulks." These scenes are significant in establishing from the outset the relatively petty nature of Magwitch's criminal offense and his position as the victim not only of Compeyson's more culpable machinations, but of a fundamental class bias within the British criminal justice system. As in the novel, Magwitch, being the older and hence presumably more hardened criminal, is sentenced to fourteen years' imprisonment, while the genteel Compeyson receives only half this sentence.

Unlike the novel, however, the film presents Jaggers as Magwitch's barrister and gives him a thematically important courtroom speech in which he argues that, contrary to appearances, Magwitch is the "natural gentleman" of the two and Compeyson the "natural rogue." Whereas in the novel it is chiefly through the figure of Joe that the idea of the natural gentleman – and the contrast with the "made" or artificial gentleman, Pip – is developed, in the film it is Magwitch who embodies this theme from the beginning and who, despite his subsequent links to criminal and other "low" environments, retains this identity until the end.

The themes of class conflict and injustice sounded in this opening sequence continue once Magwitch arrives in Australia. After the compulsory graveyard, food-stealing, and recapture episodes involving Pip that motivate the rest of the story have been established, the film follows Magwitch on a convict ship to New South Wales and installs him in a penal colony. There he undergoes brutal mistreatment and flogging from his tyrannical warders and from a particularly sadistic trustee named Tooth. Sympathy for the convicts is established by showing them as an oppressed class and depicting episodes of homosocial solidarity or "mateship," including Magwitch's kindness toward a young Irish convict who is condemned to die. In a flashback scene at the end of the first hour's installment, Magwitch remembers his own childhood and, recalling Pip's kindness to him on the marshes, undergoes what we take to be a conversion experience, complete with vibrato background music and close-up shots of the convict's rough but smiling features. From this point on, Magwitch's essential goodness will never be in question.

A second major change that the film makes in the original story is to have Compeyson turn up in Australia along with Magwitch. In fact, Compeyson's continued scheming and Magwitch's often ineffectual attempts to counter or forestall him comprise the bulk of the remainder of the film, up to and almost including the final scenes. The Compeyson–Magwitch opposition provides the basic structural binary of the film and extends the underlying class issues set forth in the opening scenes. For example, in another test of mateship, Magwitch refuses an offer of freedom extended by the prison commander if he agrees to serve as hangman for a group of condemned criminals that includes the young Irishman he had befriended. Compeyson, however, readily accepts the offer, hangs his "mates," and goes free.

Two years later, Magwitch is released from prison on probation and is "assigned" as an unpaid laborer to the estate of a wealthy landowner and free settler named Tankerton. The scene of Magwitch's release from prison has iconic significance comparable to the facial close-up of the earlier "conversion" scene. Magwitch emerges from the prison clean-shaven and trimly attired in boots, bandanna, and a broad-brimmed hat, free from the menacing filth and grime of the penal colony and the hulks. Moreover, he has acquired a distinct Australian accent. In effect, he has become a version of the ideal national type – the rugged frontiersman with his "open manly simplicity of character" (quoted in Ward 1958: 63) who is mythologized in many early Australian narratives and who acquires canonical formulation in historian Russel Ward's well-known study, *The Australian Legend*.

Ward argues that "the" [*sic*] Australian national character, with its comradely independence based on group solidarity, its distrust of authority, and its rough and ready capacity for improvisation, sprang largely from a confluence of convict, working-class, Irish, and native-born sources. Ward's thesis has been widely criticized as (among other things) essentialist, masculinist, and too narrowly focused on Anglo-Celtic culture. Despite the limitations of this construction of Australian national identity, the Magwitch of *Great Expectations: The Untold Story* conforms closely to the "type" described in Ward's book.

A major subplot in the story involves Compeyson's seduction of and eventual elopement with Tankerton's daughter, the only heir to his estate. As Compeyson's former accomplice and fellow prisoner, Magwitch is torn between the convict's code of silence about past criminal activities and loyalty to his generous master, to whom he stands in a relationship of devoted and faithful service. Magwitch eventually chooses loyalty to his master, but not in time to prevent Compeyson from winning the daughter's affections. Interestingly, Magwitch never emerges as a sexual rival to Compeyson. Indeed, another striking feature of Magwitch's character is his chaste demeanor. We learn that he longs for domestic happiness, but that he remains loyal to Molly, the wife from his "broomstick marriage" back in England more than twenty years before.

Magwitch's goodness renders him an almost entirely passive figure through much of the middle of the film. Were it not for the chance he is given to fight with Tooth, who reappears, Orlick-like, as Compeyson's henchman, Magwitch would have difficulty retaining his place as the film's protagonist. As Compeyson's accomplice, Tooth in effect replaces Magwitch in this role and becomes his filmic double. Tooth's grimy face and generally scruffy appearance link him visually to the penal-colony scenes earlier in the film and contrast strikingly with Magwitch's trim outfit and freshly scrubbed look. The dirt of criminality appears to have been washed from Magwitch and to have settled conveniently on the person of his villainous opponent.

Eventually, Magwitch serves out his sentence and begins to acquire property of his own. He discovers gold, inherits Tankerton's estate, and becomes a wealthy sheep-farmer. However, as an "emancipist" or former convict, he is still held in disrespect by many free settlers. Meanwhile, as Magwitch prospers in Australia, back in England Pip broadens his experience of the world. We see him visiting Miss Havisham, fascinated by Estella, and bound as an apprentice at the forge. Significantly, Pip remains a child throughout this sequence of events and well into the fourth hour of the film's serialization, with the same cute, tow-headed actor continuing to play his part. The fact that he remains a child for so long into the film makes it easier for the viewer to accept Magwitch's nostalgic idealization of the orphan boy and lends plausibility to his project of sending the money that will allow Pip to rise above his station.

In fact, Pip turns out not to be such a bad sort after all. The film devotes scant attention to portraying his moral deterioration, and he therefore stands in little need of rehabilitation at the end. Although momentarily deluded by his dreams of Estella and the life of genteel extravagance in London, he is quickly won over by the earnestness and probity of the returned convict. After only a brief moment of snobbish reluctance, he soon joins in the plans to help his benefactor escape and avoid the snares set for him by Compeyson, who has also returned to London.

With Magwitch's return to England, the film begins to move toward an end. In so doing, it rejoins more directly the plot of the novel, and, as a result, both similarities and differences between the two become more apparent. One area in which the film makes several interesting changes is in its treatment of romantic and sexual relations. If Magwitch remains chaste all the time he is in Australia, other characters in the film prove to have been more sexually active than they are shown to be in the novel. We learn that Compeyson and Miss Havisham have been lovers and that Molly has been the mistress, not just the housekeeper, of Mr. Jaggers. In a surprising turn of events, Molly learns from Compeyson that her "broomstick" husband has been alive all these years and that Jaggers is responsible for concealing this information from her. This news leads to a confrontation in which she denounces Jaggers, refuses to continue sharing his bed, and declares in the strongest terms her loyalty to Magwitch, thus preparing the way for an eventual reconciliation between them. Meanwhile, in a parallel development, Estella learns the story of her birth and, as a result, breaks off her engagement with Drummle, leaving a fresh opening for Pip.

The film's ending contains its deepest surprise and its most radical departure from its Dickensian source. After the failed escape plot and Magwitch's recapture, we witness a touching hospital scene in which first Molly and Estella and then Pip bid farewell to the dying Magwitch. As he leaves, Pip confirms that he has booked passage for himself and for the two women on a ship bound for New South Wales. Next we see a simple wooden coffin being loaded onto a wagon. The film then shifts abruptly to a stagecoach and the sound of laughing voices. Inside are Jaggers and Wemmick, but the reason for their laughter only gradually becomes clear. As they chuckle about body-snatching and doctors making false declarations, the camera cuts to the third passenger in the coach. It is Magwitch, on his way to join Pip, Molly, and Estella at the seaport.

The joke here is not only on the authorities, who have been fooled by the lawyer's clever trick, but also on the viewer-reader who already "knows" the ending to the novel and has been caught out by the film's unexpected final twist. For viewers familiar with the conventions of Victorian fiction, there is an added dimension to the film's surprise ending. Shipping unwanted characters off to the colonies at the end of the story is a familiar device in nineteenth-century English novels. However, in a film that aims to dramatize Australian nationhood, this device has quite a different meaning. Rather than expelling Magwitch and the others as undesirables within English civil society, the film embraces them and sends them home (in Magwitch's case) or (in that of the others) to their proper desti-nation. Nor do they return penniless. Whereas in Noonan's *Magwitch* the colonial gold ends up back in England, Burstall's film makes sure that Pip carries off with him to Australia a strongbox stuffed with banknotes and other portable property.

The film makes light of Magwitch's criminal past and confirms him as the "natural gentleman" proclaimed by Jaggers at the outset. He is an Australian gentleman, moreover. His flat vowels and elided consonants stand in marked contrast to the English voices in every speaking context. He not only sounds distinctly Australian; he also embodies many of the "typical" Australian qualities proclaimed by Russel Ward: mateship, ingenuity, and defiance of authority. The idea of Australia as a community of virtuous law-breakers even wins the endorsement of Jaggers and Wemmick, the film's final homosocial pair, who jokingly suggest in the stagecoach that they may end their careers as transports to New South Wales.

As a narrative of nationhood, *Great Expectations: The Untold Story* provides a selective and rather sanitized account of Australian convictism. In so doing, it not only repeats aspects of the Australian legend, with Magwitch as its idealized national type, but it manages to skirt other, more conflictual issues that came increasingly into focus as the 1988 Bicentenary approached. Although it does a good job of addressing problems of class conflict and injustice, both in England and in the colony, it does not attempt to deal with issues of multiculturalism, Aboriginal land rights, or the status of women – though Molly's denunciation of Jaggers may represent a partial exception with respect to the last of these. Generically, the film negotiates between its literary debt to Dickens and its cinematic debt to Hollywood. Its Australian sections in particular, with their bushrangers, saloons, and choreographed fight scenes, owe much to Hollywood westerns, but always with a local inflection.

As a postcolonial revision of *Great Expectations*, the film makes a stronger intervention than Noonan's *Magwitch*. It writes back against the "English book" both by virtue of the changes it makes in Dickens's plot, especially the ending, and by its affirmation of distinctively Australian qualities as opposed to those of the dominant, English-identified group. The film pays homage to Dickens through its faithful adaptation of many scenes from the novel as well as through its use in a new medium of Dickens's characteristic formal mode: serial presentation. At the same time, however, it departs productively from its source, resituating Dickens's novel more firmly in a global context and forcing it to speak, along with its most memorable character, in a different accent. Or, to put it more directly in Bhabha's terms, *Great Expectations: The Untold Story* confirms the inaugural power of the English book while at the same time enacting its transcultural displacement.

REFERENCES

Great Expectations: The Untold Story. 1987. Written and directed by Tim Burstall. Australian Broadcasting Corporation.
Bhabha, Homi. 1993. *The Location of Culture*. London: Routledge.
Demarr, James. 1893. *Adventures in Australia Fifty Years Ago*. London: Swan Sonnenhein.
Ward, Russel. 1958. *The Australian Legend*. Melbourne: Oxford University Press.

5   Dickens's "The Signalman" and Rubini's *La stazione*

Alessandro Vescovi

Only recently has Italian academic criticism started to produce significant studies of Charles Dickens's fiction. Yet, despite this lack of academic attention, Dickens has proved a strong seller in the Italian marketplace. Writing recently on Dickens and the Italian cultural scene, Carlo Pagetti has listed a number of novelists, from Edmondo de Amicis to Italo Calvino, who owe something to Dickens (in Bonadei and de Stasio 2000: 13–30). Francesco Casotti even claims that "in Italy Dickens is not only popular but . . . he has become also a permanent feature of the Italian cultural background" (1999: 22). So far nobody has tried to explain why a Victorian writer can be so popular in Italy, where Trollope or, to a lesser extent, George Eliot are almost unknown. I suspect it depends on the fact that Dickens is often considered a children's novelist. In fact, with the exceptions of Collodi and Salgari, whose pirate stories are considered unfit for girls, Italian literature lacks children's novels. Dickens is therefore often resorted to as a present for boys and girls on their tenth to fifteenth birthdays. In Dickensian characters Italian teenagers can find a dramatization of adult life in a reassuringly faraway world. Once grown up, Dickens's characters enter the Italian cultural metabolism and become archetypes, the "permanent feature" mentioned by Casotti. It is probably no coincidence that the other Victorian bestseller in Italy is Lewis Carroll.

    The best known instance of this popularity is Carlo Fruttero and Franco Lucentini's 1989 comic rewriting of *The Mystery of Edwin Drood* as their novel, *La verità sul caso D.*, a popular success also in its English translation, *The D. Case* (1992). Dickens's popularity has also extended to film. In 1997 Paolo Virzì directed the prize-winning *Ovosodo*, which, though set in the 1990s in the Tuscan port city of Livorno, explicitly acknowledges its debt to *Great Expectations*. With *The D. Case* and *Ovosodo* I want to group Sergio Rubini's highly acclaimed 1990 film *La stazione*. Starring Margherita Buy and Ennio Fantastichini, the film won the Fipresci Prize in Venice (1990) and also the Kodak Cinecritica Prize. In English-speaking countries it was released as *The Station* in 1991. The connection between the film and Dickens's story was first drawn to my attention by Marialuisa Bignami.

Though an original story, *La stazione* bears a striking resemblance to Dickens's best known *Mugby Junction* story, "Branch Line no. 1. The Signalman." The relationship between *La stazione* and "The Signalman" can be paralleled to that between Chaplin's *City Lights* and Dickens's Christmas story "The Cricket on the Hearth." In each case the films use some elements of the original Dickensian story, but reset the material in modern times with a plot of their own devising. In the case of *La stazione* the resemblances center on the shared railway setting, the thematic focus on cross-class encounter, and a set of details and incidents common to both Dickens's narrative and the film's drama.

Italian cinema in the last two decades tends to be treated as a period of decadence in contrast to the heyday of the 1960s and 70s when Fellini, Antonioni, and Visconti were producing canonical masterworks like *8½, Blow Up,* and *Death in Venice*. The heritage of those masters was heavy. Only a few productions in the last twenty years, notably Olmi's *La leggenda del santo bevitore* (Legend of the Holy Drinker, 1988) and Amelio's *Il ladro di bambini* (The Children Snatcher, 1992), are generally allowed to have something of the cachet of the old masters. But both were low-budget films, which did not achieve the vast success they deserved. Critics tend to connect the decline of Italian cinema with the birth of commercial television. In fact, the national film industry has recently started to invest in the more rewarding TV fiction, and carefully avoids the risk of experimenting with new ideas. As a result, the most recent generation of directors has been forced to find its own way in new directions, most notably in comedy, not rarely with enticing results. Comedy has, of course, always been the genre that propped up the Italian national film industry. But recently humor tends to surface even in overtly tragic stories. The best known instance of this tendency is Roberto Benigni's 1997 Oscar-winner, *La vita è bella* (Life is Beautiful) which achieved enormous renown. But the same comic emphasis can also be seen in the work of less internationally well-known directors like Nanni Moretti and Gabriele Salvatores – another Oscar-winner, thanks to *Mediterraneo* (1990).

La stazione stems from the same milieu. Rubini, thanks to the financial help granted by Italian law to "first works," adapted the story from a successful play of the same title by Umberto Marino, who also contributed to the screenplay. The principal actors in the film, Buy, Fantastichini, and Rubini himself, had also performed in Marino's stage version. The performers' characteristic light humor marks one of the significant differences between the film and Dickens's short story.

"The Signalman" is one of the most reprinted and reviewed of Dickens's short stories and was originally published in the Christmas issue of *All the Year Round* in 1866, entitled *Mugby Junction*. What is noteworthy is that Dickens himself had narrowly escaped death in a railway accident a couple of years before he wrote this story (which is not the only one dealing with railway casualties in *Mugby Junction*), and that the incident was probably due to a signalman's carelessness. This biographical information explains why, unlike other Dickensian revenants, the signalman's ghost appears in a bleak and tragic situation, exciting no laughter on the part of the reader. The protagonist of the story is a railway clerk who works in a "lonesome post" in a "deep trench" (Dickens 1985: 79), along a railway line and is haunted by a ghost. Such a phantom seems always to appear in coincidence with a fatal accident, as we learn from the distressed man's words. The narrator descends to visit the signalman three times on three different nights and upon his third call he finds the corpse of the signalman "cut down by an engine" (89). What strikes the narrator is that the driver of the fatal locomotive makes the same gestures and speaks the same words that the signalman had attributed to the ghost.

Dickens sees in the alienating work a real specter that threatens the life of the signalman and describes it with the conventional ghost-story machinery. Marino uses a different plot for the same theme, a theme for which Dickens's example holds true after more than 120 years. What is remarkable is that Marino uses an early Dickensian character to play the role of the protagonist. Like Fruttero and Lucentini's *Edwin Drood*, the bleak situation finds an outlet in a comic treatment of the subject. Domenico is comic and sad at the same time and with the simplicity of a Dickensian Barkis wins Flavia's heart. In fact the station-master has the mannerisms that are ascribed to the most famous Dickensian characters. He speaks with a strong regional accent, frowns, does everything in the most methodical way. When he talks to the woman he behaves exactly like Joe Gargery would. Danilo, the villain, is a kind of Uriah Heep, a social climber who woos a rich man's daughter. The unhappy ending of the film could not go so far as to see him succeed. He fails as Uriah did, thanks to the courage of the signalman, who does not die, but will live on, almost as tragically, with his useless grind.

La stazione is set in a lonesome place in Puglia, the nearest village being four kilometers away. Most trains just go by and never stop. Since the film derives from a play, unity of place and time is largely respected in the plot, which covers the events of one night. Domenico, the station-master, works alone and spends his night beside the fire, trying to kill time by learning German and timing small events that punctuate his night duty. Outside, the pouring rain beats incessantly, the noise never ceases and remains in the background even during indoor dialogues. The plot is rather simple: Flavia, a beautiful young woman from Rome in an evening dress, runs away from the party at a nearby villa as she overhears a conversation that makes her understand that her fiancé, Danilo, is aiming at her father's money. She would like to leave, but the next train will only be arriving the following morning at six a.m. The abandoned man, seeing his scheme endangered, drives to the station and tries to persuade Flavia to return to the villa, where they are expected. She refuses to follow him and remains at the station. Flavia and Domenico are thus forced to spend a few hours together and make each other's acquaintance during the night. Eventually Danilo appears again, probably drunk, and becomes violent, even trying to kill the station-master, who had helped Flavia to resist him. The station-master is smaller and weaker, but more cunning and luckier and takes the upper hand. Time has come by now for Flavia to take her train to Rome and leave.

Though sharing the same plot, several differences separate the film from the play. Domenico is more or less the same in both. But the film lays more emphasis on his television, a symbol of contemporary trash culture, as well as on his family, his mother, and girlfriend. Flavia and Danilo, however, are significantly altered. They quarrel for different reasons in the film. Originally their split was due to a pornographic film Danilo was watching at the party. In the film there is no mention of pornography. Instead, the break is motivated by Flavia's realization that Danilo is really using her to get at her father's money.

But plot is not the key element in *La stazione*, just as it is relatively insignificant in Dickens's story. In both, it is the railwayman himself who forms the main feature. It is worth noting in this context that none of the changes from play to film concerns the station-master and his job. In fact, the film preserves everything the play took from Dickens, retaining the railwayman as the core around whom distinctly secondary characters are plotted. In all three, story, play, film, what is central is the meeting of two classes. In Dickens those classes are represented by the socially higher narrator and the lower railwayman. In the play and the film, dramatized, not narrated, the narrator's function is taken over by Flavia, whom the station-master respectfully addresses as *signorina*. But in all three, the interest rests with the railwayman and his world. Both the narrator and Flavia belong to worlds outside the railway station, worlds that are referenced but not described, significant only as positions from which the real subject, the railway world, may be perceived.

Dickens's narrator describes himself thus: "In me, he merely saw a man who had been shut up within narrow limits all his life, and who, being at last set free, had a newly-awakened interest in these great works" (79). In fact the original reader of *Mugby Junction* knows from the start that the narrator is a kind of *flâneur* who has suddenly decided to stop at Mugby on a rainy night and to report some of the stories he had come across there. About Flavia, similarly, we learn only that she is the daughter of a banker and that she makes pottery: both pieces of information, like other details of her life, merely function to create a contrast with the station-master's own life. At a certain point, for instance, a train passes by on its way to Frankfurt and Domenico explains how his own father planned to go there to visit a German friend with whom he had fought during the war. The old man never went, but his son says that he will one day. Flavia, who has studied in a German school in Rome, knows the city and patronizes Domenico's inexperience. Later she wonders how it can be that all the postcards in the office come from Italian spa towns. The reason is that travel expenses to such places are covered by the national health service, Domenico explains humbly, much to the astonishment of the woman.

The strongest resemblances between the film and Dickens's story center on the life of the workingman. He is always seen at sunset, or during the night. Dickens describes his workplace as a "deep cutting" (79) with water dripping down the steep walls. A zigzag path leads from top to bottom, where the sleepers run. On one side of the line stands the "massive architecture" of a tunnel with a "gloomy red light" (79). On the other side the railway disappears in the dark. *La stazione* is also set in the middle of nowhere. The few trains appear out of the dark and disappear as they came. The camera eye and ear underlie their almost supernatural apparition in various ways, with slow-motion, low-degree shooting and uncanny sounds. Moreover, the man beside a train is always viewed as a small object endangered by the huge black form. There is even a sequence, when the station-master runs toward a train to switch the points in order to put it on another line, where it seems that the train might overrun the man. During this desperate run the noises blur and the train is hardly visible in the mist by which it is surrounded. Similarly, Dickens's narrator does not describe the death of the signalman from his point of view, but from the train driver's, according to which it is likely that the doomed signalman's senses failed to perceive the coming of the fatal machine, the same impression the spectator gets from the points scene.

The train produces on Flavia and on the spectator exactly the same sense of fear as described by Dickens's narrator: "a vague vibration in the earth and air, quickly changing into a violent pulsation, and an oncoming rush that caused me to start back, as though it had force to draw me down" (78). Both in the short story and in the film, these are metaphors of how the machine overpowers man.

In both Dickens and Rubini the signalman is scrupulously exact in the discharge of his duties: Dickens writes that "No man in England knew his work better" (89), while a colleague of Domenico asks him "How can you say that? You are always so very accurate." Both men seem to enjoy their talk with the unexpected guest, but always keep an eye on their instruments and always control what happens on the line. Very often they are interrupted by a ring or a blinking red light and have to make signals to passing trains and communicate with other invisible stations, the only difference being the use of telephone instead of the telegraph.

Both protagonists are compelled by the monotonous routine of their work to seek diversion in learning a foreign language. Dickens ironically comments "If only to know it by sight, and to have formed his own crude ideas of its pronunciation, could be called learning it" (80). And the film shows us that process. Domenico sits in front of an old-fashioned German grammar-book and spells slowly with a strong Italian accent: "*Tonis Mutter ist eine Frau.*" Having accomplished the task of reading, the man proceeds to translate: "Tony's mother is a woman" and then reads the next line: "*Tonis Vater ist nicht eine Frau*" and slowly translates "Tony's father is not a woman," upon which he comments: "Hardly surprising, being the father."

The difference between the narrator's ironic dismissal of the station-master's efforts and Rubini's comic exemplification typifies the difference in tone between the story and the film. Dickens's story insists on the bleak and gloomy atmosphere of the signalman's world and work. But Rubini's station-master is more like Sam Weller, to whose social class he belongs, than the Dickensian signalman, educated "above his station" though he had "misused his opportunities" (81). In part, this change in register comes from the way in which the new dramatic plot affects the original tale. Marino and Rubini deploy humor to deflate the potential for a princess–pauper romance between heiress and workman. And the film prefers its unhappy ending to the predictable romantic closure even at the cost of implausibility. It is unlikely that Flavia would actually be permitted to leave as she does without being questioned by the police: Danilo is left unconscious on the floor after a fierce fight. But the film could not keep Domenico and Flavia together any longer without becoming melodramatic. The ghost plot did not have this problem, but it did exact a death. The short story heaps together a number of oppressive elements concerning the work, the setting, and the mysterious apparitions. As the narration flows toward the end, the only outcome that is consistent with the climactic development is the death of the railwayman.

The shift from ironic to comic, even farcical, representation also surfaces in Domenico's already mentioned hyper-precision and watchfulness. Both railwaymen have to make entries in certain ledgers and respond to the call of mysterious red lights that flash from time to time. While the signalman is portrayed as a serious man earnestly discharging his duties, Domenico becomes comic because of the enormous energy he puts into comparatively easy work. Answering Flavia's questions about the timetable, he lists a number of trains with their departure platform, midway stations, and final destinations in a single breath, a most exhilarating scene. Domenico does not realize how comic he is. The overall effect is humorous at first and bitter upon afterthought, like other Dickensian situations, such as the blind girl's naivety in "The Cricket on the Hearth," whose innate goodness and chronic blindness make her think that her father is rich and respected and that the despotic landlord is a kind, good-hearted man.

Dickens's railwayman responds to Marxian analysis. He is alienated from his work and this alienation is the deep cause of his death. Though he does his best, he knows he will not be able to avoid the casualty on the line. Moreover, he is not in command of his actions, which are decided by bells and flashing lights (Vescovi in Bonadei and de Stasio 2000: 111–22). In Rubini's film the protagonist is also alienated by work that he feels to be completely useless. In a dramatic sequence he says that he has tried to alter some of his duties. Nothing has happened in response, but he was reported. "If you make a mistake you get reported, but as for usefulness, your work has none." These words, the most dramatic in the film, are not very different from those pronounced by Dickens's distressed signalman, when he feels powerless in front of the impending accident:

"If I telegraph Danger, on either side of me, or on both, I can give no reason for it," he went on, wiping the palms of his hands. "I should get into trouble, and do no good. They would think I was mad. This is the way it would work, – Message: 'Danger! Take care!' Answer: 'What Danger? Where?' Message: 'Don't know. But, for God's sake, take care!' They would displace me. What else could they do?" (87)

Though certainly not new and revolutionary as it was in mid-Victorian times, the train is still one of the biggest machines we daily encounter in Italy, where trains remain the commonest means of transportation after the car. The railway is therefore apt to symbolize the power of technology over man. In Italian imagery the train often figures as a symbol of the uncanny or even of evil. In the nineteenth century young Giosue Carducci, who would become the first Italian Nobel Prize winner in 1906, wrote an "Inno a Satana" (Hymn to Satan, 1863) whose protagonist is the diabolical train. In 1972 the popular Italian singer Francesco Guccini recorded a ballad "La locomotiva," where the steam engine is called a "strange monster" and paralleled to a "young colt." In addition, in Italy, building model trains is one of the most popular hobbies. I know no man between twenty and forty who did not own a model train as a child. Thus trains, both beloved and feared, are particularly apt to be used in Italy as ambivalent symbols. In such a context Dickens can at the same time model the sort of light humor advocated by the escapism of contemporary Italian film, and yet also serve to satirize the evils of contemporary social life.

REFERENCES

Bonadei, Rossana and Clotilde de Stasio. 2000. *Dickens: The Craft of Fiction and the Challenges of Reading*. Milano: Unicopli.

Casotti, Francesco. 1999. "Italian Translations of Dickens." *The Dickensian* 95: 19–23.

Dickens, Charles. 1985. *Selected Short Fiction*. Harmondsworth: Penguin.

Pagetti, Carlo. 2000. "Hard Times / Heart Times / Art Times: Carlo Dickens's Moral Fable for Our Times." Bonadei and de Stasio 2000: 13–30.

Vescovi, Alessandro. 2000. "The Bagman, the Signalman and Dickens's Short Story." Bonadei and de Stasio 2000: 111–22.

6   Bill Murray's Christmas Carols

Murray Baumgarten

Convention has it that the translator betrays the text: the Italian bon mot
sets *traduttore* (translator) against *traditore* (traitor), finding as the difference the change from *u* to *i*. How much more so, convention notes,
when a classic fiction is turned into a Hollywood film. I want to argue
against this received wisdom, using as my proof-texts two films of the
comedian, Bill Murray. Each film is a translation and adaptation of
Dickens's *A Christmas Carol*: not inferior versions of a sacrosanct original
but powerful reconceptualizations in their own right of Dickens's powerfully theatrical original. *Scrooged* (1988) purges the *Carol* of the Victoriana
customary to adaptations, bringing to twentieth-century life the experiences of healing and renewal commented on by Dickens's early readers.
Murray's later film, *Groundhog Day* (1993), crystallizes the issues of time
and identity of *A Christmas Carol*, just touched on by *Scrooged*. In so doing, *Groundhog Day*, less true to the original narrative, is perhaps truer
to the central themes of Dickens's tale. In them we discover gateways to
Dickens's text hard to come by in other forms.

Scrooged

Scrooged (1988) was directed by Richard Donner, and written by Mitch
Glazer, who later supplied the script for Alfons Cuaron's *Great Expectations* discussed by Pam Katz in chapter 9. His script tells a tale of the
consequences of isolation and separation on the personality of the main
character, Martin Cross, played by Bill Murray. In the course of the story,
we discover that the roots of his inability to relate to others lie in childhood
trauma. When he was five, his mother left home on Christmas Eve as a
result of a fight with his overbearing father. She wishes her son a merry
Christmas, blows him a kiss, and disappears from his life. Young Martin
grows up watching television – what he was doing when his parents had
their family argument – and is hard put to differentiate between his life
and those of the characters he watches. Perhaps for that reason, he is as
an adult an appropriate president for a television studio, an intimidating,

violent executive who wants to terrify viewers into watching the shows he stages for his network.

Cross springs on his staff a promotional video for the network's presentation of *A Christmas Carol*. He has put it together himself, and it represents the acting out of anger that characterizes his view of life. The video consists of a series of violent episodes that recount the political, social, and environmental catastrophes of the era. There is acid rain, a freeway shooting, an airplane in flight blown up by terrorists. These images of mayhem all culminate in the mushroom cloud of an atomic explosion, with Cross's superimposed head narrating, "Don't miss Charles Dickens's *A Christmas Carol*: your life might depend on watching it." The structural irony of the film plays out his statement: Cross's own life is transformed because he watches *A Christmas Carol*. But in his case, seeing cannot become believing until he learns a new way of experiencing visual reality. The master of illusion, Martin Cross, will discover the reality of the repressed through the encounter with the fantastic beings of Dickens's tale and the violent impact of a fired employee, Elliott Lowdermilk (Bob Goldthwait). Lowdermilk, ejected from his office at Cross's command on Christmas Eve, arms himself with a shotgun and seeks revenge.

The psychological exploration of Martin Cross begins with the self-imposed isolation and spiritual alienation central to Dickens's novel. But this Scrooge becomes not withdrawn and miserly, as in the original, but angry and violent. In foregrounding Cross's angry and violent response to experience, *Scrooged* restages Dickens's tale as a strikingly contemporary moral parable. Cross's penchant for violence yields an equal and opposite reaction when he first meets Claire (Karen Allen), the woman with whom he will be reunited in love at the climax. When they meet, she closes the door of a store on him, and he is knocked down. The ensuing lumps on his head produce the nickname she gives him, and Lumpy he will be from this time on. Not only does he dish it out, he has to learn to take his lumps, notably from the Ghost of Christmas Present (Carol Kane). She appears as a pink angel (with significant cleavage) who takes every chance to beat him, sometimes quite savagely. In effect, she softens him up for the transformation that will occur when he discovers his own mortality.

Scrooged stages a doubled psychological reading of Dickens's tale. Not only does the film include sections of film-within-a-film dramatization of *A Christmas Carol*, it also parallels the dramatization with Cross's experience, which adapts Scrooge's. At the film's climax Cross, having discovered a new way of seeing, knowing, and understanding, enters the televised dramatization of Dickens's tale and speaks for its values of generosity, kindness, and connection. Now he acts out all those values and meanings he has consistently undermined through the violence of his earlier behavior. What he has previously manipulated, through his illusion-making power, turns upon him and transforms his understanding of illusion. And Cross's intervention and entrance into the television dramatization of Dickens's tale breaks the boundary between life and art. The film ends with Cross leading the actors, stagehands, and TV crew in song.

Cross's hard-bitten realism, which has motivated all his actions as a violent studio executive manipulating illusion for financial gain, is transformed by his encounter with the Ghosts of Christmas Past, Present, and To Come. His ensuing discovery of his own mortality, made possible through the illusion and fantasy the ghosts provide, transforms him. In leading the cast of the Dickens tale in celebrating Christmas on stage Cross also celebrates his own new identity. As his brother, who is viewing the televised event, comments at the end of the film, Martin Cross has become the King of Christmas. No more "Bah! Humbug!" here. It is a psychological transformation but, even more, a filmic joining of character and audience in a visual and auditory expression of communal connection. In this way, *Scrooged* moves from generic violence to generic musical theater. Through the doubled tale a dominating anger has been healed, and an isolated character has found connection.

Groundhog Day

Groundhog Day (1993), considered by some critics the most significant American film of the late twentieth century, was directed by Harold Ramis and written by Danny Rubin. Ramis is the director of undistinguished low-level comedies like *Caddyshack* and *Vacation*. And Rubin has done very little of any note before or since *Groundhog Day*. Their joint mediocrity would seem then to argue for crediting the considerable achievement of this film to the extraordinarily talented leading man, Bill Murray. However, whether due to Murray or to the creative team as a whole, *Groundhog Day* must be treated as a deep and complex comedy. While completely satisfactory as popular entertainment, it is also a thematically and psychologically complex narrative, involved with intersecting themes of time and identity that easily lead us back not only to Dickens's *Carol* but to Goethe's *Faust*, the great work of modern culture about time. The latter connection, if only by association (though as we shall see it is much stronger than that), underlines the seriousness, the philosophical exploration, of Dickens's magnificent tale, in which both these texts share. In contrast, *Scrooged*, for all its merits, seems cartoonish, almost an animated film, drawing heavily on caricature. (There is even a reference to a typical encounter between Bugs Bunny and the cartoon farmer Elmer Fudd.) *Groundhog Day*, however, focuses its difficult, central romance around the problem central to Romanticism, the discovery of the complexity of the phenomenon of time.

This discovery of time is ubiquitous in Romantic literature, so much so that only later could people have enough distance from that fact to pay it significant attention. Romantic tales are characterized by the jumbling of time. Rather than starting at the beginning and going to the end, they routinely start in the middle, and then move backwards and forwards at the same time. Think of E. T. A. Hoffmann's tales, or one of Wordsworth's long poems. Thus they leave the reader to sort out and put in chronological order the sequence of events. In refusing chronological order, the Romantics were undoing a common-sense notion that time is made up of "discrete parts as sharply separated as the boxed days on a calendar" – perhaps still the prevailing popular view – and nudging toward the notion that "private time was real time and that its texture was fluid" (Kern 1983: 33). Furthermore, they insisted that while public time symbolized by the calendar might flow in one direction, private time "was as capricious as a dreamer's fancy" (34). Romantic time became, then, not a series of lumps or milestones but a stream of consciousness. And it did not flow in one direction, but was reversible under certain conditions, as Einstein was to prove in what became the foundation of modern physics. Sometimes, as is the case for example with *Groundhog Day*, chronology is strictly adhered to. But the same sequence is repeated over and over, each time varying slightly, with the result that the very idea of sequence is unsettled. (Similarly, in *Scrooged*, the realistic sequence of Martin Cross's life is interrupted by the fantasies that he sees and which are as real as everyday life to him.)

In response, the Victorians attempted to reorder the jumble of Romantic time-tales into chronological sequences. Wilkie Collins, for example, elaborated a mode of detective fiction that leads from a confusion about sequence and timing to a denouement in which order is brought to both. Similarly, it was the Victorians who codified the genetic understanding of time, leading to the discovery of evolution, so dependent on the sweep of history over long periods and archaeological time. But in retelling these stories chronologically, the Victorian versions tended to reduce fantasy to realism, depriving narrative of much of its literary magic.

The *Carol* of the 1840s then, while it surveys the early Victorian economic scene, is formally and thematically much more significantly attuned to the vision of Romanticism. In its conventions, its themes, and especially in its theatricality, Dickens's *Carol* echoes Goethe's *Faust*, which Dickens knew and loved in Gounod's operatic version (Dizikes

1992: 2–3), as well as through his friendship with Thomas Carlyle, the Victorian authority on (*inter alia*) democracy, German Romantic thought, and the French Revolution. Both *Faust* and *A Christmas Carol* depend upon a theatrical technology deriving from the popular experimental shows of their era, including the phantasmagoria, picturesque theatre, and diorama (Falx, 1978: chapter 4). These were technologically innovative multimedia presentations, utilizing photographs and magic-lantern projections, combined sometimes with human actors, often staged in specially constructed buildings, to create theatrical illusions that included ghosts and moving pictures as well as three-dimensional effects – all this fifty and sixty years before Edison invented the motion picture, but following hard on the heels of Daguerre's invention of photography. In fact, Daguerre became one of the most important of the host of entrepreneurs who popularized photography by means of these wildly popular, illusion-creating magic-lantern shows. But both Dickens and Goethe created imaginative works slightly ahead of the illusion-making technology of their time. And it is not surprising that the means to produce the full theatrical expression of both works has perhaps only been possible in the modern film. John Jordan notes that Dickens's "story itself is already a multi-media production, especially the scenes where Scrooge is made to witness a series of visionary tableaux in which he can not participate. It is almost as if Dickens were writing a story to be told by media not yet available in the Victorian age" (1993: 6).

Unlike many ghost stories which are mere thrill-and-chillers, the apparitions central to both Dickens's and Goethe's work, thanks to what we would nowadays call "special effects," de-realize routinized views of time and transform them. (That's where Einstein comes in.) A sense of time as change *and* stasis central to *Faust* and *A Christmas Carol* informs both *Groundhog Day* and *Scrooged*. Similarly preoccupied with time, the films invite us to rethink Dickens's tale in terms of the challenge Faust delivers to Mephistopheles in the scene in his study.

> If ever I should tell the moment:
> Oh, stay! You are so beautiful!
> Then you may cast me into chains,
> Then I shall smile upon perdition!
> Then may the hour toll for me,
> Then you are free to leave my service.
> The clock may halt, the clock hand fall,
> And time come to an end for me!

Here Faust tells Mephistopheles that he will willingly forfeit his soul if he ever finds such satisfaction in a moment as to ask ever-changing time to stay its course.

But that is exactly what Phil Connors does ask in *Groundhog Day* as the film, in effect, quotes the *Faust* passage near its conclusion, when Rita Hansen discovers the ice-sculpture of her Connors has made.

RITA It's lovely. I don't know what to say.
CONNORS I do. No matter what happens tomorrow or for the rest of my life, I'm happy now 'cause I love you.

The discovery of self, and erotic fulfillment (this is a Hollywood film), both depend on and coincide with breaking from and through clock-time to a vantage point at which time's course is stayed.

In *Groundhog Day* and *Scrooged*, then, just as in *Faust* and *A Christmas Carol*, the vehicle of the moral education of the hero is the reconception of time. In all four, the figures from the spirit world have a demonic aspect and yet also teach the lessons of moral reform, including generosity of spirit and sympathy, both central Romantic ideals. As variations on the ghost story, they generate a plot which goes backward in order to go forward, and in the process wittily interrogate "realistic" notions of time and space. The central figures of these works, Faust and Scrooge, Martin Cross, and Phil Connors, begin isolated and imprisoned in their routines. They make contact only with the world of economics, and, hence, illusion. From the claims of ordinary humanity they defend themselves with ideological assertions of privilege. Faust asserts his knowledge and genius as a man of learning. Scrooge sticks to his money-making routines. Cross and Connors by their violent sarcasm put everyone around them in their place, below them in the social economy of the TV pecking order.

Like Martin Cross, Dickens's Scrooge has grown up solitary, and neglected. We suspect no less of Faust and Connors. In all four characters, arrogance is overwhelming. What the old woman says of Scrooge is also true of Faust, Cross, and Connors: "He frightened every one away from him when he was alive." This arrogance toward both men and women blinds the four men to the other dimensions of experience, keeping them focused on their own increasingly routinized behavior. They devalue the humanity of everyone in the apparently mundane worlds around them as they elevate themselves. The arrogance with which the four insist on their own perspectives links them to a process in which each will have to discover the importance of exactly those values which they have hitherto denied. Values which they have repressed by insisting on a unidimensional sense of time they have constructed for themselves, to the exclusion of any other. For Scrooge, time is routine, and that routine is centered on money. Both for him are not a matter of spending or of speeding up the process of circulation but of hoarding, and Scrooge is not so much capitalist as mercantilist miser. This is also the role Cross plays out in the corporate hierarchy in which he works, and the role Connors has created for himself on his TV station. For Faust, time is so constant a process of striving as to put significant change out of reach. For Connors and Cross, only TV time is real. When the camera focuses on them in an isolating head-shot, they become endowed with a greater-than-life presence. For all four, then, their narrow view of time, and the tunnel vision it induces, has become naturalized into the only landscape they can experience. All they see is the time-world they have created.

All four fictions depend on special effects to elicit the repressed dimension of time. Here, however, I want to concentrate on *Groundhog Day* since its relation to the *Faust/Carol* paradigm may be harder to recognize than the closer copying that transpires in *Scrooged*. In the film's set-up, the protagonist, a television weatherman for a Pittsburgh television station, goes with his crew to witness the annual forecasting ritual at a nearby small town, Punxatawney, Pennsylvania. There, on 2 February, the local groundhog emerges from his nest. If he sees his shadow, the winter will last another six weeks. If not, spring is around the corner. It is worth noting that Groundhog Day, which falls on 2 February, coincides in the Christian calendar of feasts with the ancient celebration of the Purification of the Virgin, which also commemorates the presentation of the infant Jesus in the Temple in Jerusalem. Candlemas, as it is often called, is also the occasion when all the candles to be used in the church for the coming year are blessed. The religious feast like the secular holiday thus centers on the interplay of light and dark, the markers of deep time, in that form having originally been a pagan folk festival and witches' feast, before it was transformed by the Catholic Church. Susan Anderson has called my attention to the importance of 2 February as one of the female/chthonic holidays working throughout the year contrapuntally to the major male/Christian holidays. All of them, like St. Lucy's Day, traditionally the darkest day of the year, 13 December, or Halloween (31 October), are concerned with a natural cycle of light and dark counter to the more openly conducted cult histories of fall and redemption.

The typical television weatherman, Phil Connors is handsome and dynamic but, off-camera, he lacks any ability to accept the independent existence of other people. His effort to seduce the beautiful news reporter, Rita Hansen, who accompanies him on this outing, leads to a peculiar time-warp. Just as Scrooge is compelled to revisit the past, so Connors is forced to relive each and every incident of the day until he can "get it right." Time stops, and scenes repeat themselves incessantly, as part of his learning process. When he finally manages to speak fully to Rita and acknowledge her independent existence, he is rewarded. Lust turns into intimacy and love, and time can move forward once more, in the scene with the ice-sculpture cited earlier.

The film thus reinforces the ways in which theatrical representation reconceives the everyday sense of time and becomes the vehicle for moral education. Like Cross and Connors, Faust and Scrooge learn by literally *seeing* time, and hence its meanings. They learn to re-view and therefore to read, and reread, what they have made of their lives, just as Phil Connors and Martin Cross get to relive their lives as – what else? – movies. For all four, the reinvention of time happens because they are able to spatialize time, to see time in space, and thereby discover the full meaning of time's flowing stream, something which, on behalf of modern culture, Einstein recalibrated as relativity.

In *A Christmas Carol* it is by means of the visual re-experience of the past and pre-vision of the future, in juxtaposition, that Scrooge can release himself from his time-prison. Inevitably, then, Scrooge's conversion alters not only his attitude toward his fellow human beings but necessarily his attitude to time, celebrating that crucial moment which makes him aware that time can move both back and forth. It is not an accident that it is his discovery of himself at the moment of his death as the pre-converted Scrooge that turns the tables. At the beginning of the last spirit's visit, Scrooge discovers his colleagues "on 'Change" are reluctantly planning to attend a funeral. The man who has died has been a miser; their judgment of his heartlessness leads one to remark that "'Old Scratch' has got his own at last." (112). The devil, we realize as does Scrooge in this scene, has at last taken possession of the man who has been one of his all along – as if, like Faust, he had made a bargain with Mephistopheles long ago. And as for Faust, the vehicle of his self-discovery is encapsulated in the act of seeing, which now takes place in a new dimension.

It is at that instant that he wants time to stop so that he might mend it. And that is also, paradoxically, the moment when he discovers the need to change himself. The vehicle of that change is the realization of time's flow and the understanding that only by changing within time can one stand outside it. It is to this doubled consciousness that the fiction leads him as well as its readers – and it invites Scrooge, as well as Connors and Cross, and the reader to reenact it.

In her fine essay "Spectacular Sympathy: Visuality and Ideology in Dickens's *A Christmas Carol*," (1994), Audrey Jaffe emphasizes how qualities of spectacle shape the tale. Her analysis delineates the problematic of representation in the *Carol* and at the same time pursues the psychological impact on the protagonist of the representational process. "The scenes Scrooge is shown 'speak' to him," she argues, "positioning him as spectator and as desiring subject" (260). This notion of spectator connects her essay to discussions by Edward Eigner and Uli Knoepflmacher of the ways in which Dickens's book depends on elements of pantomime, masque, and other older theatrical forms (Eigner 1989; Knoepflmacher 1983). By staging time out of time Scrooge's visions lead him back to his boyhood and then forward to a new understanding of himself in which different phases connect to each other. By the end of the tale, he has seen himself in a Past, a Present, and a Future, rather than in an endless, undifferentiated cycle of unchanging money-making. Not only does this echo the theme of rereading and lead us back to the question of the conception of time at the heart of these works, it also locates the Wordsworthian project informing them, for *A Christmas Carol* is about how to make the child the father of the man. In effect, it is about the ways in which to stage time as a meaningful spectacle.

Faust's situation is the mirror-image to Scrooge's, and thus helps us understand not only Scrooge's predicament but also that of Cross and Connors. At Christmas Scrooge, self-focused, is transformed by looking through the window of time and discovering the existence of the Eternal. Faust, at Easter, is granted immortal life – that is, the chance to continue in the same way for ever – unless he finds one moment, an *Augenblick*, so wonderful he would ask time to stop. In honoring Christmas in his heart, keeping it all the year by living in the Past, Present, and the Future, Scrooge discovers not eternity – he has already had that endless duration in his money-making routine – but a break with duration and an escape from ongoing, unending time into immortality. But Faust discovers that even in the promise, and realization, of immortality, he cannot escape the longing for the Eternal. Both Faust and Scrooge thus encounter a moment, differently inflected but sharing in common its function, as a mirror-image of Eden. The result is to make them break with repetition, with the immortal routine of their lives, which is now unbearable. Plunging into the ongoing routine of time, both Scrooge and Faust refuse to accept repetition as destiny.

This reframing of time, shared by *A Christmas Carol* and *Faust*, is the very stuff of film, which is no small reason, perhaps, why Dickens's tale has become not only much adapted but a household word. It is in film, preeminently, that we experience the "new refutation of time," to steal Borges's title. Film reinvents real time as reel time. It not only freezes frames but it can also flow equally well backward and forward, dependent for comprehension on a double joinery of montage and suture. Montage: the creators' juxtaposition of discontinuous images into an artificial but convincing coherence independent of ordinary space–time continua. Suture: the complement to montage, the audience's work of filling in the connections among images, making the logical bridges which turn projection into narrative. As film freezes, sunders, reconnects spaces of time, it paradoxically also renders mobile and fluid the fixed sense of everyday time allowing other possibilities for liberation.

Thus film freezes and frees, both Cross and Connors. This is particularly true of *Groundhog Day*. Repeatedly, Connors, horrified at the endless repetitions of his life, attempts to kill himself. Whatever he tries, be it stepping in front of an ongoing truck, staging a car crash, or jumping from a window, fails. Invariably, the next morning he awakens to Groundhog Day once more. It is only when Connors confronts his arrogance – which has kept him from realizing and acknowledging the fullness of the life around him – that he learns to live in more than one narrow dimension. Connors, the TV reporter, is preparing to edit film that will cover the groundhog's appearance. Instead, film, as it were, takes over and edits him, splicing and looping his performances into narratives he cannot control or make sense of, until like Scrooge, at once the seer and the seen, he moves from the death-in-life of repetition to the possibility of significant change, to the ideas which Einstein has helped us acknowledge and film has helped us see, and feel: that time is a stream in which we too are located and that our location in relation to that of others is crucial with regard to how we perceive them.

It is obvious that both of Murray's adaptations, the simple, clearcut *Scrooged* and the covert, complex *Groundhog Day*, articulate that Victorian sense, so strongly argued by *A Christmas Carol*, that by working on the self we can change, even transform it, and so discover the true life of community. But they also redeploy the Romantic discovery of time, dramatizing for their protagonists, and viewers, that moment when time goes forward and backward, the moment when we discover that neither seeing nor the experience of time are absolute qualities. Rather, both are not only transitive but reflexive. It is only as we take into account the seer as well as the seen, and our location in time as part of its stream of movement, that we discover the relativity of our lives and being: what stands before us then is the self-in-its-community. That is what Goethe's and Dickens's texts persuasively suggest but which Murray's films, as film, can so convincingly show.

REFERENCES

Dizikes, John. 1992. "Dickens and Opera." Paper read at a colloquium at University of California, Santa Cruz, CA.
Eigner, Edward. 1989. *The Dickens Pantomime*. Berkeley: The University of California Press.
Falx, Neil M. 1978. "Written Pictures: The Visual Arts in Goethe's Literary Work." Ph.D. Dissertation, Yale University.

Jaffe, Audrey. 1994. "Spectacular Sympathy: Visuality and Ideology in Dickens's
    A Christmas Carol." *PMLA* 109: 254–65.
Jordan, John. 1993. *A Little Book About A Christmas Carol*. Santa Cruz, CA: The
    Dickens Project.
Kern, Stephen. 1983. *The Culture of Time and Space 1880–1918*. Cambridge, MA:
    Harvard University Press.
Knoepflmacher, Uli. 1983. *A Christmas Carol by Charles Dickens and Other Victo-
    rian Fairy Tales*. New York: Bantam.

7   Screen memories in Dickens and Woody Allen

Robert M. Polhemus

Love is now the stardust of yesterday,
The music of the years gone by.
                                    Mitchell Parish

Psychoanalysts have loosely defined screen memories as forms of remembering whose content works to disguise or divert from conscious thought some strong, still painful, dangerous, or shameful emotional event or current, usually from childhood. I want to compare revealing screen memories in the work of Charles Dickens and Woody Allen, and in doing so point out the rich irony in the unfolding history of that word *screen*. What meant something that keeps you from seeing somehow turned into a site and apparatus of light that lets you view what before you never could. A means of deflecting attention, keeping the heat off (a *firescreen* is one of the earliest OED definitions of *screen*), or hiding something from public scrutiny and even your own consciousness becomes the center of cinematic projection where you can see illuminated the new featured subject. These different meanings of the same word can stand for a basic principle underlying the creation of much art and its power of enlightenment: *what needs a screen needs a screening*.

Artists often use the screens they construct around their emotional obsessions to project fantasy images that let you see into the buried, but volcanic, desires that shape people and culture. Taking a specific example of how this process can work, I want to focus on the compound word, image, metaphor, and concept *stardust*, with its emotionally potent overtones, and then show how Dickens and Allen feature it in some highly charged moments in their art. They both hide and reveal themselves in stardust, and they show how others do too.

The poetic oxymoron *stardust* reminds you of both the fading splendor and the poignant waste of the past – the residue of glory. It conveys both brightness and that which blurs vision. It can stand for the inevitable dimming of the leading lights in time and memory and suggests an emotional shower of ashes from exploded stellar hopes. It can also call up a longing to retrieve the sense of buoyant distinction that love can bring. But though you look up to see a star loom and twinkle above, the *dust* floats all around you. (Among the meanings of *dust* that Dickens invokes are *tiny particles of dirt, powder, refuse, industrial waste*, and even *the moldering remains of mortal flesh*.) Try to catch a star, and sooner or later you're liable to be choking on so much psychological stardust.

By looking at some figurative stardust floating down from Dickens, the star of Victorian fiction, to Woody Allen, the little dickens of late-twentieth-century filmmakers, I mean to bring to light key patterns out of which they formed their creative visions. As it happens, a stardust path does run from *Great Expectations* to Allen's *Stardust Memories*. Taking off from Dickens's great expectations that end in stardust, Allen shows that stardust means something more than dreamy erotic nostalgia and that he, like Dickens and lots of other men, uses it to screen the replacement of an older woman by a younger. Both of them fused intimate autobiographical memories and materials into their work while denying it or covering their tracks. Each felt and rendered time's transformation of erotic relationships into ironic romantic memories and bitter present realities. Both feared aging women, and both disliked and portrayed the petrifaction of energy, passion, and love in wives and marriage. Both, in art and life, were drawn to daughter figures, sister figures, and enticing younger women. And both, after the age of fifty, joined with women not half their age, presumably as a means of fighting time, preserving vitality, and keeping fresh their powers of expression. The screen of their stardust memories projects light on both Dickens and Allen, on the flow of artistic imagination, on the development of twentieth-century film-world culture, and on the shape of modern social history.

The biographical imperative

Relating an artist's life and work is a notoriously tricky thing to do and must usually be hypothetical. Still, thinking about how, why, and what autobiographical signs appear in an artist's work helps you see what generates it, how it functions, what needs it fulfills, how it may touch and move people, and why they might care about it at all. The events and urgencies of life can show how imagination develops and how it grapples to preserve and extend human consciousness. Whatever disparagers of biographical criticism and probings into personal psychology may say, a biographical imperative surely drives most modern artists and art. It drives audiences too. In the era of modern media, knowledge of an artist's work and life runs together, and that mixture often informs the way you see the artwork (it is as false to say that the knowledge you have of the life stories of Dickens or Woody Allen or Proust or Virginia Woolf doesn't affect the way you read and see them as it would be to say that knowledge of your mate's history doesn't affect your sex life).

Artists' projections of their own desires, psychological conflicts, wish-fulfillments, and obsessions usually give their work its deepest interest and meaning. Most feel that they try to put the truth as they know it into their work, that in it lies their special experience, that it's distilled from their deepest life, and, even, that their artistic expression gives form to the history of their being. Two examples from Dickens and Allen make clear the imperative to merge fact and fiction.

1. After the death of his beloved teenage sister-in-law Mary, Dickens imagines, in *The Old Curiosity Shop*, the famous thirteen-year-old girl Little Nell, whose goodness offered hope for moral redemption in a pa-triarchal world of aging, tired faith. Almost two decades later, he hap-pened to fall in love with a teenager named Nelly and reportedly even took Nelly Ternan to see Nell's bedroom in the building he imagined as "the old curiosity shop."

2. Fifteen years after filming the outrageous affair of the middle-aged writer and the teenager in *Manhattan*, Woody Allen took up with a school-girl he eventually married. Artists may have love affairs and they may write about love affairs, but both the love and the story come out of fusing men-tal processes and the play of memory.

Seeing stars and stardust: I

Stardust, as the famous lyric says, is "the memory of love's refrain," the retrospective "consolation" in a "song" – in other words, it flows into, and out of, art. In *Great Expectations* Dickens names the girl his narrator loves *Estella* (deriving from the Latin *stella*, meaning *star*). Both early and late, the story shows Estella as Pip's own Venus, the morning and evening star upon whom he projects all the yearning of his life. In childhood, working-class Pip, hired to come and play for the warped amusement of rich Miss Havisham, first sees the haughty girl moving in somber settings pierced by striking light (David Lean's 1946 movie version of *Great Expectations* features and makes you see the dark radiance that surrounds Pip's first visions of Estella). Estella appears as a figure above and beyond him, the star of his desire, a beautiful, cold image that from then on haunts what he calls "the innermost life of my life" (chapter 29).

Behind...was a rank garden with an old wall...I could...see that the rank garden was the garden of the house, and that it was overgrown with tangled weeds...and that Estella was walking away from me even then. But she seemed to be everywhere...I saw her walking...at the end of the yard...She had her back towards me, and held her pretty brown hair spread out in her two hands, and never looked round, and passed out of my view directly...I saw her pass among the extinguished fires and ascend some light iron stairs, and go out by a gallery high overhead, as if she were going out into the sky. (Chapter 8)

The boy's star-struck memory of Estella becomes Pip's stardust. (Lean's film even gives us a quick shot of him later in bed musing on Estella, gazing straight up, bathed in celestial nightglow.)

Crucially, however, in Pip's mind and narrative, Estella is fused with her "mother-by-adoption," aging, crazy Miss Havisham, the jilted, victimized, vengeful bride of decay who lives amid the dust and rot of a ruined marriage feast. After Pip first sees Estella "going out into the sky," he immediately hallucinates that Miss Havisham is hanging over him – literally:

It was in this place and at this moment, that a strange thing happened to my fancy...I turned my eyes – a little dimmed by looking up into the frosty light – towards a great wooden beam...and I saw a figure hanging there by the neck. A figure all in yellow white, with but one shoe to the feet; and it hung so that I could see the faded trimmings of the dress were like earthy paper, and that the face was Miss Havisham's. (Chapter 8)

This extraordinary link in Pip's imagination between the "starlet" above him and the desiccated bride animates the vision in *Great Expectations* – a vision that pioneers both a cinematic and psychological "screen" world.

The life of the two figures – the repulsive older woman and the attractive young girl – runs together in Pip's typical visual projections:

Whenever I watched the vessels standing out to sea...I somehow thought of Miss Havisham and Estella; and whenever the light struck aslant, afar off, upon a cloud or sail or green hill-side or water-line, it was just the same – Miss Havisham and Estella and the strange house and the strange life appeared to have something to do with everything that was picturesque. (Chapter 15)

The novel's most shocking imagery (and Dickensian screen memory) bursts out with the burning of Miss Havisham near the end (Chapter 49). The grown-up, disillusioned Pip revisits the scene where he first saw Estella in "the sky" and then fantasized the hanged old bride. In a reverie, he walks again in "the ruined garden" in "the dying light," when he suddenly hears Miss Havisham cry out. An amazing, fiery climax follows in which the old lady and her trappings turn to ashes and dusty death:

I looked into the room where I had left her...I saw a great flaming light spring up. In the same moment, I saw her running at me, shrieking, with a whirl of fire blazing all about her, and soaring at least as many feet above her head as she was high.

I had a double-caped great-coat on, and over my arm another thick coat. That I got them off, closed with her, threw her down, and got them over her; that I dragged the great cloth from the table for the same purpose, and with it dragged down the heap of rottenness in the midst, and all the ugly things that sheltered there; that we were on the ground struggling like desperate enemies, and that the closer I covered her, the more wildly she shrieked and tried to free herself; that this occurred I knew through the result, but not through anything I felt, or thought, or knew I did. I knew nothing until I knew that we were on the floor by the great table, and that patches of tinder yet alight were floating in the smoky air, which a moment ago, had been her faded bridal dress . . .

I doubt if I even knew who she was, or why we had struggled . . . until I saw the patches of tinder that had been her garments . . . falling in a black shower around us . . .

Though every vestige of her dress was burnt, . . . she still had something of her old ghastly bridal appearance; for they had covered her to the throat with white cotton wool, and as she lay with a white sheet loosely overlying that, the phantom air of something that had been and was changed, was still upon her. . .

[S]he began to wander in her speech, and . . . said innumerable times in a low solemn voice, "What have I done!" And then, "When she first came, I meant to save her from misery like mine." And then, "Take the pencil and write under my name, 'I forgive her!' " . . .

I leaned over her and touched her lips with mine, just as they said, not stopping for being touched, "Take the pencil and write under my name, 'I forgive her.' " (Chapter 49)

In speculating about what screen memories this fantastically suggestive scene might hold, it's worthwhile noting: 1. the connotations of grotesque eroticism in Dickens's choice of imagery and details in this most memorable embrace between a man and a woman in all his fiction (clothes burned off, union in fire and nakedness, and then his kiss of farewell for the old woman begging forgiveness); 2. the desire of many men to free themselves from what they feel to be the burden of clinging old brides who mirror their physical deterioration, remind them of the chains of the past, show them the inexorable threats of passing time and ebbing vitality, and spoil their dreams of some bright little star.

Pip, at the very end, after many years, in a twilight reverie again, revisits the old place. Nothing is left, "but the wall of the old garden."

[T]he stars were shining beyond the mist, and the moon was coming, and the evening was not dark. I could trace out where every part of the old house had been . . . I had done so, and was looking along the desolate garden-walk, when I beheld a solitary figure in it . . . I saw it to be the figure of a woman . . . "Estella!"

The freshness of her beauty was indeed gone, but its indescribable majesty and its indescribable charms remained . . . [W]e went out of the ruined place, and, as the morning mists had risen long ago . . . so, the evening mists were rising now, and in all that broad expanse of tranquil light they showed to me, I saw no shadow of another parting from her. (Chapter 59)

Seeing stars and stardust: II

Next to the mood and imagery of Dickens's ending, I want to juxtapose the lyric of "Stardust," that most famous and widely recorded ballad of the twentieth century, music by Hoagy Carmichael, words by Mitchell Parish (1929). Note how the "now" of the first line is, like the end of the novel, the "dusk of twilight time."

> Love is now the stardust of yesterday,
> The music of the years gone by.
> Sometimes I wonder why I spend
> The lonely night dreaming of a song;
> The melody haunts my reverie
> And I am once again with you,
> When our love was new
> And each kiss an inspiration.
> But that was long ago –
> Now my consolation is in the stardust of a song.
> Beside a garden wall when stars are bright,
> You are in my arms. . .
> Tho' I dream in vain
> In my heart it will remain.
> My stardust melody.
> The memory of love's refrain.

Whether or not Mitchell Parish was directly influenced by Dickens (I think he was), Pip's nostalgic stardust memory of Estella has obviously influenced and shaped the imagination of love – as Woody Allen shows.

Seeing stars and stardust: III

The image of Estella beside the garden wall flows into the "Stardust" lyrics and then Allen makes the song a part of *Stardust Memories* (1980), his quasi-autobiographical, quirky, wonderful dark comedy. The film focuses on Sandy Bates (Woody Allen), a highly neurotic film director, and it features "Stardust" in a striking scene of erotic reverie. Bates, at a retrospective weekend conference devoted to himself and his films, is shown floundering among women and unsure where to go next with his art. His inner and outer life, both present and past, jumble together, and memories and images from his love life and work pour wildly through his on-screen psyche. His art and life get mixed up, and desire looks the same in both: A narcissistic, creative male is drawn to accomplished women with movie-star beauty and charisma; he longs to find in them intimacy, freedom, sexual turn-on, and aesthetic inspiration. He looks for a lasting romantic relationship, but also for fresh, serial erotic relationships too. He needs love, devotion, and danger. He wants coherent identity with the past but also something new. Reveries of the fascinating Dorrie (Charlotte Rampling), his absent, beautiful, vulnerable, manic-depressive ex-lover and muse, dominate his inner retrospective even as he looks for ways of replacing and moving beyond her. He remembers that Dorrie, an aspiring actress whom he met on the set of a movie called *Suppression*, freed him for a time from his repressive, mind-forged manacles. The magnificent "Dorrie" flashbacks last only a few minutes, but they give the film its emotional depth – and its title.

What makes life, so cruel and ridiculous, worth living? Sandy explicitly faces that question and then imagines a stardust memory when he felt the joy that justifies the absurd pain. He remembers a morning with Dorrie. Before, in a flashback, Allen with brutal jump cuts of Dorrie's face in close-up and her comments about psychiatric hospitalization, had shown her visually shattering and going to pieces. Now, he focuses the camera on the movie-star-gorgeous Rampling and fills the soundtrack with the music of the great Louis Armstrong singing and playing "Stardust" ("I am once again with you, / When our love was new / And each kiss an inspiration").

The so-called "male gaze" of Sandy/Woody, the director, takes her in as she's reading, prone on the floor, in a room filled with light. There's a brief shot of him casually eating and idly looking at her. It's a sequence of calm radiance. She looks up, catches his eye; affection and contentment play over her face. She goes back to reading. The camera holds her for a time, then switches back to the filmmaker, and he smiles. The focus quickly moves back to Dorrie reading. Then she looks up. Armstrong's *Stardust* keeps on pushing happiness. The camera stays on her. She moves her leg slightly to the rhythm of the music; sexuality is starting to flow. The amusement, the engagement, the staring, and the erotic desire of the director subtly begin to animate her expression. She herself is gazing, taking in the man across the room, taking the lead, putting the shot of the primly eating, erotically hungry little man in perspective, moving before your eyes from object to subject in a glorious moment that the film captures and the director treasures.

"But that was long ago." The movie shows Sandy wanting to preserve that screen experience by trying to repeat it with others – with a neurotic violinist, for example, and with a Mia-Farrow-like film star, her children in tow. Woody Allen, in this "autobiographical" character and film, gets at a conflict in himself and in many others when, in the course of a movie, he fantasizes women as both interchangeable and irreplaceable – somehow unique figures of memory who nevertheless blend into one another, each of whom he does and *does not* wish to transcend. A man like Sandy Bates may want to hold on for ever to a young woman he has loved, but that desire might lead him to find other young women on whom to focus and preserve his stardust memories – in life and/or on film.

In the movie Sandy's friend calls Dorrie a very crazy person who has only two good days a month, but for those two days she's absolutely fabulous. Allen, in an authorized biography by Eric Lax, says exactly the same thing of Louise Lasser, his second wife and his leading lady in *Bananas* (1971): "Even the two days are almost worth it because two good days a month with Louise were better than a good year with most other people" (Lax 1991: 170). The book praises Louise but reveals how her troubled life inspired the portrait of Dorrie. In a delicate "interview" sequence, Sandy both probes and kids Dorrie about her intense bond with her powerful, attractive father (her mother, like Louise Lasser's, was institutionalized). Sandy jokes knowingly about incestuous impulses and the erotic pull of father–daughter closeness. Later, when Dorrie falls into a paranoid phase that hospitalizes her, she accuses Sandy of being attracted to a thirteen-year-old relative of hers. She screams at him not to deny it; she knows the look and mood, because she had the same libidinous conspiracy at the same age with her father. Sandy tries to calm her mania, but to anyone looking at this now, knowing of Allen's life to come, his long liaison with Mia Farrow, and her rage at Woody's erotic relationship and marriage to her adopted daughter Soon-Yi Previn, the prophetically ironic nature of the scene is uncanny.

One more ironical twist in *Stardust Memories*: In a secondary role among the glamorous movie folk, Louise Lasser shows up, playing Sandy Bates's fat, dowdy, drab secretary and looking like a time-battered afterthought – a modern, burnt-out Miss Havisham in the steno pool.

Seeing stars and stardust: IV

Certainly, as Julian Fox puts it, "The idea of an older man–younger woman benefiting each other is a consistent theme in Woody's work" (1996: 79). In *Manhattan* (1979), forty-something Ike Davis, another semi-autobiographical artist played by Allen, hangs out with a long-legged, ravishing seventeen-year-old girlfriend Tracy (Mariel Hemingway). She looks like the perfect romantic fantasy for an anxious male in mid-life crisis. Like a sexually mature Alice in Wonderland, she's the center of goodness and hope in the movie's brittle, jaded intellectual world. A spiritual trophy girl, she also likes to "fool around" and "fuck" Ike without making any serious demands ("no harm, no foul"). And Ike loves to mentor her; he teaches her, for instance, what old movies are really good. Allen, however, projects onto the teenager not only the characteristics of the good student, but also those of a good *mother*: uncritically accepting, loving, nurturing, devoted, full of good health, and happy to support his fantasy life.

The main stardust memory of the film is Ike's recall of the girl's countenance. In one scene, all alone, he talks into a tape recorder about what things make life worth living (à la Sandy Bates). Some of them are Groucho Marx, Louis Armstrong, Ingmar Bergman movies, and Cézanne's fruit, but last and most important is "Tracy's face of course." It's the face of a teenage Madonna inspiring aesthetic faith and moral hope memorialized electronically and, in the movie, its beauty replaces the faces of Ike's former lovers, the older women played by Diane Keaton and Meryl Streep, who wind up screened out and stardusted.

People can't keep a secret, says Freud; look closely at them, listen carefully, watch what they do, think, and act out, and the truth of their nature and deep desire reveals itself. The memorable images of Tracy and Dorrie on Woody Allen's screen do not make you think of lasting marriage to a woman who exists and changes with passing time. Rather he shows you lovely pictures from remembered erotic interludes that open up across generation gaps the possibilities of continued revitalization in and through starry-eyed girls. In *Crimes and Misdemeanors* (1989), Cliff Stern (Woody Allen), a disillusioned, struggling, miserably married filmmaker, loves taking his prepubescent niece Jenny to see old movies. The girl is the one person to whom he can give unconditional, uncritical love and approval. In the first part of the film, he takes her to the movies, teaches her things, amuses her, confides in her, has fun, and says he's "crazy about her." They discuss the movies and enjoy each other's company. He also gives her advice ("don't listen to what your teachers say, look at them, think what they look like – that's how you'll know what life is like"). Unlike most of the characters he meets, she respects him. Then later he takes the grown-up Halley (Mia Farrow), a TV producer, to the movies, tell her things, has fun, and is crazy about *her*. When Halley leaves him, he again takes Jenny to the movies and has fun with her, mentoring her in front of a movie palace. He continues to see old stars on the screen with a young girl. This companionship, in the midst of absurdity and moral abominations, carries a seed of hope in the film. In other words, with Allen, what you see is what you get and, usually, *will* get. Stardust memories, for Woody Allen, are bound up with the silver screen, movie celebrity, and the temporal fixation of youth and beauty that film can capture and that cultures value.

What exactly are these stardust memories in Allen's films screening? It looks like they share with Dickens and his Pip a strategy of holding on to great expectations by eroticizing nostalgia and bringing it forward in speaking "pictures" (*Great Expectations*, chapter 53) that can dissolve the barrenness of the present and the monstrousness of the past in a fountain of youth. They hide and reveal the fear of impotence and also the ruthlessness of back-to-the-future drives and impulses.

Seeing stars and stardust: V

Allen (né Allen Konigsberg) had trouble with his mother Nettie, a sharp, tough woman who, it seems, slapped him around a bit, found him annoying, and was never for him the "good-enough mother." In a flash, she could turn the milk of human kindness to salt. But when he was three, she did take him to his first film, *Snow White*, and he found at the movies what he was looking for. According to Allen, when the small boy ran up to touch the huge figures on the screen, Nettie had to grab him and drag him away. True or not, this scene makes a parable. You have the fascination with moving pictures, the mixture of film and life, and a woman he wanted to get away from so he could find Snow White or some beautiful, wicked stepmother.

When he was eight, his new little sister Letty came along like his own personal Shirley Temple to lift his spirits. His relationship with her helped fix and figure the pattern of his desire on screen and off (*pattern of desire*: the way you keep hoping things should and might be). He found himself looked up to by an adoring female; things could change for the better. The girl brought out the best in him, loved him, and let him be a good big brother, care for her, and play the benevolent authority. He could identify with her, take her to the movies, teach her what the world and films were really like, and find what he wanted to be reflected in her pretty eyes.

What would it mean to love your sister more than your mother? It could mean that you might always worry about a Letty turning into a Nettie. Later, you might from time to time want a new girl – as Allen's *Manhattan*, *Stardust Memories*, *Crimes and Misdemeanors*, *Husbands and Wives* (1992) and *Deconstructing Harry* (1997) all show. Replaying intimacy with a younger female looks like the role of a lifetime for Woody. That may sound like psychological regression, but in fact, for good or ill, it represents a drive and pattern to keep moving forward out of a felt dilemma of soul-searing, dying relationships. And it was the role Dickens screened for himself in *Great Expectations*.

The big picture on Dickens's screen

I want to return to the enduring significance of the fire and the stardust in Dickens's vision, because they combine to make a burning paradigm that sheds light on modernity and its media. You see in the way Woody Allen's art and life reflect on that stardust flameout, how much recent film history and sociology of the movie world have in common with Dickens's vision. Once I read in the burning of Miss Havisham signs of both Dickens's hostility and his reconciliation to his own mother. In the dying words, "Take the pencil and write under my name, 'I forgive her,' " I imagined him scripting a pardon for the real woman whom he judged, in the wake of her support for prolonging his child-labor nightmare in the blacking factory, a mother insensitive to his talents and feelings. Dickens, I thought, in projecting maternal guilt and a way back to maternal love through writing, revealed the nature of his own muse and, beyond that, a big reason for the genesis of art (Polhemus 1990: 154–62). But though all that may be partly true, it sentimentally screens Dickens's fantasy – and a hugely important fantasy in Hollywood and all of filmland – of getting rid of an old wife and not having to lie with her anymore.

What happens if you identify the main generating figure in his imagination here not as his mother, but as his wife Catherine, from whom, just two years before beginning the book, he, the laureate of domestic virtue, had publicly and shockingly separated? Traumatically, amid withering gossip and his own shadowy maneuverings, Dickens left his wife to begin a long, secret, guilt-tinged liaison with eighteen-year-old Ellen Ternan, a girl younger than his eldest daughter (Tomalin 1990: 96–182). It looks as if, with his nuptial split on his mind, he was projecting wildly in *Great Expectations*. If so, then the image and effect of burning up a withered bride living in a dead past of erotic obsession can symbolize both a private conjugal catastrophe and a male cover-up of historic proportions. Out of his own marital predicament, it appears, he imagined one of the most memorable deaths by fire since Lot's wife, looking back at Sodom, was blasted into saltash. And that is how I now read the passage: the fire-struck Miss Havisham *is* a new Lot's wife.

Havisham and Estella represent a modern instance of what I call the Lot complex: the interaction and developing relationships in history, art, culture, and psychology between older males and younger females. In the Bible's Lot story (Genesis 19), God saves Lot, his wife, and his two daughters from the fire-and-brimstone holocaust of Sodom, but Lot's wife looks back, gets burnt to a pillar of salt, and the daughters, thinking Lot the last man left on earth, decide to "preserve seed of our father." They get him drunk, seduce him in a cave, and bear his sons. Among the progeny are Ruth, King David, Solomon, and – depending on your faith – even Jesus Christ.

It's a perplexing, disturbing myth, full of irony and ambivalence. And in the era of great change and progress in women's lives of the last two centuries, you can see again and again both direct allusions to the story and deep traces of its malleable life and power. Its patterns, figures, and imagery can and do illuminate projected male desires of lasting potency, growing female agency and fears about it, the ambitions of young women and older men to share power and intimacy, and the social and personal dilemma of aging, displaced wives and mothers. In light of modern gender history, Christ's admonition, "Remember Lot's wife," takes on new meanings – some of which you can see by the glare of Miss Havisham's fire and Estella's soft starlight.

What comes through in a "Lot's wife" reading of Havisham is a man's selfish fear of age, of a madly cloying woman, and of the debilitating effect she might have on him and his future – including his dreamy hopes to star anew in some romantic love play. Stated baldly, that's anything but a pretty vision, but it matters greatly and obviously has sinister dimensions. The old lady is burnt like a sacrificial offering, and the man in good conscience can immerse himself in stardust and get on to a new "meaningful relationship" with a younger "significant other."

Stardust memories are screened reveries of eternal youth that can burn up lives. The angst of men getting older, unsure of their sexual prowess, embarrassed by the paralyzing grotesqueries of tedious conjugal demands, and desperate for a chance at rejuvenating new alliances has helped form the sociology of our world. One reason is that the gist of Dickens's erotic dilemma and fantasy imprinted itself spectacularly on the hugely influential, on- and off-screen, movieland world of the twentieth century. It helps now to see Lot complexes and *nouveaux* Lots like Woody Allen in the twilight of Dickensian stardust.

Dickens cast his own wife in the role of Lot's wife and, middle-aged, found himself joined with a daughter-like figure in the half-light of Victorian dissimulation. He met Ellen Ternan, an aspiring actress who seems somehow to have embodied for him both a muse and a fetish of his own continuing dramatic power. Taking up with her and changing his life was, he felt, an emotional necessity; on it depended his continuing creativity. But his moral vulnerability in acting that way bothered him.

A sweet, desexualized Lot theme had long held Dickens's imagination. He seems at a young age to have transferred the primary focus of his love for a female from his mother to his sister, and that virginal image of a love object and that emotional change from an older woman to a girlish appear in most of his fiction. In *David Copperfield* he coined his revealingly Lottish term "child-wife." Honoring the civilizing influence of the iconic *girlchild* that Victorian moralists used to sublimate the genital libido, Dickens imagined what he felt in himself: a constructive Lot complex, under control, on the side of virtue, pushing innocently toward progress through patriarchal responsibility nurtured by daughterly goodness.

A complex, however, like the rest of inner and outer life, changes over the years, and changing psychology changes your art. For a long time, Dickens had been able to compartmentalize his real-life marriage and sex life from his fantasies of ideal young females. But when his marriage went up in flames, sparks from it set Miss Havisham on fire and brought on the dubious stardust twilight surrounding Estella, Nelly Ternan, and himself. Somewhere in his psyche he realized his disgust with the wife of the past and the force of his need and desire for a ripe, daughterly woman.

In 1857, after his infatuation with Ellen had begun, Dickens, without first telling his wife, had the door blocked up between his dressing room and what had been the marital bedroom in Tavistock House, his London home. He shut Catherine out. A few days later he left the house at two in the morning after a quarrel with the jealous, frantic old wife – according to Dickens, wildly and continually jealous, like Miss Havisham. (For accounts of this crucial episode see Tomalin 1990: 108; Kaplan 1988: 378, and Ackroyd 1990: 798–9.) In chapter 38 of *Great Expectations*, Pip visits Miss Havisham and describes himself in bed falling into a waking mania over the old woman whose existence frustrates his hope for the love of Estella:

She was on this side of my pillow, on that, at the head of the bed, at the foot, behind the half-opened door of the dressing-room, in the dressing-room, in the room overhead, in the room beneath – everywhere. At last, when the night was slow to creep on towards two o'clock, I felt that I absolutely could no longer bear the place as a place to lie down in, and that I must get up. (Chapter 38)

The passage, odd in its context, makes sense as a projection of hysterical moments in the collapse of Dickens's marriage. It gives you the emotions of a guilty man spooked to near battiness by a desperately unhappy woman who won't let go. I read it, then, as evidence that links Dickens's life to his art (note the dressing room and the wee small hour of two a.m. figure in both life and fiction).

But so what? Why bother to speculate about a connection whose exact nature you can't finally know? One answer is to try to see how

Dickens's creative mind works, but another is that reading him this way lets us see a crucial pattern in the history of literature, of movies, and of sex and gender. The odd parallels, for instance, between the Dickens–Catherine–Nelly and Woody–Mia Farrow–Soon-Yi triangles are more than coincidental. Part of the dirty little secret code in the doomed turn of Lot's wife back to Sodom ciphers conflicted male feelings about sex life. Men may want to be free to touch and love new partners, but even more they also may want to get away from the sordid humiliations of stale, undesired sex with oh-so-familiar mates and the pride-searing pressures of obligatory erotic performance. In the petrifaction of Lot's wife, in Dickens's vision of the hot morbid clutch of Havisham and Pip, in Pip's touch of Estella in the shadows, in Woody Allen's stardust vision of the lovely Charlotte Rampling acting out the part Louise Lasser had once played in his life and in his casting of Lasser as a plain-Jane functionary in the film, I find narrative art not only covering the desire for new girls, but finding ways to screen repressed male resentments and anxieties at the conjugal imperative of having to get it up and keep it up – to put a not-so-fine point on it. Embedded in the tone and the symbolism of *Great Expectations*'s bizarre burning and in the hostility for ex-wives in movies like *Manhattan* and *Deconstructing Harry* a century later lies an ordeal of the bed we might dub "pre-Viagra falls." This is a big, if unsavory plot, part of the sacrificial old wives' tale that, in various forms, runs surreptitiously in the imagination of modern culture from Dickens's vision through Allen's.

Men and women invent and project wonderful, ingenious cover stories about and around sex, erotic desire, the need for love, and intergenerational relationships – fictions that can change and shape reality. But *all* stories, as Pip's burning embrace and then his reunion with his stardust girl show, are cover stories – or, in Woody Allen's case, screen adaptations.

REFERENCES

Ackroyd, Peter. 1990. *Dickens*. London: Sinclair-Stevenson.
Carmichael, Hoagy. 1946. *The Stardust Road*. New York: Rinehart & Co.
Dickens, Charles. 1989. *Great Expectations*. Oxford: Oxford University Press.
Fox, Julian. 1996. *Woody: Movies from Manhattan*. Woodstock, NY: Overlook Press.
Kaplan, Fred. 1988. *Dickens*. New York: Morrow.
Lax, Eric. 1991. *Woody Allen: A Biography*. New York: Knopf.
Polhemus, Robert M. 1990. *Erotic Faith*. Chicago: University of Chicago Press.
Tomalin, Claire. 1990. *The Invisible Woman: The Story of Nelly Ternan and Charles Dickens*. London: Viking.

Part III

8   Writing after Dickens: the television writer's art

John Romano

In considering the topic of Dickens and film, I cannot help but begin in the first-person singular. It is after all the singularity of my point of view that I began my professional life with the academic study and teaching of Dickens, and with *Dickens and Reality* (Columbia University Press) in 1980. Shortly afterwards I fell into bad company and drifted into the career of writing for movies and TV. I am not sure that I have ever managed to reconcile the two lobes of my brain, labeled respectively "Dickens" and "film." The scripts I have written mostly depict (as Hollywood movies and television mostly *do* depict) lawyers and doctors and cops, in contemporary urban settings. Occasionally someone has asked me to adapt Dickens for the (American) screen, and I have declined on the grounds that the British do period pieces better. As for "updating" a Dickens novel, the 1999 movie of *Great Expectations* which translated the story and characters to contemporary Florida and Manhattan cast a kind of pall over the whole idea. Its failure at the box office was a tribute to the literary acuity of the mass audience.

And yet, setting aside the idea of adapting Dickens directly, I have often had the sense that Dickens's art has a sharp and specific relevance to the scripts I do write – the sense that he was a pre-visionary teacher of the arts of screenwriting, and, indeed, of filmmaking, that were to arise in the century after him.

This is a familiar claim. One hears, fairly often, that "if Dickens were alive today he would be writing for Hollywood." What is usually meant by this is true enough. It is arguably true, for instance, that Dickens was preeminently an entertainer, and often in the aggressively affective, sensational way we associate with Hollywood products. More particularly, comparisons can be drawn between the art of his periodical publication and contemporary serialized television, sitcoms, and one-hour dramas. In both cases, the newest installment is eagerly awaited by the public, and the success of the narrative can be regularly measured by the writer or producer (by sales in Dickens's case, by Nielsen ratings in American TV). It is even the case that, in both forms, the writer-producer can make adjustments, as in the famous instance of Dickens sending Martin Chuzzlewit off to America to bolster faltering periodical sales; nothing could be closer to the Nielsen-chasing of TV producers when a series is in trouble.

But the comparisons can be taken further, extending not only to the form or to commercial relations, but to substance and sensibility as well. Both periodical Dickens and episodic TV are quintessentially middle-class. We are told that when the monthly installments arrived, they were not infrequently read aloud, by "Father," to the middle-class family gathered in the parlor, just as families now gather in front of the television in the living room. A significant irony may be added to this: the typical set of situation comedy being itself a living room, there arises the irresistibly comic (but also suggestive) image of families watching families, the living rooms of art and life intimately reflecting each other. Classically, commercial American television does not open a window on the world so much as it takes the picture window and, swinging it around within the living room, provides a medium by which the American middle class views itself.

This intimacy is essential, not only to the goals and practice of the narrative art of television, but to that of Dickens as well. It is intimacy that provides the aesthetic opportunity which may then be exploited. Because his art is already fixed in, *belongs to* the culture of the middle-class home – a claim that couldn't be made, for instance, for the fiction of Flaubert or James, or the films of the French New Wave or Dogma 95 – the artist of the Dickens/TV persuasion can undertake a full-fledged and thorough indictment of the values of the middle class, an insider's critique of its mores, its hopes and dreams and fears, as long as he keeps to the bargain, and entertains and amuses as he goes. One recalls here the epigraph that Dickens had planned, until John Forster dissuaded him, to affix to *Martin Chuzzlewit*: "Your homes the scenes, yourselves the players here!" (Forster 1927: I, 296). The novel which followed paints a dismally telling portrait of the emotional life of families, a web of dysfunctionality that would be staggering even on today's daytime talk-shows – or, more to the point, would seem right at home there.

The aesthetic advantage, the opportunity which derives from writing for and from within the middle class, is one of which as writers and producers of TV we are quite fully conscious. My own awareness of it began in my days on the writing staffs of the shows of writer-producer Steven Bochco in the 1980s, such as *Hill Street Blues* and *LA Law*. Steven Bochco himself once described the combination of elements which were essential for the kind of TV he was creating, and in doing so offered a not-bad description of what makes up that vaster thing, the art of Dickens.

His goal was to combine a sharp instinct for issues of social justice on one hand, with a broad, consciously lowbrow sense of humor on the other, and then infuse the two with an abiding sense of how surprising and interesting ordinary human beings really are. Under that aegis, we undertook (on *Hill Street Blues* in particular) to expose to our wide audience the dark side of urban reality, as Dickens did in *Oliver Twist* or *Bleak House*, as seen from a political point of view that might be described as Centrist-Liberal-Reformist – a politics not very different, that is, from Dickens's own. But the putting on the screen of "ordinary human beings" seems to me more Dickensian still, and merits a brief excursion into TV history.

By the 1980s, the three genres of TV drama, lawyers and doctors and cops, had already been well established. Indeed, they had prevailed since the advent of regular series TV around 1950. The advent of the new shows of the 80s – not only the aforementioned Bochco shows but perhaps also Bruce Paltrow's hospital series, *St. Elsewhere* – did nothing to change the dominance of that inherently limited threesome. Instead, the difference they made was internal, and their characteristic move was to "go home" – that was the phrase we used – with the doctors, or lawyers, or cops. This meant, to begin with, *literally* going home, where the characters left behind their public role, the only one earlier TV had ever explored. Audiences were notably struck when *Hill Street Blues* went home with its police chief, played by Daniel Travanti, to find he was being hounded by a foolish ex-wife for alimony payments on which he was frequently late, and that he regularly attended meetings of Alcoholics Anonymous, and that he was having an affair with a woman from the Office of the Public Defender. None of this was visible in the quite ordinary surface Travanti presented in his role as a typical "TV" police chief – we had to "go home" to expose it. And much that was found, especially in the homes of ordinary beat cops, the "uniforms," was deliberately banal rather than tragic or melodramatic. Dickens was, of course, a past master of the Art of Going Home. One thinks of Rumty Wilfer in *Our Mutual Friend*, or Wemmick in *Great Expectations*, or of Mr. Richard Swiveller in *The Old Curiosity Shop*. These are clerks, nobodies, non-entities ignored by novelists before Dickens, and indeed by television before the era I am describing.

Now, there was a pronounced critical response to what we were beginning to do with our characters, and to the attention we were paying to the minutiae of their lives, rather than to the "big moments" of catching criminals or solving cases. This response was often to dismiss it, even in praising it, as "quirky" and unreal, whereas all we were doing was following Bochco's directive to observe and record the astounding ways in which people actually do behave. The charge of unreality was of course one that

Dickens himself faced, and the defense he offered was much the same. "What is exaggeration to one class of minds," he wrote in the Preface to *Martin Chuzzlewit*, "is plain truth to another . . . I sometimes ask myself . . . whether it is *always* the writer who colours highly, or whether it is now and then the reader whose eye for colour is a little dull?" Elsewhere, he claimed that, alluding to one of his quirkiest characters, "Mrs. Nickleby herself, sitting bodily before me in a solid chair, once asked me whether I believed there ever was such a woman" (cited in Ford 1955: 134.) In this respect, those of us writing these shows were consciously Dickensian, and no one should be surprised to hear that we used the word ourselves to describe what we were doing.

But Dickens's imperative to render the ordinary extraordinary, the unfamiliar aspect of everyday things, has a further resonance for the TV I am describing. We did not only go home with Captain Furillo but showed his official police function, too, in a way different than had been done previously. To understand the difference, we may begin by observing that a policeman, any policeman, is a terribly interesting human being. He stands at a particular conjunction of society's goods and ills; stands, that is, at a windy corner where the violent, the criminal, the institutional, and the merely respectable intermingle, often in his own individual being. For this reason policemen interested nineteenth-century novelists intensely. Balzac comes to mind, and also Dostoevsky, along with a whole host of characters in Dickens, up to and including Bucket, and less remarkably but somehow more affectingly, the haunting "Mr. Inspector" in *Our Mutual Friend*. So much is common knowledge; what is striking is how uninterested contemporary novelists of the serious sort are in the policemen and women of our own time. It is a personality, a profession, a general topic left alone by Major Novelists, left to the writers of genre mysteries or potboilers, and, naturally, to the writers of movies and TV. It is not too much to say about the most interesting cops on television – one should add to *Hill Street* the even more complex creations of David Milch in his series of the 1990s, *NYPD Blue* – that they are continuators, and worthy ones, of the earlier novelistic tradition. Lieutenant Sipowicz, of *NYPD Blue*, interested writer David Milch for the same reasons that Stavrogin in *Crime and Punishment* interested Dostoevsky: both as a window into the social construction of justice and punishment as instanced in one individual, and as an individual himself.

I began by saying that Dickens stands, in some respect, over my shoulder as I write movies and television. It might be instructive to conclude with an actual moment from the trenches, as it were, of the creative life of such writing. The moment came when I was writing, along with Jeffrey Lewis and David Milch, what was to be the final episode of *Hill Street Blues*. My task was to write a penultimate scene – it was to be a very emotional one – in which a professional "snitch," a street-character named Sid, attempts to comfort Lieutenant Buntz, an overzealous, sometimes vicious homicide detective who had just been discharged from the force, and with whom Sid is sharing an apartment. There is a good deal of strong but unspoken affection between the men, in their lonely apartment late at night. And Sid stumbles and struggles over what to say to his friend, who is unhappy at having lost his job as a cop, plainly the only profession to which he's suited. I likewise stumbled and struggled over the writing of the scene, and came out with the following:

> SID
> Hey Norman. Norman. You're a good guy, cop or no cop. You're the best guy I know. Understand?
>
> BUNTZ *gets up, pulls on his coat.*
>
> SID
> Hey. What're you doing?
>
> BUNTZ
> Gonna take a walk. Try to decide what to do with the rest of my life …
>
> SID
> *(moved)*
> Want company?
>
> BUNTZ
> No, Sid …
>
> SID
> Okay but I'm gonna wait here 'til you get back, though.
>
> BUNTZ
> *(after a beat, grateful)*
> Thanks.
>
> *And* EXITS.

I thought, knowing the actors, that the scene would play well enough to make its point; indeed I was confident enough to show my partner. Milch looked at it, read it over, evincing neither pleasure nor displeasure – meaning, to my practiced eye, that I hadn't quite hit the mark. He then made a correction, an addition, actually. The scene played exactly as above, except that, instead of actually going at the end, Buntz is stopped by Sid at the door, with a final sheepish request …

> SID
> Norm? If you're going by a convenience – one of those orange-flavored big pops?
>
> NORM
> *(looks at him)*
> If I remember.
>
> SID
> Only if it's on the way.
>
> BUNTZ EXITS.

The orange pop, the *irrelevant* orange pop, struck me then, as it does now, as the one truly fine touch in the scene, and perhaps in the show (the episode was eventually nominated for an Emmy for its writing). It would be hard to explain to a beginning student, and to many a critic as well, the value of that orange pop, except to say that its irrelevancy is itself the point. It is what plants the tragedy/pathos of the scene in a very ordinary reality indeed, a reality in which, as it were, it can shine. One thinks of Auden noting in "Musée des Beaux Arts," that tragedy takes place "while someone else is eating or opening a window or just walking dully along / . . . and the torturer's horse / Scratches its innocent behind on a tree." But one thinks more, and most of all, of Dickens himself.

In Dickens the behind-scratching is never far to seek, and that is so, even when the scene is not especially pathetic or tragic. George Orwell, in his essay on Dickens, observes that the "unnecessary detail" is the "outstanding, unmistakable mark of Dickens' writing" and gives the perfect comic instance. Mr. Murdstone is in the habit of ending David Copperfield's lessons every morning with a dreadful sum in arithmetic. "If I go into a cheesemonger's shop, and buy five thousand double-Gloucester cheeses at fourpence halfpenny each, present payment," it always begins (Orwell 1968: 452–4.) As Martin Price insisted in his important essay, "The Irrelevant Detail and the Emergence of Form" (1971), what is typical in Dickens is the Dickens detail, the double-Gloucester cheese.

The permission the artist gives himself to mention double-Gloucester cheese is, after all, permission to let the story take place in the real world. And that is, in turn, permission to *matter*, to move us, not only to laughter or to tears, but as persons engaged creatively in the act of reading, or watching TV. It is in enabling writing to matter that Dickens makes his greatest contribution to the television-writer's art.

REFERENCES

Ford, George H. 1955. *Dickens and His Readers*. Princeton, NJ: Princeton University Press.

Forster, John. 1927. *The Life of Charles Dickens*. London: J. M. Dent. 2 vols.

Orwell, George. 1968. *The Collected Essays, Journalism and Letters*. New York: Harcourt, Brace. Vol. I.

Price, Martin. 1971. "The Irrelevant Detail and the Emergence of Form." *Aspects of Narrative*. Ed. J. Hillis Miller. New York: Columbia University Press. 69–91.

9   Directing Dickens: Alfonso Cuaron's 1998 *Great Expectations*

Pamela Katz

"Let desire be your destiny." (Tagline for the movie poster)

Adapting a literary classic to the screen is a no-win game. Intellectuals hate you. And the non-literary public has no idea what the big deal is about. So what is it that attracted the young Mexican director, Alfonso Cuaron, to attempt something like this, knowing that the critics lie in wait, eager to prove that Hollywood is once again behaving in a shameless manner toward high literature? Here are the answers Cuaron gave me when I put that question to him.

Cuaron was approached for the 1998 Twentieth Century Fox version of *Great Expectations* largely because he had already directed, with great success, the adaptation of another beloved classic, *A Little Princess*. He began his career in 1991, with a Mexican feature, *Solo con tue pareja* (Love in the Time of Hysteria). This promising first film landed him a gig on the prestigious television series, *Fallen Angels*. Next in line was *A Little Princess*, the success of which (both box-office and critical) procured him a strong foothold in Hollywood. Coincidentally, part of Cuaron's preparation for *A Little Princess* included multiple screenings of David Lean's adaptation of *Great Expectations*. What he had yet to learn was that his *Princess* would be far more Dickensian than his *Great Expectations* ever had the chance to become.

When Cuaron first received the script by Mitch Glazer, he was daunted by the title alone. He loved the book, and now knew Lean's film by heart. These were two mighty predecessors and Cuaron was savvy enough to tremble. Nevertheless, he says, it was his Mexican background that gave him the nerve to accept this difficult challenge.

In Mexico, *Great Expectations* is *not* required reading in school. It does not hold the same revered place in a literary canon. Cuaron had read it many times, but just for pleasure. His approach to the film was significantly colored by this cultural difference.

I had none of the incredible solemnity about the great Dickens. I just liked him! But suddenly, I found myself working on a project that *everyone* had an opinion

95

about. Was it "good" to adapt Dickens or "bad"? Did one *have* to be faithful, or was that the entirely wrong approach? I didn't obsess about being faithful. It was more important for me to find a way to use film images to portray the themes and atmosphere of the book.

Before he even opened Glazer's script, Cuaron already knew he was strongly drawn to the quintessential Dickens landscape – a sharply defined, class-driven, nineteenth-century moral universe. And while he was aware that any Hollywood film would focus on the romance between Pip and Estella, he still hoped to include the background of a class-shaped society in the modern film. This would be, he told me, more in the Spanish tradition of tales about the journey from rags to riches.

Turning the initial pages of the script, Cuaron found the story reset in modern times, the marshes of England replaced by the Florida gulf. Pip is renamed Finn (Finnegan Bell). He and his sister's husband Joe are local fishermen, with a side business in lawn and garden care. Finn is a boy with artistic talent, although he initially has no hopes of becoming an artist. Magwitch the convict becomes Arthur Lustig, an escaped convict and Mafia murderer, who forces Finn to help him before he is recaptured. Soon after this defining event, Finn meets Miss Havisham, now Miss Dinsmoor, as well as Estella (still Estella) when he and Joe are asked to come and take care of the ruined garden at "Paradiso Perduto" (the new name for Satis House.) Finn is invited back to play with Estella over a period of seven years. Estella then leaves for Paris, and a heartbroken Finn works on Joe's fishing boat for years, until a secret benefactor offers him, *not* a mysterious fortune, but an one-man art show in New York, (which replaces London), a loft in Tribeca, and a plane ticket. In New York, he finds Estella again and, in cyclical patterns, either has his heart broken, or has wild sex with her. Lustig eventually reappears and reveals that he is Finn's artistic patron, the man who purchased all the paintings at his show. In a sequence which can only be dubbed *Great Expectations* meets *GoodFellas*, Lustig is pursued by enemy thugs, and ends up dying in Finn's lap after being stabbed on the subway. Finn then goes to Paris and there (we hear in voice-over) he has great artistic success. Returning to Paradiso Perduto years later, he finds Estella, now with a young child, and, as in the book, they give the appearance of reuniting.

Glazer's screenplay focused almost exclusively on the theme of unrequited love. Tugging quite forcefully on this single thematic thread, he transformed (or updated?) it into the very requited form of "erotic obsession." That was no surprise for Cuaron, who had been around Hollywood long enough to know that it would have to be some kind of steamy romance, or the budget would go way down. As to the erotic update, Cuaron says up front that it is impossible to make a contemporary film of a book about young people in love *without* sex. "If Dickens were writing today, he would have more sex in his own novels too." As long as Finn was still pining away for Estella, the occasional physicality between them wouldn't lessen his romantic agony. Cuaron's Mexican films deal predominantly with sensuality; the "sexier" version of the Dickens story appealed to him. Sex without love, in his opinion, can be even more painful than no sex at all. He vigorously resisted my argument that every time a piece of classic literature is adapted, repressed or unrequited desire will be translated into sexual display – as if there is no movie audience in the world that can go 111 minutes without any, so to speak, satisfaction.

For Cuaron, the greatest concerns were in another area. In this script, although Finn was poor and Estella rich, there was absolutely no attempt to incorporate the social and cultural backdrop of this hierarchy. Cuaron had hoped for more, even in the context of a full-blown romantic drama.

I knew that if I had my way, I would have made a film of this novel in a more picaresque way, without focusing so much on the romance. It could have been more like *Candide*, a "coming of age in society" story. But I felt that this script still had the potential to include this aspect. For example, I loved the world of the Gulf fishermen, and I had many ideas about how to elaborate on Finn's and Joe's lower-class world.

But there was opposition to this element from all sides. Cuaron was amazed to learn how fervently "most Americans will deny the problems of class in their own country." Cuaron knew that his efforts in this arena would have to be quite subtle. Nevertheless, intrigued by the legendary romance, he was convinced he could "sneak in" more of the broad social meaning of the book.

His first step was making Finn into a credible contemporary character. Pip's passivity would not fly on the screen. Cuaron liked Glazer's solution for the "sudden fortune" of the book. Finn would become an artist, replacing the arbitrary wealth of the nineteenth century with the twentieth-century equivalent: celebrity success. But however clever, this was a hard lump for this classic tale of rags to riches to swallow. Transforming the nineteenth-century Pip, a sensitive boy destined to life as a blacksmith, into Finn, a poor but happy contemporary boy with evident artistic talent, brings us to one of the crucial areas of this adaptation. The entire plot of Dickens's *Great Expectations* revolves around the inability of people to change their station in life. But, unlike Pip, who must rely on chance, screen heroes require the free-choice feature in their make-up, or they self-destruct. Even in this "artist" version, Ethan Hawke still complained about the passivity of his character, and Cuaron had to walk a fine line between helping the young actor identify with his part and destroying the basic structure of the plot, which relies on Finn's inability to make things happen on his own, whether Estella's love or professional success.

Choosing the art world to replace the arbitrary class society of the book worked well. As a sphere in which money and caprice can buy fame and fortune, art could keep the element of surprising success, while simultaneously giving Finn's character the potential to "deserve" it. If Finn's "free choice" is the penalty the story has to pay (and Cuaron agreed with this assessment) he felt it was worth it.

What seems odd is that the attempt to make Finn a believable twentieth-century figure made no parallel change in Estella. Despite her Donna Karan wardrobe, the film's Estella is hardly a modern woman at all. As a powerful woman of the 1990s, surely a profession would only have enhanced her attractiveness to men. So why wasn't she appropriately updated?

Cuaron laughed when I brought this up, accusing me humorously of spying on the rewriting process. As it turns out, Estella *did* have a profession in the original script. And an intriguingly relevant one: an art restorer. But the studio felt that her profession was "not necessary" for the story and, due to the demands of time, it fell to the cutting-room floor. Cuaron misses it, and so does the film.

As a result, Estella's "modernity" focuses only on her sexuality, and yet the story hinges upon the idea that she consistently rejects Finn's desires. The result is a sexy leading lady with nothing to do, except *not* have (too much) sex with the leading man. This paradox made Cuaron's job virtually impossible.

The scene which best illustrates his ingenuity in responding to this dilemma involves Estella's visit to Finn's New York apartment. Here, she asks: "Will you paint me?" Criticized as a cliché, this painting scene is actually the place where Cuaron makes his most impressive attempt to marry the atmosphere of the novel to the taut requirements of a Hollywood film. In this scene, the characters touch each other, without actually touching. Sex without sex. Desire without contact. Communication without words. For Cuaron, this was Estella's call for help, her admission of vulnerability, again, in silence. Paint me. Redefine my image. And although Estella is obviously flirting with Finn, and driving him crazy with desire, she is also giving him the opportunity, for once, to control the situation. He is the artist, she is the subject: this is the first time she lets him, so to speak, be on top. He can finally do what he wants with her body. She can make love to him without admitting it. Thus, in an utterly contemporary setting, Cuaron used the metaphor of painting, in order to emulate, on the screen, Pip and Estella's legendary contrast between feeling and action.

This painting scene, in fact, is far more sensual than the film's actual (and obligatory) sex scene. Here, Finn and Estella run home through the rainy streets of Manhattan, in a scene which must be dubbed *Great Expectations* meets *The Graduate*. This is followed by a scene where they finally consummate their lifelong passion in a night of wild sex. Estella leaves, and the cycle of Finn's agony begins anew. Estella is once again untouchable, but now the game is getting tedious. She's not that untouchable. Cuaron's painting scene, the one where nobody touches, is not only sexier, it's more satisfying. The "virtual" touching fits perfectly into the psychology of Estella and Finn's relationship, proving that from time to time you can "have it all" when it comes to film adaptations of literature.

Despite the insistence that Gwyneth Paltrow's Estella did not need much updating beyond the loss of her virginity, the studio did change its mind about the prominence of her role in the film. And they did so rather late in the game. Although shooting had already begun, a new demand was placed on Cuaron's shoulders: "More Gwyneth," because Paltrow's career had exploded near the beginning of the shoot. Her box-office appeal was soaring to unprecedented heights, driven by the two seemingly disparate forces of the highbrow movie *Emma* and the Calvin Klein advertising campaign. "A brilliant actress, and a delight to work with, this was hardly a painful suggestion," Cuaron says affectionately. But the last-minute demand also entailed much rewriting on the set, complicating an already difficult production.

These changes decimated Cuaron's plans to explore the other, less romantic themes in *Great Expectations*. "I had an idea for a sequence about the fishermen in Florida. At that time, they were going broke and working at McDonald's. But no one was at all interested in this class element except me. And once we began rewriting scenes for Paltrow on the set, well, that was it." From this point on, any spare moment had to be handed over to the assured box-office draw of Paltrow.

Thus Cuaron was compelled to transform the film into a vehicle for Gwyneth Paltrow long after the script had been conceived, and several scenes had already been shot. Despite the script's thin characterization of Estella, Cuaron used powerful images to enhance Paltrow's already compelling screen presence, and he and Glazer wrote several new scenes. But after shooting was completed, the marketing folks threw him a curve ball that Dickens himself, no stranger to commercial concerns, would have had trouble catching.

Estella had to be nice.

The first audience previews revealed that "Estella was not sympathetic." Audiences didn't like her. When I suggested that Estella is not meant to be liked, Cuaron said: "Try saying that when Gwyneth Paltrow is playing the part!" A nice Estella: the only thing that would be more difficult would be casting Meg Ryan as Medea.

This new requirement involved several changes. First, the soon-to-be famous scene in the back of the taxi, when Estella is once more abandoning Finn. Here she tries to explain, in a short paragraph, *why* she is such a cold person. *Why* she is incapable of love. It sticks out. It doesn't belong, this attempt to sum up the psychology of a complex character in four lines of dialogue. It's the nadir of the no-win game. And as I learned, it was shot later, one of those last minute script Band-Aids that screenwriters and directors hate most of all.

Confident that Estella's character had already been very well drawn, Cuaron originally shot the scene in silence. Estella departs in a taxi, leaving a forlorn Finn on the cold, rainy, and dark streets of New York. But previews showed that people did not understand her, and demanded an explanation. "Understanding *why* she is 'like that' was said to make her more sympathetic," Cuaron relates, because if the audience doesn't "like Estella," there goes the box-office potential.

Making Estella nicer knew no end, quite literally. It was actually the final scene of the film that caused one of Cuaron's largest struggles. In his version, Finn and Estella take hands and stare out at the water, while her beautiful daughter plays nearby. The glowing image of Finn and Estella hand in hand gives a very definite indication of their future life together. The fight was all about Estella's golden child. What's with the kid? I mean, how romantic is that? Now we *know* she had sex with someone else besides Finn! And besides, stepchildren are messy. Mothers are messy. Cuaron was pressured to lose the little girl, and to film Finn and Estella running into each other's arms, kissing romantically without a care in the world, and in close-up, please! But with his instinctive and fierce attachment to the real ending of the book, Cuaron fought for his version, and, for once, prevailed.

On some notable occasions, Cuaron did manage to use his directorial imprint in order to heighten those scenes that at least had the potential to explore the issue of class. Finn's now quite attractive sister voluntarily leaves Joe for another man, and a better life. Although the screenplay painted the sister as hard-hearted, Cuaron directed the scene in such a way as to illustrate her conflicting emotions. It is clear that she loves her brother, and that this choice is made with mixed feelings. Without changing a line of the script, Cuaron managed to make her ambivalence keenly felt, lending her character a complexity not on Glazer's or Dickens's pages. Cuaron also wanted to reveal that blue-collar people have no less warmth or responsibility than the upper classes, only fewer choices. In a few brief scenes, Finn's sister starkly reveals the trapped sensibility of those without money, education, or opportunity.

Another scene which particularly stands out in this regard is the one where Joe surprises Finn by coming to his one-man show in New York. At first unforgivably snide to Joe (who appears in a cheap, rented tuxedo), Finn is then pained by his own cruelty toward the kind man who raised him. All this is communicated in silence, Finn's remorse, Joe's eternal understanding, the disastrous wardrobe. As written, it could have read as a simple portrayal of Finn's cruelty. In Cuaron's hands, we watch the two worlds of poor and rich, working class and elite, collide with pathos. The power of this scene reveals Cuaron's own passion for the theme of class.

Finally, the film is, simply, a stunning visual achievement. Given all the dramaturgical difficulties, Cuaron was happy to have one of the few people with whom he could communicate his truest vision of the story, and without the limitation of words. Longtime collaborator, Mexican cinematographer Emmanuel Lubezki, worked his usual magic. When the words fail to communicate, the pictures win the day. The bright, blinding light of the Gulf Bay bounces off the water, only to be held back by the covered windows of Paradiso Perduto. Anne Bancroft's Miss Dinsmoor is first found dancing to "Besame Mucho" (the song title is also the name of Cuaron's own film company) while crumbling fabric keeps the sun out of her house with faded tenacity. Coming in from the bright outdoors, our eyes adjust along with Finn's to find Dinsmoor's face in a grotesque close-up, mirroring the desperation of her surroundings. With the help of production designer Tony Burrough, Lubezki shows us the supernatural decay of Dinsmoor's household so fiercely you can almost smell it. Each location has a dominating color: the dark and dusty brown corridors of her house contrast with the warm daylight outside. In New York, we go quickly to blue and yellow as taxis glide down the glistening streets of the big city. The sparkling spots of illumination in Finn's fancy art gallery contrast with the gritty neon light of the New York subway.

Locations, such as Dinsmoor's house, Finn's loft, and the art gallery, are always shown in wide shots, but sliced by sharp shafts of light and, again, a distinctive use of color. In contrast, faces are seen in tight close-ups, where Lubezki's camera lingers, often in silence, allowing the audience into characters' emotions through the expression of their eyes. The ever elusive Estella often wears memorable sunglasses – to keep out the glare of the Florida sun, as well as anyone (like Finn) who wants to find a way into her heart.

Finn's voice-over dominates the film and, in like fashion, we see most of the film through his eyes. His vision of Estella is particularly stylized. Her face is usually photographed in an extreme (and extremely flattering) close-up: it always appears suddenly, by Finn's side, and then just as suddenly leaves. This surreal touch makes her seem more like a figment of Finn's imagination than a solid human figure. Her reality rests in his mind alone.

Using the camera to represent Finn's point of view allows us into the slanted reality of his love-soaked consciousness. In this way, the film uses something close to the literary technique of magical realism. This cinematic effect is most starkly revealed in the scene where Finn is abandoned by Estella for what he believes to be the last time. When he looks up into the sky in despair, we cut immediately to Estella's face in the window of an airplane. It is intentionally unclear as to whether we are sharing his inner vision, or if we are seeing something completely outside Finn's point of view. Such surrealistic departures echo the literature of Latin America more than England. In these lush images we see how adept the Mexican Cuaron is at using film language to portray the visualization of desire. The pictures capture the universal and timeless phenomenon of desire far more convincingly than the hard plot of the film.

At the end, when birds fly through Dinsmoor's roofless house, we are treated to a sensual familiarity with a location (Miss Havisham's house) that is enshrined in the imaginations of countless people over more than a hundred years. Lubezki allows us to enter – and he does so with mastery.

Toward the end of our conversations, I asked Cuaron if it would have been different if he had made this film in Mexico.

Well, that was a running joke on the set between me and Emmanuel [the cinematographer]. We said if we were adapting this book for a 1950s Mexican melodrama, what would we change? And you know that scene where he runs to Miss Dinsmoor's house and is shouting up at the window to Estella? He's shouting "I did it all for you!" If that had been a Mexican scene, he would have been drunk, there would have been a group of Mariachis playing behind him, and he would be singing, instead of shouting. That was the main difference between an American and a Mexican version – ours didn't have any Mariachis.

Perhaps that's why Cuaron returned to his native Mexico to make his next film. The subject is the contemporary erotic tale *Y Tu Mama Tambien* (And Your Mother Too). Like Pip, Cuaron returned home to assess the ups and downs of his lucky fortunes. After making a more personal film, he gained strength and wisdom, and came back north again. In the winter of 2001, I found Cuaron putting the final touches on his latest American film. I thank him for stealing precious moments out of the editing room – and for discussing his work with unusual grace and candor.

10   Playing Dickens: Miriam Margolyes

A conversation with John Glavin

Your career has been uniquely associated with Dickens's work. You have per-
formed Dickens on the radio, on film, and on the stage. Is there a Dickens
character that you would like to play that you haven't yet done?
Yes, I very much want to play Mrs. Gamp.

In the mid-1990s the BBC decided to do *Martin Chuzzlewit* (1994)
and the director was Pedr James. I wrote him and I asked if he would
interview me. And he said that I wasn't on his list, but he would come
and see me in *She Stoops to Conquer*, which I'd asked him to do. I was
playing in London, in the West End, at the time. He came to see it. I was
playing Mrs. Hardcastle. And I didn't hear from him again. And then I
rang him up, *as* Mrs. Gamp. I said, "See her again, sweetums." And he
came to the phone and he was amused and he said, "Alright. I'll come
and have lunch." But he said "I think you're too young."

When I arrived at lunch, the make-up lady was there and he said,
"Could you make Miriam up to look the age of Mrs. Gamp, that I think
Mrs. Gamp should look, which is about sixty." Which was about ten years
older than I really was at the time. And she said, "Oh yes! You just do
this and this," and she said what you do. And then we talked. It seemed
to me that he was afraid that I knew more about Dickens than he did
and that he thought I would unbalance the production by being sort of
bossy, and saying, "Well I think it should be done . . ." Which, of course,
I would never have done because I'm too professional. You just don't
do that. It doesn't help. You just do what the director wants. You can
suggest things and it's up to him to make the choice. Because when you
work in television or film, you put yourself in the hands of the director.
That's what you have to do. Sometimes you don't agree with it and you
can argue your point, but he has to have the final say. And there's no
questions about that.

He said to me, "You know, everyone tells me that you should be Mrs.
Gamp. And I'm getting irritated with everybody telling me." And I said,
"Well, I would love to do it." And he said, "Well, you're a very good
radio actress," and he put the stress on radio. And I thought that was

very insulting, because I'm not just a radio actress. And he knew that. He'd just seen me giving a very highly praised performance in a West End play. He just didn't want to have me in it. I mean he just didn't want to. He chose an extremely fine actress called Elizabeth Spriggs, who has a glorious record in English theater. She's a wonderful actress but in my somewhat jealous opinion, it wasn't one of her best roles.

I've always thought of Mrs. Gamp as short and fat like me, with very little neck. Elizabeth is tall and stately. And Mrs. Gamp was a little butterball of a woman, like me, with no neck. Like me. I am Mrs. Gamp. It is the central tragedy of my professional life that I didn't get to play her. So one day, if they ever do a remake of *Martin Chuzzlewit*, I hope I'll play that.

Other than that, I'm omnivorous. I want to play every Dickens role I can. I'm not in the *David Copperfield* [1999], but there are not many parts that I could play in that. I mean I'm not right for Peggotty. I'm not right for Betsey Trotwood. So you have to have a certain humility about things. I'm not going to be able to do everything. I would love to do Clara Murdstone, absolutely love to. But it's a question of what people will ask you to play. Zoë Wanamaker is playing that, and she will be completely perfect. I do think that being fat is both a plus and a minus. I think that you have to accept that you're physically limited. I am physically limited in what I can do. But there are many fat characters in Dickens.

That's a particularly Dickensian thing, that Dickens's characters have such defined shapes. It is quite wrong for me to be Betsey Trotwood when she is clearly an angular creature. That's why Maggie Smith is perfectly good casting. But I was wonderful on radio when I played Betsey Trotwood. It's one of my best pieces of work. And the reason I think that I got it so well was that when she was talking about her husband she cried. And that gives Betsey another layer.

You see you have to find the note. Most people have lots of notes. And when you're acting, you've got to be another person. So, I try to do that, literally, I look into the text and if there's another texture there – another layer – then I've got to try and embody that. I don't think it's coming from me. I think it's all in the text. And my problem with critics is that they don't go to the text enough. If you go to the text, you'll find everything that you need. You don't need to bring in suggestions from somewhere else.

And I don't know that there's much difference really, in doing any character – Shakespeare, Dickens, Chekhov – because the way you work on it, for me, is the same. You try to find the truth of it, whatever it is. I always had more fun doing Dickens than anything else. I think that's because his prose is so astonishing. He uses a word – words pop out. And I am just dazzled by that. I mean for me it's Migs in *Barnaby Rudge* at the moment. And that "Mim" of hers, I just can't get over it. Where did he find that? It's so cunning and clever and it just releases a whole comic area for me. Because what it implies is that she's trying to be refined. Because mim, you think mimsy of course, but "Mim" is what someone would say who did not want to say "Mum" . . . because Mum is common. So immediately it's just there and it's done for you in one word.

At about the same time you did Age of Innocence *for Martin Scorsese and* Little Dorrit *for Christine Edzard. Could you talk about the differences?*
Funnily enough there are some similarities because they're both geniuses and they're both intensely focused on the work that they're doing, so you do feel as if you're under a beam of light when you're working for both those individuals. Scorsese is an easy person to work for. Christine in a way is much more demanding. Martin stood back from it, he wasn't so much a hands-on, he wouldn't say "turn there, do that." Christine was very much more an *auteur* in that way. He would leave it to you as to whether you turned or not. He would just come in between each take and make a very, very small comment, or nothing at all. So he's not breathing down your neck. Whereas Christine . . . and I wouldn't put it like that, because it's not that she breathes down your neck because it's revelatory what she says and asks of you. But it's much, much harder to do. He's much easier to work for.

Do you think there are some Dickens novels that lend themselves better to adaptation than others?
He's a filmic writer. I mean, it's scenes. It's in scenes. You can see them. They're all wonderful. I just wish they'd do it better. I just wish that they'd give Dickens his thing and not try and impose. I'm not a writer, and I'm not a television expert. But I do think that Dickens paces his novels quite cleverly, and very consciously, and they move. They have their own trajectory. And I think that if you try to impose another graph on it, you distort it, the work. I think his long scenes should be allowed to be long scenes. And his short scenes should be short scenes, rather than scriptwriters playing around with it. But they all do. They will and they will.

Are you thinking of any particular examples where you think that it wasn't Dickensian enough?
I loved *Our Mutual Friend*, but I do think that they didn't get the class thing right. And that's a constant problem in most of the Dickens things that I see. That the upper-class people don't speak like upper-class people and the lower-class people don't speak like lower-class people. They all

have that terrible kind of in-between nothing. Especially the younger ones. The young women. Gaffer Hexam's daughter spoke like a lady. If she speaks like a lady, there's no reason why Eugene Wrayburn shouldn't marry her. I mean she should "tawk like 'at. Oderwise, 'ere's no point, is 'ere?" Lizzie should be rough.

Doesn't Dickens sort of fudge that? Doesn't he make her from the start a sort of lady-in-waiting?
Well, he does do that because he's uneasy with the young sexual women. He doesn't classify them. Like Nancy. But then that's your job, the actor's job. You've got to be very dextrous vocally. You've got to be adroit. And actresses today aren't. They're not taught to be at drama school, perhaps. Or they don't hear. Class distinctions are flattening out to some extent, today even in England. But I think it's crucial to show it in Dickens, because that's what he was writing about. He was a social climber and I think that informed all of his work. And that's part of the tension in Dickens, that he is both critical of the establishment and wants to be part of it, like all social climbers.

It is in the rhythms of his characters. And in the vocabulary. I mean, he allows his comic characters to be clearly cockney or country folk, or whatever. But he doesn't allow the characters with gravitas to have it. And I suppose you could say Lizzie Hexam is a kind of heroine, so she's not allowed to sound off. Off is what we call muck speech.

Famously that's the case with Oliver. When you read Oliver Twist, *on the radio, what did you do?*
I think I gave him a slightly sort of countrified sound. [*Her voice gets a little higher with a little more cockney.*] I think he was sort of like that, I'm not quite sure, but I think so. Just a little bit of something like that. Just slightly.

So he could sound more like Dickens himself?
Well, no, accent changes. As it certainly did for Dickens. I mean, he must have had a rough sound to start. But everybody who heard him when he read said that his voice was wonderful. That it was a rich and sonorous sound and it certainly used received pronunciation, otherwise people would have remarked on it. But this was a little boy who had grown up in Portsmouth and then went down to Chatham, so I think he would have had a slightly country sound. But he probably didn't sound cockney.

But what a formative time in his life was that time when he was at the blacking factory, getting up at four in the morning, walking across

London to work. Through the most noisome, unsavory, and scary parts of London. Seeing prostitutes fucking up against a wall, and drunken people spewing out, and pickpockets...he saw all that. Actually saw it. I think of it a lot, that amazing thing, every day walking right across London. From Camden Town to the Strand, it's a long way.

Is that part of why Dickens seems to be such a natural for the screen?
Yes, because I think Dickens had the eye. And when he saw things he saw it the way that a child sees things. It's an in-taking gaze. Everything went in. He never stopped seeing things. And that detail is astonishing. He was trained as a journalist, of course. That accuracy is there, as well. It's the mature accuracy plus that open gaze. You know when children look at things they just see it. Well, he did that. He never stopped.

Could you talk a little about your one-woman Dickens theater piece?
The show wasn't meant to be a one-person show. It was devised and first performed, in Edinburgh, as a two-person show. And I had a wonderful chap named David Timsen who worked with me. And it was the two of us. And he played Bumble and I played Mrs. Corney, and he also played Charles Dickens and, it's been so long I can't remember, but a number of others. It was a twosome, absolutely equal. Then he got married and didn't want to come to America, unless he got a very large sum of money, which in an Equity-waiver theater you don't do, which is where I first performed it. So I had to do it alone, because he wouldn't come. And that's how I got to play Mr. Bumble because my Mr. Bumble let me down. I was jilted.

The whole show had to be rejigged in a week. I will never get over it. It was the most terrifying, abhorrent, ghastly time of my life, because I had done a show with huge success in Edinburgh which I had hoped to replicate here. Instead of which, we were working to the last minute with me trying to remember...you know, learning all of these parts and rejigging the show. And what happened was we tried to hire another person to take it over and he performed on the first night. He was so terrible we had to sack him. And then I had to do it on my own.

He was fired after the first performance. It was a preview thing. And the producer was Norman Lear, who was the producer of the series I did that wasn't a success, but he was lovely and I love him and he was terrific to me. He said, "You can't do with that guy. You gotta forget it. He's outta here. Send him back, pay him off, I don't care, but just forget it." And so there we are. We had to start again in a week. And I did Mr. Bumble after a week. And I said "I don't want to do it! I don't do drag!"

But it worked, you see. It was amazing. So it wasn't meant to happen, but it was meant to happen. I will still go on doing that show as long as people ask me to do it. And I am asked all the time to do it, so I will keep on doing it. And people say "Don't you want to change it?" NO! It's done! That's the show. It won't change.

It's just as Sonia Fraser and I wrote it. Sonia collaborated with me in writing it, and she directed the show, both in England and America. Her vision made the show work. Every actress needs a director, most especially in a one-woman show.

Part IV

11   Cinematic Dickens and uncinematic words

Kamilla Elliott

The field of novel/film studies is troubled with a central critical paradox. On the one hand, scholars declare film's integral formal, narrative, and historical connections to the novel, especially the Victorian novel. Sergei Eisenstein decrees the Dickensian novel "cinematic" (1949: 195). Christian Metz argues that film took over the social function of the Victorian novel (1977: 110). On the other hand, scholars argue that film and the novel are inherently opposed as "words" and "images." The same Eisenstein, and most film aestheticians following him, insist that any type of verbal narration in film is "uncinematic" (Stromgren and Norden 1984: 173). Nowhere is this paradox more marked than in the claim that Dickens is "cinematic" but that words are not. What, after all, is "Dickens" apart from words? This chapter argues against both claims: that Dickens is cinematic, and that words are not.

The opening of David Lean's 1946 film of *Great Expectations* exemplifies this paradoxical theoretical claim. The film begins with a shot of the novel, *Great Expectations*, opened to chapter 1. John Mills, who plays the adult Pip, reads the opening paragraph in a clipped, dry voice-over: "My father's family name being Pirrip, and my christian name Philip, my infant tongue could make of both names nothing longer or more explicit than Pip. So, I called myself Pip, and came to be called Pip." The circling self-referentiality, repetition, and clutter of subordinate clauses renders the prose tedious and confusing, flowing at the speed of sound in a medium that operates at the speed of light, so that the viewer is relieved when a scouring wind rises and turns the pages rapidly in a parody of flip-book animation, which then gives way to the more sophisticated and dynamic animation processes of film. The scenes that follow are deliberately wordless, showcasing film's visual and aural vivacity. A silhouetted Pip runs pushed by a howling wind along the shoreline to a shadowy, ghoulish graveyard, where he is menaced by waving troll-like trees and creaking branches, which grasp at him like arthritic witches' arms. When we next see text from the novel, it is on the gravestone that records the deaths of Pip's parents. Unlike most films that open with shots of their founding text, this film does not return to show the novel closing at the end: the novel is dead and buried by the middle of the film's first scene, commemorated on the gravestone with Pip's parents. This film thus both inscribes and dematerializes the novel on which it purports to be based, in much the same way that academic criticism claims Dickens and the Victorian novel as cinematic ancestors and yet, paradoxically, denies the paternity of their words as uncinematic.

Cinematic Dickens

Montage, film historians claim, allowed film to be born as a new art rather than to be defined as a compilation of arts or, worse still, as a technological recording device for other arts (Bordwell 1997: 13). Together with outdoor scenes, so the story goes, montage freed film from its designation as a flatter, less vivid, soundless, and colorless form of pictorial theater. Most important of all, scholars tell us montage created a new kind of language, a visual syntax that freed film from dependence on verbal narration. And montage, they insist, derived from scenic and visual shifts in the Victorian novel.

Even A. B. Walkley of the London *Times*, who in 1922 expressed skepticism regarding Griffith's claim that Dickens was his source for montage, perceives a connection between montage and the Victorian novel more generally:

Mr. Griffith found the idea to which he clung thus heroically in Dickens . . . he might have found the same idea almost anywhere . . . Newton deduced the law of gravitation from the fall of an apple; but a pear or a plum would have done just as well. The idea is merely that of a break in the narrative, a shifting of the story from one group of characters to another group. You will meet with it in Thackeray, George Eliot, Trollope, Meredith, Hardy, and, I suppose, every other Victorian novelist. (Cited in Eisenstein 1949: 205)

There are, however, several problems with this history of film and its connections to the Victorian novel.

Given its roots in photography, magic-lantern shows, public spectacles, theater, painting, *tableaux vivants*, and various optical toys, it is highly doubtful that film required the invisible visualities of the Victorian novel to discover its own visuality. Indeed, art historians have repeatedly and convincingly demonstrated that any visual "cinematic" propensities in Victorian novels are readily traceable to prior and contemporaneous visual and dramatic arts, arts which influenced both novel and film directly. Rhoda Flaxman has shown that, while visual description in the Victorian novel "often yields an effect we moderns call cinematic," it derives from older visual arts (1987: 9–10). Moreover, Griffith's cinematographer Billy

Bitzer attested to drawing on Victorian paintings to create his composi-
tions, with nary a mention of Dickens's prose (Gunning 1991: 250). Even
more tellingly, Dickens credits the theater for his own use of "montage":

It is the custom on the stage, in all good murderous melodramas, to present the
tragic and the comic scenes, in as regular alternation, as the layers of red and white
in a side of streaky bacon . . . sudden shiftings of the scene, and rapid changes of
time and place, are not only sanctioned in books by long usage, but are by many
considered as the great art of authorship. (1966: 168–9)

When one considers that Griffith was both playwright and stage actor before he turned to film, it is improbable that the technique filtered through
to him directly from the novel without any influence from theater.

Why, then, do both film and literary critics continue to press the
Dickens/cinema analogy and the primacy of the novel/film link over film's
debts to other arts, like painting and theater? Both mythologies thrive,
despite considerable contradictory evidence, because they serve each side
of the literature/film rivalry. On the literary side, designating Dickens in
particular and the Victorian novel more generally the immediate ancestors of film forges a history of narrative that creates a continuous line
from oral poetry through the rise of the drama and subsequently the rise
of novel through to film and television. Such a lineage gives the literary
camp film credits, positioning literary scholars as experts credentialed to
discuss films as well as written texts, and to do so using literary methods, methods that tend to favor literature over film whenever they are
discussed in conjunction with each other.

And yet this anachronistic analogy has not been overthrown by film
studies, because it also supports film's bid for cultural and representational dominance. The myth of the cinematic novel, intriguingly, asserts
that film grew out of the Victorian novel – though not from its words
and not from its illustrations. Such an argument creates a mythical virgin
birth for film, in which film derives only invisible visualities and immaterial structures from the novel. Were film to acknowledge its debt to the
novel's actual words and illustrations, or to other arts, like painting and
theater, its birth would appear far more mundanely derivative. The film
camp represents the partially cinematic novel as an incomplete precursor
of the purely cinematic film, establishing a hierarchy in which any film
trumps any novel, since all films are more "cinematic" than even the most
cinematic fiction. The anachronism of the cinematic Victorian novel thus
makes film the glorious fulfillment of what is only a seed of promise in
the novel, rather than representing itself as the feeble offspring of a more
potent narrative parent. The literary camp does not counter this aspect of
the filmic myth, because parenting film makes Dickens modern and even

timeless. It bestows on him seminal and prescient powers that allow him to be read not only as our contemporary, but as ahead of his own time, prophetic rather than antiquated, eccentric, or sentimentally nostalgic.

Uncinematic words

The move to denigrate words as uncinematic and, as far as possible, to rid cinema of them has been important to establishing the myth of film's virgin birth from the novel. By and large, film aestheticians and historians have tended to see language of any kind in film as hampering and competing with film's language of montage, an indication of filmic immaturity or filmmaker ineptitude, a reluctant concession to narrative necessity, a contamination of the pure art of film by literature. I want to question the claim that words are uncinematic through a consideration of intertitles (also called title cards, subtitles, leaders, and captions) in so-called 'silent' film adaptations of Dickens's novels. While my readings are limited to these adaptations, they do have more general applications to a considerable body of Anglo-American (melo)dramatic films made in the same period.

Purists from the earliest days of film to the present have perceived the pinnacle of filmic representation as one entirely free from verbal language. James Card rhapsodizes over "silent films so eloquent in their pantomime that they needed no intertitles whatsoever – no dialogue, no explanatory titles, just pure, uninterrupted images. What a boon to international distribution – no language barrier anywhere!" (1994: 60). Ralph Stephenson and J. R. Debrix assert, "In silent cinema, the written captions were always an alien element and never combined with the visuals into an artistic whole" (1978: 207). This sense that intertitles comprised a contamination of film by literature was strong during the silent period. In 1928, the Ukrainian theorist Leonid Skrypnyk complained, "Cinema has to humiliate itself and seek compromises. Intertitles constitute the first major compromise" (20). A reviewer in 1929 referred to intertitles as "literary hemorrhages'" (Milne 1929: 101). Intertitles, the argument runs, were a temporary crutch, a compromise with literature, while film fumbled toward its manifest destiny, its own "visual" language, the editing between shots that could create a purely visual narrative and syntax apart from words. In this argument we see that not only does montage free film from theater, but also from the written word of the novel.

Film historians argue unilaterally that, the more film developed its visual language, the less it required and used verbal intertitles. The evidence, however, overwhelmingly contradicts this claim. While some early and late silent films do indeed manage without intertitles and, while there is a temporary reduction in the length of intertitles between the early silent period (before 1908) and the middle silent period (1908–17), in the late silent period (1918–26), when the celebrated visual "language" (editing) is firmly established, in the vast majority of films, intertitles are far more prolix and appear much more frequently than before film "language" took root. Bafflingly, film historians do not contest these facts: those who address intertitles do confirm that they grew more verbose and frequent; they simply ignore the critical paradox.

Dickensian adaptations provide succinct illustrations of the more general phenomenon that intertitles grew longer and more frequent. Vitagraph's 1911 *A Tale of Two Cities* uses between eleven and twelve intertitles per reel of film; the later 1926 adaptation of the novel (titled *The Only Way*, after the 1899 stage version) bears an unusually high number, even for this period – thirty-five per reel. Since many cards are narrative titles and not just stage dialogue, the higher number cannot be explained simply as the result of adapting a play. Moreover, length as well as frequency increases in the late silent period: the curt cards of the 1911 *A Tale of Two Cities* give way to florid and verbose cards in the 1926 version. For example, 1911's "The first stain of the revolution" becomes 1926's "And whilst St. Antoine danced the Carmagnole, never did the moon rise with a milder radiance on a quiet corner in Soho"; 1911's "To the guillotine" elongates to 1926's "In the black prison of the Conciergerie, the doomed awaited their call to the Guillotine." Another pair of mid- and late-period silent films adapting the same Dickensian novel show similar tendencies: the 1912 Thomas Bentley *Oliver Twist* bears between seven and eight intertitles per reel, while the 1922 First National version carries eighteen per reel. Again, the cards are not only more frequent, but also more loquacious. 1912's "Rose saves Oliver, who is adopted by Mrs. Maylie," becomes "Bill's murderous purpose was thwarted by the Providence of a just God and Oliver quickly recovered from the slight wound in his shoulder." (Intertitles often vary from print to print in the silent era. I have seen other versions of intertitles for this film: here, I cite the intertitles from the British Film Institute's copy.)

Not only does the argument that film "language" decreased the need for intertitles in late silent films fail to hold for a majority of films, the idea that film editing is a purely visual language is also contradicted by a closer look at intertitles in late silent films. The very word, intertitles, suggests intercutting; indeed, some of the first editing practices were between intertitles and single-shot scenes. The earliest film in which I have found intertitles (two years earlier than any other film scholar to date has located) is W. R. Booth's 1901 *Scrooge, Or Marley's Ghost*. The first extant intertitle reads:

Scene II.
Marley's Ghost
Shows Scrooge Visions of himself in
CHRISTMASES PAST.

It is followed by two vignettes, one of a woman and boy together and one of a young man kissing a girl, representing somewhat obscurely Scrooge's rescue from boarding school by his sister and his broken engagement. The film continues to alternate cards and scenes: thus between words and scenes lie some of the earliest origins of film editing.

This kind of editing has been overlooked, I believe, not only because of the low status of language in film aesthetics, but also because editing between intertitles and filmed scenes points to montage practices based in verbal language rather than freed from it. To set the stage for this argument, a brief consideration of mid-silent titular practices (1908–17) is in order. In this period, intertitles continue to function as scene headings or verbal explications of filmed scenes, increasingly appearing only to represent what images could not specify or what would require too many images to delineate. This becomes clear when we look at Vitagraph's 1911 *A Tale of Two Cities*. Intertitles append names to faces and, within that naming, state the legal relations of characters ("Doctor Manette, his servant Defarge, and his infant daughter, Lucie"). Similarly, words make spaces places ("In England"; "In Paris") and specify passages of narrative time ("Eighteen years after the events of Part 1"). They represent words spoken by silently moving mouths ("Take this estate for the benefit of the people"); convey the silent thoughts and plots of characters ("The Marquis, now hating Darnay, sends a criminal to London to accuse him of being a spy"); explain the significance of a scene ("Darnay acquitted") or an absence from a scene ("The Marquis' companion fails to appear"). Titles pull the general from specific images ("The starving populace"); provide an adjectival narrative tone ("An ominous summons"; "A joyful reunion"); and offer moral commentary on an action ("The aftermath of the crime. The wrecked home").

But this rigid division of narrative labor between intertitles and filmed scenes led increasingly to complaints of narrative disruption, resulting in new intertitular practices in the late silent period aimed to ease the transitions between intertitles and filmed scenes. As one writer in 1921 put it:

Picturegoers of to-day who can recall the early days of the kinema industry will retain memories of the crude and ugly explanatory sub-titles that once disfigured the silver sheet. In those days the sub-title was regarded as a necessary blemish on the face of the film, and no attempt was made towards either literary or artistic improvement. (Anon. 1921: 21)

During this period, intertitles were illustrated to ease the transition between pictures and words, and texts (like letters) were legible in the scenes. Dialogue cards increased in proportion to narrative cards, so that words would appear to come from the scenes rather than from an omniscient narrator. But for my argument here, the most relevant effort made to remedy disjunctions lies in changing editing practices between intertitles and filmed scenes. Far from film language replacing verbal language in the late silent period, there develops a complex interweaving of intertitles and scene shots to form hybrid verbal-visual "sentences." In Maurice Elvey's 1920 film of *Bleak House*, a scene shot between two intertitles is not simply an illustration of the words but part of a complex visual-verbal sentence:

INTERTITLE But the third morning of the elopement brings bad news...
Shot of a distraught Captain Rawdon holding a letter; close-up of the letter's text revealing his disinheritance
INTERTITLE ... and the sheriff's officer tracks Rawdon and executes his warrant.

The narrative here is primarily verbal, using the text of the letter to explicate the intertitle's "bad news." But the shots between the intertitles also illustrate and dramatize the character's reaction to the news, so that the narrative import is by no means entirely conveyed by words. More importantly, for all the rhetoric addressing the visual and musical rhythms of montage, in these sentences the montage is guided primarily by verbal syntax.

Frequently in the latter part of the late silent period, intertitles carry less of the narrative and create more purely rhetorical and rhythmic effects. The last two intertitles of the 1924 *Little Dorrit* contain only dependent clauses, between which are sandwiched shots of Little Dorrit's wedding to Arthur Clennam: "Beyond the sombre shadow of the Marshalsea..." and "And that was one hundred years ago." The shot of the wedding thus forms the main "clause" of the "sentence"; words state only a vague place and distant time and have a primarily rhetorical and emotive effect.

In some cases, incomplete sentences begun by intertitles are completed by pictures alone. When Dot asks John where he found the Old Man in the 1923 film of *The Cricket on the Hearth*, we see a shot of John replying, but no intertitles represent his words. Instead, the scene fades to black and opens on a new outdoor scene depicting John's discovery and conveyance of the Old Man. An intertitle concludes only: "– and he slept all the way here."

These rhetorical rhythms are not limited to dialogue cards, but extend to narrative cards as well. Omitting actor credits for Manette and Defarge that appear on two of the cards, *The Only Way* contains a sequence that runs:

INTERTITLE Then, sixteen years . . .
Long shot of the Marquis and guests feasting
INTERTITLE . . . Years that to Evrémonde recorded only the passing of Time
Midshot of the Marquis and guests
INTERTITLE Years that so changed another, that even, freed from the Bastille, the twilight of his mind held him prisoner
Midshot of Manette holding a shoe and staring vacantly at camera
Long shot of a concerned Defarge, Lorry, and Lucie standing near Manette
INTERTITLE Years that burned the hatred of a decadent aristocracy into one having reason to hate
Midshot of Defarge speaking

At a time when most intertitles are end-stopped, the absence of punctuation at the end of these cards positions the shots more particularly as punctuation. The semantic and syntactic relationships of the sequence are thus established by the run-on sentence of the intertitles, rather than by narrative relationships between images (looker and looked-at, actor and reactor). Here intertitles function as rhetorical pacers, adding the emphasis and force of dramatic pauses. In this way, images come to take on aural properties as well as visual ones. But again, the shots do not have purely aural and rhetorical functions: they also illustrate the words, even empirically "proving" their hypotheses.

The evidence that Dickens is not cinematic and that words are, even in that bastion of cinematicity, montage, is clearly overwhelming. Yet the two interdependent mythologies persist regardless, because both literary and film camps use them to foster interdisciplinary rivalries and word/image rivalries within film itself. The evidence of these hybrid titling practices points to new ways in which Victorian novels and films, as well as the words and pictures within films, can be explored, indicating that, far from destroying a fruitful connection between Dickens and the screen, putting to rest the myths of cinematic Dickens and uncinematic words will open rather than close down paths for analysis.

REFERENCES

Books
Anon. 1921. "The Art of the Sub-Title." *The Picturegoer* May: 21.
Bordwell, David. 1997. *On the History of Film Style.* Cambridge, MA: Harvard University Press.
Card, James. 1994. *Seductive Cinema: The Art of Silent Film.* New York: Knopf.
Dickens, Charles. 1966. *Oliver Twist.* Harmondsworth: Penguin. Originally published 1837–9.

Eisenstein, Sergei. 1949. "Dickens, Griffith, and the Film Today." *Film Form: Essays in Film Theory*. Ed. and trans. Jay Leyda. New York: Harcourt, Brace & World, Inc. 195–255.

Flaxman, Rhoda L. 1987. *Victorian Word-Painting and Narrative: Toward the Blending of Genres*. Ann Arbor, MI: UMI Research Press.

Gunning, Tom. 1991. *D. W. Griffith and the Origins of American Narrative Film*. Urbana: University of Illinois Press.

Metz, Christian. 1977. *The Imaginary Signifier: Psychoanalysis and the Cinema*. Trans. Celia Britton, Annwyl Williams, Ben Brewster, and Alfred Guzzetti. Bloomington: Indiana University Press.

Milne, Peter. 1929. No title. *Photoplay*. Jan.: 101.

Moynahan, Julian. 1981. "Seeing the Book, Reading the Movie." *The English Novel and the Movies*. Eds. Michael Klein and Gillian Parker. New York: Frederick Ungar. 143–54.

Skrypnyk, Leonid. 1928. *Narysyz teorii mystetstva kino*. Kiev, Ukraine: Derzhavne vyd.

Stephenson, Ralph and J. R. Debrix. 1978. *The Cinema as Art*. Harmondsworth: Penguin.

Stromgren, Richard L. and Martin F. Norden. 1984. *Movies: A Language in Light*. Englewood Cliffs, NJ: Prentice-Hall.

Films
1901. *Scrooge: Or, Marley's Ghost*. Dir. W. R. Booth. R. W. Paul. UK.

1911. *A Tale of Two Cities*. Dir. William Humphrey and Stuart J. Blackton. Vitagraph. USA.

1912. *Oliver Twist*. Dir. Thomas Bentley. Hepworth Films. UK.

1913. *Scrooge*. Dir. Leedham Bantock. Zenith Films. UK.

1920. *Bleak House*. Dir. Maurice Elvey. Ideal Films. UK.

1922. *Oliver Twist*. Dir. Frank Lloyd. First National. USA.

1923. *The Cricket on the Hearth*. Dir. Lorimer Johnston. Biograph/Paul Gerson Pictures. USA.

1923. *David Copperfield*. Dir. A. W. Sandberg. Nordisk Films. Denmark.

1924. *Little Dorrit*. Dir. A. W. Sandberg. Nordisk Films. Denmark.

1926. *The Only Way*. Dir. Herbert Wilcox. UK.

1946. *Great Expectations*. Dir. David Lean. Cineguild. UK.

12 Dickens, Eisenstein, film

Garrett Stewart

Dickens was born for film. That's the truism. The further truth that film was born from Dickens is the burden of the most famous genealogical essay in the literature of cinema, by the renowned Soviet director and theorist Sergei Eisenstein. The accomplishment of that essay, and certain motivated blind spots in its attention, is the topic of this one. Though never thinking to film a Dickens novel, Eisenstein understood the cinematic strategies – if not the deeper logic – of the novelist's construction as never before. His observations offer an endlessly fertile point of departure for what I would call a filmic grasp of Dickensian prose.

The trouble comes mostly with filmed Dickens. What movies repeatedly ignore in his writing, as they milk locations for his "atmosphere" and dial up his dialogue, is exactly the shared basis of the two media, film and prose fiction: their common reliance on the very dynamo of narration. This is the structural engineering of storytelling itself, operating in Dickens's prose from the level of syllable and word to sentence and paragraph. In stylistic matters, adaptation is usually the graveyard of appreciation. Occasional screen exceptions, to which we will come round in the end, only cement that general verdict by contrast. For what Dickens secretly willed to film is exactly what no copyright could ever have protected: a whole new mode of kinetic sequencing in which juxtaposition is submitted to continual resynthesis. Such oscillating effects take shape in ways that Eisenstein, given his allegiance not only to a dialectical or conflictual model of thesis/antithesis but to its frequent figurative resolutions, might have appreciated more fully than he did.

The present essay attempts, therefore, a comparative media analysis rather than anything resembling the triumphalist narrative of advance and transcendence proposed in Eisenstein's three-tiered title, "Dickens, Griffith, and the Film Today" (1944), where the last refers mostly to the recent glory days of Soviet avant-garde practice. D. W. Griffith's transfer of Dickensian technique into a different medium is only two thirds of the story Eisenstein tells; the rest concerns the outdistancing of Hollywood craft by Soviet artistry. For all of Eisenstein's sincere admiration and detailed celebration of Dickens, it is crucial to note how the Victorian storyteller's narrative technique becomes, toward the climax of the essay, mostly a marker for conceptual limitations in Griffith.

To see beyond this deployment of Dickens requires a return to what I will be calling the filmic rather than the cinematic elements of his work, a dimension of his writing that goes mostly unnoticed by Eisenstein. Filmic Dickens locates the rapid layered succession of his verbal as well as imagistic effects, whereas cinematic Dickens concerns larger, more readily staged (and filmed) blocks of description and plotting. The ideal Dickens movie would have been shot by Griffith at the height of his powers; that's Eisenstein's slightly patronizing gist. My point is that the ideal Dickens movie might have been shot by Eisenstein himself, keyed to the increments and upheavals not only of shot sequence but of disjunctive frame advance: that is, the jamming together of images that fail to cohere either as continuous space or action. Not adding up as expected, these jostling images must instead be thought through. Hence the interpretive element in that collision of frames so central to Eisenstein's program.

Some preliminaries, then. Montage: the piecing together of discrete images to make a film sequence. Call it editing. Writing: the piecing together of discrete word forms to make a verbal sequence. Call it syntax. But each depends on a preceding level of serial juxtaposition. On the screen, automatically recorded and then projected photographic frames displace each other to induce the look of movement. On the page, alphabetic characters compact into words and accumulate toward grammar. Concerning the rudimentary units of the filmic image, however, Eisenstein was interested more in tension than in sheer succession, explosive contrasts that recombine under pressure into new meaning. Image slams against discordant image to produce a metaphoric third term. It is the prose equivalent of this counterpoint and resolution that he consistently overlooks in what we might call Dickens's word advance. Eisenstein's attention to Dickens rests at the macro rather than micro level, again cinematic rather than filmic. For Eisenstein, that is, Dickens anticipates film narrative mostly in his obsessive descriptive details (especially in close-ups), their intercutting, and the broad formats of parallel plotting.

This deliberately leaves to one side exactly what Eisenstein prides himself on in his own filmmaking practice: namely, "conceptual montage," where editing is designed not for sheer sequencing but for higher-order integration, where disjunction leads to "a new qualitative fusion out of juxtaposition" (1957: 238). This intellectual synthesis is what Eisenstein found missing in Griffith, as implicitly in Dickens before him. A clear sense of Eisenstein's limited homage to Dickens – as in fact a rallying cry, by contrast, for his own avant-garde invention – only slowly emerges over the course of an unfolding three-stage argument. First, as Eisenstein demonstrates at length, Griffith may well have taken Dickens as a model in matters of both emphasis and suspense, from shot to sequence level, in everything from melodramatic close-ups to parallel storylines. Second, the practice of Soviet montage, in learning from Griffith all that it did in the first flush of enthusiasm for Hollywood technique, must acknowledge a similar lineage. Third and finally, as detailed in the closing pages of the essay (often forgotten by literary critics), these popular origins of cinema had nevertheless to be left behind in the articulation of a revolutionary aesthetic. Dickensian fiction claims attention mostly, for Eisenstein, as the long outgrown seed of a modernist initiative fully realized only in another medium.

The reason to revisit this position has little to do with celebrating either the prescience or the influence of Dickens, let alone with smoking out the patronizing undertone of Eisenstein's famous appreciation. It is simply to see what Eisenstein's bias led him to miss. One of the unfollowed leads in his essay is easy to spot. Instead of alluding to the Chinese ideogram as model for cinema's composite signifier, as he had done in earlier position papers, Eisenstein refers this time to the work of Russian linguists in accounting for the ways in which their concept of the rudimentary "word-sentence" (237) of primitive utterance operates, like the "montage cell" of film (236), as the "embryo of syntax" (237). But by this point in the essay, Eisenstein is three pages beyond his last mention of Dickens (234) – who was never for him a linguistic experimenter anyway (a view to be partly explained by the problem of Russian translation, no doubt) – while still eighteen pages from the end. The linguistic anchor for his theory of montage collision as an advance on "parallel editing" (the simple intercutting between separate narrative strands) would seem to have left Dickens, let alone Griffith, far behind.

This is where we need to put on the brakes. For what seems important about the pressurized nature of the "word-sentence" as a model for the explosive character of Soviet montage also typifies the tensed density of Dickensian phrasing in its syntactic overspill from word to word, its potential splitting even of syllables and linked sounds. I will begin with the most circumscribed examples I can find, at the level of word borders and their phonetic friction. Turning on the sibilant (or *s* sound), the slippages in question range from eroticized sentimentality, at one pole, to outright farce at the other. Late in *Little Dorrit*, we are let in on the hero's abiding image of Amy Dorrit as a "youthful figure with tender feet going almost bare on the damp ground, with spare hands ever working" (1.27). (All references to Dickens's novels refer to chapter, or in the special case of *Little Dorrit*, to chapter within volume, rather than to page.) Aural juxtaposition captures the virtually fetishistic association of vulnerable body parts in the slide from "almo*st bare*" to the phonetic skid and resynthesis of "spare." Or take the comic variant of such phonetic flicker in *Dombey and Son*, when the bumbling Mr. Toots plants an uninvited kiss on the cheek of Susan Nipper. Rebuffed, "the bold Toots tumbled staggering out into the street" (390), with Toots's "stumble" heard in the toppling forward of the *s* from his own improbable last name. Imitative pratfall syntax: sound in echo of sense. Another account comes to mind. In this alphabetic "montage by collision" (Eisenstein's preferred format) and its resulting grammatical implosion, this dialectic of difference, wording bursts forth into a new third term. Toots + tumbled staggering = Toots stumbling.

In a novel like *Dombey and Son*, a harmless erotic lunge of this sort is set in contrast to the lifeless energy of such implacable forces as business and railroads. Eros vs. death. *Dombey and Son* is the first great fictional treatment of the railway revolution. It is no accident that it was the industrial locomotive which was later to become a central symbol – and dynamic prototype – for Soviet cinema: the disorienting machine of modernity rescued for the streamlined aesthetics of modernism.[1] In this light, it is revealing to note the emphasis placed by Eisenstein on the preindustrial stagecoach-eye-view in *Oliver Twist*'s racing panorama of commercialized London street life (217), what he might have called a tracking shot, achieving as it does only the nonsynthesized seriality of urban clutter. By the coming of the railway a decade later, a similar tracking procedure has grown all the more driven and ironic.

In *Dombey and Son*, both words and syntax capture the speed of the new railway with such an uncanny aptness that they become filmic almost by default: descriptive flashes that seem at first atomistic, then serial, then fused in a transformative rush, artificially synthesized by the relativities of speed and position. The following is a description from the grieving Mr. Dombey's point of view, in mourning for his dead son. The despoiled cityscape is so completely focalized through his perspective that it becomes almost an hallucinatory "subjective shot," whereby the train sweeps him onward like "a type of the triumphant monster, Death" (20). The whole paragraph is triggered by a preposition ("Away!") that seems to vibrate halfway between description and imperative. Grammar then grinds its way through several more prepositions in present-tense series: raw momentum without sensed destination. This began three paragraphs back with the locomotive, in a single sentence, "burrowing among . . . flashing out into . . . mining in through . . . booming on in . . . bursting out again" (20). And here is the subsequent surge of force and disorientation:

Away, with a shriek, and a roar, and a rattle, plunging *down into* the earth again, and working *on in* such a storm of energy and perseverance, that amidst the darkness and whirlwind the motion seems *reversed, and to tend* furiously backward, until a ray of light upon the wet wall shows its surface flying past like a fier*ce* stream . . . sometimes pausing for a minute *where a crowd of faces are, that in a minute more are not*; . . . (20; emphasis added)

The grammatical torque from past participle to infinitive phrase in "seems reversed, and to tend" administers a wrench to grammar comparable to the optical jolt described. Further, the steam-driven hissing collision of sibilants at "fier*ce* stream" insinuates the engulfing "dream" that offers the deep logic for this waking nightmare of funereal projection on the perceiver's part. All is vulnerably relativized and fleeting, as when, finally, the collective noun "crowd," taking "are" as verb, pivots on the comma and, instead of offering further predication ("are" what?), hustles a glimpsed cross-section of the waiting public away to negation in the suspended present tense of this bleak epiphany.

A more figurative variant of the funereal and subjective tracking shot occurs in the implausibly animated stasis of a later turn of phrase in *Little Dorrit*. A deserted street is described as "long, regular, narrow, dull, and gloomy; like a brick and mortar funeral" (1.27), so that static and depopulated space is converted by simile to a kind of paralyzed motion. The paradoxical effect falls somewhere between a tracking image of blank fixity and a spectral freeze-frame of immobilized procession. In the eye of its forlorn beholder, the world is caught dead in its tracks under the analytic camera of Dickens's silent cinema.

Even Dickensian dialogue, though unmentioned by Eisenstein, can undergo a serial dislocation that results in a mismatch of utterance and narrative inference. Such dislocation is thereby related indirectly to that most radical aspect of Soviet sound technique, the "vertical montage" (254) mentioned in passing at the end of his essay. Eisenstein resists the seamless realism of standard sound cinema, in particular the "mechanical parallelism" (254) of image and voice. He champions instead the pasting-over of sound upon image in a discomfiting and conceptual manner, contrapuntal rather than naturally meshed, generating a kind of aural palimpsest entirely divorced from the slavish representation of continuous speech.

In a strictly verbal medium like Dickensian fiction, a related conceptual gap may open up between the flow (or stammerings) of dialogue and the disruptive identification of the speaker by narrative tag.[2] Here is Dombey ponderously inflating himself after the birth of his son and heir in the opening chapter of *Dombey and Son*. " 'The House will once again, Mrs. Dombey,' said Mr. Dombey. . . ." Will what? Be a home? Hardly. We immediately suspect Dombey to be referring to the patrilinear

Firm, not the family hearth – as is all too clear when he finishes his swelling thought: ". . . be not only in name but in fact Dombey and Son." Under the "softening influence" of this preening self-congratulation, he adds with a revealing stutter: "Mrs. Dombey, my – my dear." The typical grammar of possession ("my") in the mouth of this capitalist bully is, only with some effort, nudged over into endearment. Emotional backsliding occurs at once, however. The voice of command returns across the self-corrected personal pronoun in "He will be christened Paul, my – Mrs. Dombey – of course," where what is taken for granted in the last idiom, "of course," is the wife's nameless status as property as well as the son's anointed one as partner in the course of all things patriarchal. Across the halting uneasiness of Dombey's speech, that is, the words of a continuous oral syntax have seemed to be stripping their gears. In Eisenstein's terms, the effect of this slippage is an overlapping or "vertical" montage in which speech and its narrative presentation are ironically syncopated rather than smoothly synchronized.

So we continue bearing down on the prose of Dickens, as filmic rather than filmable, to ask whether and where, well beyond the sweep of Eisenstein's spotlight, such prose might achieve something like a dialectical synthesis of its own, sprung from ironic disjunctures of all sorts. In pursuit of this question, we get unexpected mileage out of a concocted example of montage failure dropped on the run by Eisenstein. In its striving for the detonation of seriality into nuclear intensity, Eisenstein readily admits that the attempted "flashing unity of image" may degenerate into "a miserable trope . . . left on the level of an unrealized fusion, on the level of a mechanical pasting together of the type of 'Came the rain and two students' " (253). Pages past his last mention of Dickens, Eisenstein would seem to have no inkling of just what accidental two-headed nail his sarcastic hammer blow has hit on the head. For "came the rain and two students" is close kin to one of the signature effects of Dickensian comic writing – and directly related to his most serious symbolic effects. Usually, in non-inverted grammar, this "trope" (or "figure," here of speech rather than image) is a device called *syllepsis*, sometimes *zeugma*. It typically involves one verb governing two objects or modifiers in different senses, rather than two subjects laying claim to a lone verb (as with the "coming" of downpour and students). A classic example in Dickens's first novel, with debts to the eighteenth-century comic writers he grew up on: "Mr. Pickwick fell into a wheelbarrow, and fast asleep" (19). Compare *Little Dorrit*'s "and so to bed, and to sleep" (1.28), where the prepositional sense slides over into an infinitive verbal force.

Such sylleptic effects proliferate in *Little Dorrit*. The frequent difference that gets splayed out in such phrasing – between a figurative and a literal sense – can be carried over to a metaphysical difference between immaterial and material meanings: "[H]e would have taken my life with as little scruple as he took my money" (11.20). How can one really call such phrasing, as the schoolbooks would have it, "faulty" parallelism? The whole logic of grammar seems under interrogation at such moments. Or consider this self-referential example, again from *Little Dorrit*, about the normative constraints of script and their occasional defiance. Writing about writing, Dickens even reads the aggressive flourishes of calligraphy through the double focus of a sylleptic shift, so that the decorated capitals of certain manuscripts "go out of their minds and bodies into ecstasies of pen and ink" (11.15). It is a matter of psychic and linear transgression in a single twisted idiom (the shifting of sense from "go out" to "go into"): a case of writing overstepping its own syntactic rather than graphic bounds. At other times, Dickens takes as much delight in elaborating the divergent senses of such forked grammar by open repetition as he does in collapsing them into one split syntax, so that *Little Dorrit* also offers summary descriptions of debtors "being left behind, and being left poor" (1.36) and of a climactic banquet where, in a dreary doubling of space and time, "the table was long and the dinner was long" (11.19).

Eisenstein may have had more of a sense of this verbal license in Dickens than he lets on. As it happens, his first example of the human "close-up" in his essay links the "icy cold moral face" of Griffith's villains with the detailed physiognomy of Mr. Dombey in the early chapters, "revealed through cold and prudery" (199). At least in the English translation of Eisenstein's essay, that phrase "cold and prudery" has something of a sylleptic feel in its own right: the coldness of both house and heart at the novel's opening, chilling all desire to the bone. A later "close-up" recruits the sylleptic double-take even more directly, when Mr. Dombey, as pillar of capitalist society, is seen "stiff with starch and arrogance": uptight linen and rigid class pride seized in the same phrasal breath. What is such an effect but a "montage trope" (240) at the grammatical level – or, in filmic terms, at the level of the unreeling syntactic strip? In a single shifting phrase Dickens sparks a melding of incompatibles combusting into a third, higher-level term. Starch and arrogance: stiff f/rigidity in a single figurative close-up.

I happened to conduct a visiting seminar recently on the broader political reverberations of these sylleptic effects in Dickens, their potential for ideological doublethink, and I was reminded by a member of the audience of a perfect example from *Bleak House*.[3] It comes in the chapter "Telepathic Philanthropy" in order to skewer the addled Mrs. Jellyby and her enforced tithing of her children for contributions to the African cause: the empty inverse of colonial exploitation. In the lightly ironic words of the narrating heroine, letters sympathetic to the cause flood in "from people excited in various ways" – note the giveaway "various" – "about the cultivation of coffee, and natives." The last comma is an insufficient partition for muzzling the satiric charge that collapses agriculture into cultural imperialism. Natives do not inspire excitement on their own, but only as paired with coffee crops in the circuit of exploitation.

I am certainly not suggesting that there is anything "cinematic" about this type of phrasing in the traditional sense – unless worked up in a movie version with intercut shots of western-dressed Africans herded into makeshift chapels and rows of dock workers loading the beans. A "miserable trope" indeed for the racist economies of an enforced system. Instead, improving immeasurably on Eisenstein's "came the rain and two students," Dickens's sylleptic formats expose more broadly the kind of differential – or protofilmic – logic that spawns both literary trope and film editing alike: the undoing of strict sequence by the interplay of disjunction – and its ignited explosion of new meaning.

Though arguably filmic, syllepsis doesn't necessarily feel cinematic even when it is more visual to begin with. Take the first lawyer we meet in *Bleak House*. As Dickens's choppy prepositional satire activates the lightest form of comic syllepsis (the three senses of *with* all evoking different aspects of possession), the portrait is then capped by a legalistic oxymoron: "a large advocate with great whiskers" – rather than a great advocate with large whiskers – "a little voice, and an interminable brief." In the idiomatic paradox of an endless "brief," legal adjudication in the law courts of Chancery stands accused as a charade and a joke. The deeper "montage thinking" in this famous opening passage, however, arrives a paragraph earlier, where the mist and slipperiness of a drizzly London day offer an objective correlative for the obscurity and muddle of the law courts. And more: a reciprocal troping, so that each figures the other. "Never can there come fog too thick, never can there come mud and mire too deep, to assort with the groping and foundering condition" of legal process. The tacit metaphor is visualized as a kind of stark parallel montage, eroded into total overlap. Come the fog and the befuddlement together. That's the "trope," the *turn*, from material to "conceptual" plane, atmospheric sludge to bureaucratic muck: in a more modern idiom, from smog to smokescreens. In this dialectic of indictment, the move toward ironic synthesis – exposed commonality – erupts in the form of prose superimposition. Fog upon fog: murkiness thickening to metaphor. Yet such figural mockery carries its own inoculation. Confusion at law is as inevitable as bad weather to a Londoner, hence insurmountable. Beyond political remedy. Culture has thereby been naturalized, however bleakly. This is the very work of ideology, unraveled only momentarily here by being made brazen and overexplicit. Critique stops far short of a call to arms. This is the famous conservatism of Dickens's radical instincts in a nutshell. With the senseless Chancery litigation not only seen for what it is, but seen for the way it makes us sense it as an intractable force of nature, the system can only be ironized, not revolutionized.

So let's look, for contrast, at a genuine revolutionary image, perhaps the most famous in all Soviet cinema: the sequentially lying, crouching, and sitting statues of three marble lions rapidly intercut – and so cartooned into motion – in Eisenstein's own masterpiece *Potemkin*. Rather than a metaphor for uprising – a direct translation of image into visual pun – Eisenstein intended the image to cut deeper into the materiality behind the metaphor. For the three shots are "merged into *one* roaring lion and, moreover, in another *film-dimension*," where they operate as "an embodiment of a metaphor: '*The very stones roar*'!" (253; Eisenstein's emphasis). Such is the most fully achieved form of the synthesized image as trope: a complex double translation of sculpture into animal life, silent cinema into defiant outcry.

Those stones and that roar are Dickensian too, in more ways than one. I am thinking of gloomily animated cobblestones, the ones that pave the streets on a forlorn Sunday in *Little Dorrit*, which seem to wear a "penitential garb" (1.3) of soot. Rapid montage multiplies the sameness of these streets into a metaphor of tedium. "Nothing to see but streets, streets, streets. Nothing to breathe but streets, streets, streets." Cut, cut, cut. Synthesis achieves only the fusion of the morbidly unvaried: the multiplied dead weight of Sunday desolation. The stones that pave the streets of *Little Dorrit* are themselves separately personified in another symbolic locale of the novel, "Bleeding Heart Yard," where the slumlord Casby is able to wring "a good quantity of blood out of the stones of several unpromising courts and alleys" (1.13).

It is into the "roaring streets" (11.34) of this same mercantile and dehumanized urban world that Arthur and Amy make their marital way at the end of the novel, but not until she retrieves him from imprisonment across a strange recapitulative temporality in which the novel's long day of suffering is clocked symbolically to its finish: "And the day ended, and the night ended, and the morning came, and Little Dorrit" – vessel of the novel's redemptive vision, with her twin dwelling in spirit and flesh – at last arrives. She enters as the living incarnation, no less, of sylleptic – and here synthesizing – resolution. For not unlike those students and their rain in Eisenstein, she "came into the prison with the sunshine" (11.34). Literally, the heroine makes her final entrance at day's first light. Figuratively, she embodies in her own person the brightness she brings with her – and shortly takes back into the world at large.

After signing the marriage register, the new couple "paused for a moment on the steps of the portico, looking at the *fresh perspective of the street* in the autumn morning sun's bright rays, and then went down" (emphasis added). Where before the fragmented grammar of "streets, streets, streets" was disjunctive but interchangeable, now the vista is aestheticized into the singular painterly prospect of a "perspective." Two more repetitions of "went down" (into a life of selfless service) precipitate grammatical fragments that operate like overlapping images of the couple's dutifully-ever-after future, until normal grammar resumes for the summarizing syntax of "They went quietly down" – down to meet the "usual uproar." In the colliding vectors of "down" and "up," the only "conceptual fusion" possible is compromise, social assimilation without overriding synthesis. Immersion in the flux of humanity becomes its own reward, all revolutionary anger drained away in the middle road of benevolent pragmatism. That Dickens is conservative doesn't make him any the less dialectical in his balancing acts; it just holds him to a certain stage of inference in the allowed possibilities for transformation and resolution.

Imagined as layered sheets of simultaneous futurity, much is repaired by *Little Dorrit*'s twinned final "perspective," with the selfless couple together at last and ever after. The whole loosened and levitated syntax of this final overlapping cadenza is for the heroine, in one sense, the rectifying double vision (of now and to come) for a life previously trapped in a kind of hallucinatory limbo of retrospect. After sudden unearned wealth has released her family from the Marshalsea prison, Little Dorrit on the mandatory Grand Tour kept refiguring the decayed relics of the former Roman empire as the foregone domesticity of her life in the debtors' prison: "The ruins of the vast old Amphitheatre, of the old Temples," and so forth, through three more parallel phrases, "besides being *what they were, to her, were ruins* of the old Marshalsea – ruins of her own old life – ruins of the faces and forms that of old peopled it – ruins of its loves, hopes, cares, and joys" (11.25; emphasis added). Each scene is caught slipping past – and surrendered again – in the flitting serial syntax, which pits two time frames, epochal and familial, against each other: the olden and the "of old." Or not so much pits as superimposes them in the tracked itinerary of review. And does so across the self-dissolving phonetic evanescence of "were, to her, were r. . . ." Ultimately: "Two ruined spheres of action were before the solitary girl," the subjective flashback and the fabled historical panorama, so that "she saw them both together." By such means does parallel editing become a sustained double exposure. Here, in sum, is the mirage of the heroine's ocular and spiritual displacement – as redeemed finally by the alleviated moment of future overlay at novel's end.

It is often said that cinema exists only in the present (even a flashback being the recovery of an elapsed moment in its own replayed present). Cinema in this sense has no familiar tense structure. It is immediate, immanent. Classic fiction, by contrast, has a standard tense: the historical past. Anything else is an exception. And Dickens relishes the exception, not only in passages of reverie and rewarding forecast, as we've seen, but for purposes of irony. An example taken to extreme lengths. Why should the funeral of Dombey's son be conducted for paragraphs on end in a lugubrious present tense? Because patriarchal continuity has been truncated for Dombey, all linearity and lineage choked off? Maybe. Because death throws time out of joint – as it will later do, in symbolic projection from the mind of the bereft father, in the present-tense juggernaut of the railroad's inhuman force? Okay. But if this is what the technique comes to *mean* in the earlier funeral scene, that's not exactly its immediate feel. The disembodied present tense operates instead like a disorienting case of collapsed parallel montage in which all is going on in simultaneous superimposition. "There is a hush through Mr. Dombey's house," with the grieving atmosphere shot "through" – as if knifed rather than pervaded – by silence. So that muted shufflings only emerge by subsonic echo with "h*u*sh" itself: "Servants gliding up and down stairs r*u*stle, but make no sound of footsteps." Inverted grammar emphasizes the continuous atemporal present in the next paragraph: "After dark there come some visitors – noiseless visitors, with shoes o*f f*elt" – as soft as the feathering juncture between the last two words. "All this time, the bereaved father *sits* alone," while, in an equivalent time frame, "At the office in the City, the ground-glass windows *are* made more dim by shutters" (18; emphasis added). On it goes for pages, the prolonged mortuary present folding over each other the wake and the funeral procession and the interment and the grief, one inexorable unbroken ordeal. Only at the moment of burial (beside the boy's long-dead mother) does stress on the grave's convenient location shift weight into a future-oriented editorial present that seems filtered through indirect discourse as the clutched consolation of Florence herself: "It is well. Their ashes lie where Florence in her walks – oh lonely, lonely walks – may pass them any day." Here an earthly rather than transcendental future mitigates the hovering finality of the funereal present.

Compared with the overlapping omniscience of this ritualized day of mourning, Dickens can just as drastically reverse his narrational point of view to a lone subjective vantage. A single flamboyant example of such a point-of-view shot from *Little Dorrit* may in this sense help specify one of the most oblique of Eisenstein's unexemplified technical allusions – to the actual deployment in prose of special refracting lenses. The exemplary scene in *Little Dorrit* is set entirely by premonition. The international banker and crook Mr. Merdle has tortured his daughter-in-law with boredom during a brief visit, in which his own dialogue dips into a sylleptic doubleness, apologizing for "equally detaining you and myself" (II.24). Here is the fracturing internal montage of identity itself (as both subject and object of consciousness), just before he borrows the penknife with which to execute his suicide in the break between chapters. Exit Merdle. Exit Merdle – more to the immediate point – in the eyes of the latest uncomfortable victim of his repressed panic, who watches him, from a removed perch on her moneyed balcony and cage, as he literally passes away down the street. At which point we can indeed see the sort of thing Eisenstein may have meant by including in the "optical quality" of Dickens's "frame composition" the "alternation of emphasis by special lenses" (213). With Fanny's proleptic and unconsciously mortal sense that "this was the longest day that ever did come to an end at last," we watch Merdle recede in a bird's-eye shot filtered and distorted through her rippling tears: "Waters of vexation filled her eyes; . . . making the famous Mr. Merdle, in going down the street, appear to leap, and waltz, and gyrate, as if he were po*ssessed* of *sev*eral *dev*ils," where the blurred vision even finds its aural correlative in the thick of hissing phonetic ricochets. Prophetic cinematography, by any other name. Or think of it as prose's own "special effect," abetted by every linguistic twitch available to it. In the buckling perspective of the image, whereby she half sees in him what he feels, objectivity and subjectivity succumb to each other across the nervous wreckage of a transferred point of view.

So now, for a few moments in closing, let's take what we have seen to the movies. Not in the spirit of judged and ranked "translations" but of comparative stylistics. A "subjective shot" like Fanny's, anchored by an optical point of view (POV), is the kind of technical inflection of Dickensian prose that gets readily transposed to screen, offering directors an effective, if limited, way of dynamizing their narratives. Two years after Eisenstein's essay, David Lean achieves an ambitiously distilled moment of subjectivity in the first-person *Bildungsroman* of *Great Expectations* (1946). Succumbing to fever after the death of Magwitch, Pip is disoriented in the London street by the heaving sea of glinting satin top hats. They manifest en masse a dizzying sign of that faceless gentlemanly order into which Pip has never successfully inserted himself. Hot-flashes appear before his eyes like the rotating shimmers of a flickering hypnotic wheel (fig. 12.1), eventually blurring his own intercut image as well (fig. 12.2). All is swallowed up in the fever pace of social mobility. In the shot/reverse shot pattern, these blades of light continue to distort the hero's own POV until, once he is safe in his bedroom and falling toward

Fig. 12.1. Lean, *Great Expectations*, 1946

Fig. 12.2. Lean, *Great Expectations*, 1946

Fig. 12.3. Lean, *Great Expectations*, 1946

his pillow (fig. 12.3), the screen fades to black, and the track to silence, for a full ten seconds. As we dissolve back into the image of
Joe watching over Pip at his bedside, after an elliptically treated bout
of nursing, the film, alas, veers from the novel in giving us the moment in a full resumption of omniscient narrative – so that Joe is seen
slightly from the side (fig. 12.4) rather than as a strict POV of hard-won
recognition.

In the more cinematographically accomplished *Oliver Twist*, filmed by
Lean in 1948, a similar subjective fadeout develops across several scenes
as an actual motif of liminal consciousness. Point-of-view shooting thus
links the inward life of certain focalizing characters and sets them into
ultimate contrast with the spiritual evacuations of the scapegoated villain
Sikes. On her birthbed turned deathbed, Oliver's unwed mother drifts
into consciousness for the last time (fig. 12.5) to hold down a subjective shot that can just barely keep in focus the flickering candles of her
charity room as her own life is rapidly snuffed out (fig. 12.6). Oliver later
goes unconscious in a POV shot after a blow in the street (fig. 12.7),
and yet again after being dizzied by confrontation with his false accusers
in the police court (fig. 12.8), the camera toppling with him to the
floor this time before cutting to the next scene (fig. 12.9). In both
these latter cases, the lapse in consciousness is an elision of narrative

Fig. 12.4. Lean, *Great Expectations*, 1946

Fig. 12.5. Lean, *Oliver Twist*, 1948

Fig. 12.6. Lean, *Oliver Twist*, 1948

Fig. 12.7. Lean, *Oliver Twist*, 1948

Fig. 12.8. Lean, *Oliver Twist*, 1948

Fig. 12.9. Lean, *Oliver Twist*, 1948

Fig. 12.10. Lean, *Oliver Twist*, 1948

time as well. This is of course the most common use of the fadeout in the syntax of cinema. In its overt form as flashback transition, it is just the sort of thing Eisenstein hopes to be "excused" for finding in Dickens when unable to resist identifying a "dissolve" in *A Tale of Two Cities* (213). (To which he adds, in a speculative spirit that has certainly motivated my own discussion: "How many such 'cinematic' surprises must be hiding in Dickens's pages!")

In standard practice, of course, the dissolve is more prevalent as a flash forward across a less yawning gulf between temporally sequential scenes. In a striking example from Lean's *Oliver Twist*, however, two temporal trajectories are involved, along with a spatial arc. From a close-up on his mother's recovered locket in a lowlife setting of the detective counterplot, we quickly dissolve from the image of Oliver's dead mother to its genetic double (the pretty lookalike son), as the boy comes swooping into the foreground on a garden swing in his new pampered setting at Brownlow's (fig. 12.10). The mother's lovely static image seems sprung to breathing life in an allegory of the generations. Juxtaposition becomes fusion: image plus spitting-image synthesized in the biological transcendence of time itself. It is as if the mother – whose own death scene was inscribed by a cinematic fading of focus – were consoled *in absentia* by the complementary magic of transitional montage: releasing another life from and in her image.

Fig. 12.11. Lean, *Oliver Twist*, 1948

But turn now to one last image sequence from Lean's film: a fleeting and ingeniously Dickensian dissolve that not only avoids the subjective POV shot (as also in the disembodied transitional trope of the cameo/swing) but actively overrules it in the moment of death. I am thinking of the accidental suicide – become in the film the public execution – of the murderer Sikes, who slips into a noose wrought by his own hand. "Staggering as if struck by lightning," writes Dickens, "he lost his balance and tumbled over the parapet. The noose was at his neck. It ran up with his weight, tight as a bow-string, and swift as the arrow it speeds." After a deep-focus establishing shot of Oliver at the roof's peak, Sikes in the middle distance, and the ravening mob beneath (fig. 12.11), we cut to a close-up of Sikes's panicked face. At which moment the metaphor of "lightning" seems almost overexplicitly spelled out as a musket shot, sending Sikes's body backwards in recoil out of the screen frame (fig. 12.12). At once a disorienting shift of focus steals definition from the roof's tiles behind (fig. 12.13). All that remains within the forefront of the frame is the lethal rope rapidly snapping tight across the angled expanse of tiles (in the lower right of the frame, fig. 12.14). It does so not just as a function of the camera's disoriented depth of field in the abrupt removal of its human object, but also as a shuddering trope, all but subliminal, for the last spasms of the instantaneously removed villain.

Fig. 12.12. Lean, *Oliver Twist*, 1948

Fig. 12.13. Lean, *Oliver Twist*, 1948

Fig. 12.14. Lean, *Oliver Twist*, 1948

Fig. 12.15. Lean, *Oliver Twist*, 1948

"Tight as a bow-string, and swift as the arrow it speeds": a kind of normalized forking grammar taking the form of exaggerated parallelism. In prose, the elegantly ironic concisions of syllepsis would be out of place for this melodramatic comeuppance. As with Dickens's aggressively compressed simile of cause and effect, in Lean's film Sikes's lifeline gives out in visual simile before our eyes. All the while we hear the rope whipping over the roof until the shot cuts – on the sudden jerk of the body's dead weight – to the chimney above (fig. 12.15). This is where the movie has stationed Oliver – as if to ground its version of Dickens's final gruesome personification: "The old chimney quivered with the shock, but stood it bravely." And remained standing. Holding firm against horror as well as mechanical tension, the inanimate formation of bricks is braver than the coward Sikes. Even beyond this, the jump cut has on its own abrupt terms offered the near cousin of a metaphoric (Eisensteinian) syllepsis: came the jolt and unflinching justice together.

Through such cognitive overlays and new resolutions in Dickens's prose we encounter the two-made-one of juxtaposition as fusion, linkage as reconfigured sense, ironic disparity as triggered synthesis. Regardless of whether a given cinematic adaptation may be said to get it right, such lexical and syntactic oscillation remains the governing filmic energy of Dickensian technique: its intrinsic flicker effect and its resultant conceptual montage. This is the dictional, grammatical, and figural dialectic of his hypercharged style. This is, in short, the way we screen his sentences in the synthesizing mind's eye.

NOTES

1. See on this point Kirby 1997: 8.
2. See Lambert 1981, where the "aggressive and disruptive" effects (133) of dialogue interrupted by such narrative markers as "said Dombey" (though without the present example) are given a full hearing.
3. My thanks to Criscillia Benford, in the doctoral program at Stanford, for this example.

REFERENCES

Dickens, Charles. 1985. *Bleak House*. Harmondsworth: Penguin.
Dickens, Charles. 1985. *Dombey and Son*. Harmondsworth: Penguin.
Dickens, Charles. 1982. *Great Expectations*. Harmondsworth: Penguin.
Dickens, Charles. 1998. *Little Dorrit*. Harmondsworth: Penguin.
Dickens, Charles. 1982. *Oliver Twist*. Harmondsworth: Penguin.
Dickens, Charles. 2000. *The Pickwick Papers*. Harmondsworth: Penguin.

Eisenstein, Sergei. 1957. "Dickens, Griffith, and the Film Today." *Film Form: Essays in Film Theory*. Ed. and trans. Jay Leyda. New York: Meridian Books: 195–256.
Kirby, Lynne. 1997. *Parallel Tracks: The Railroad and Silent Cinema*. Durham, NC: Duke University Press.
Lambert, Mark. 1981. *Dickens and the Suspended Quotation*. New Haven, CT: Yale University Press.

13 Orson Welles and Charles Dickens 1938–1941

Marguerite Rippy

In July 1938, Orson Welles introduced "First Person Singular." In this CBS radio series he intended to wed the performance experimentation he had brought to the Federal Theatre Project with the income and commercial appeal that radio had consistently afforded him since his 1935 appearances in "March of Time." Over the remaining months of 1938, he produced in "First Person Singular" four radio plays based on the work of Charles Dickens, *A Tale of Two Cities* (July 25), *Oliver Twist* (October 2), *The Pickwick Papers* (November 20) and *A Christmas Carol* (December 23). Dickens thus became Welles's most frequently adapted author in 1938 (Wood 1990: 92–7). In 1939, when he was lured to Hollywood with an RKO contract, it was widely expected that Welles would continue this practice of adapting the "classics" for the "masses," and in 1940 rumors circulated about a pending production under his direction of *The Pickwick Papers*, to star W. C. Fields. This is the story of why that film never materialized.

"First Person Singular"

Following *Dracula* and *Treasure Island*, *A Tale of Two Cities* was the third text to be adapted by Welles in the series. It was an ideal choice for "First Person Singular," since it both fulfilled Welles's interest in the collapse of narrated time and offered a variety of possibilities for experimentation with the retelling of the story in first-person singular. Welles made the banker Lorry the principal storyteller, giving him the ability to collapse memory into present commentary, and offering the radio listener the sense of "intimacy" that Welles had often created through first-person narrative. The performance actually split the narration evenly among Manette, Lorry, and Carton, thereby fragmenting the listener's identification and creating a sense of three competing "authors" of this tale – two of whom, Manette and Carton, were played by Welles. Finally, it offered Welles a chance to explore his lifelong personal and professional interest in doubling: "Just as there are two Charles Foster Kanes . . . so there are two Orson Welleses, one an eccentric, difficult genius, the other a huckster and eternal television personality" (Anderegg 1999: 13). These Wellesian doubles are themselves doubled in Dickens's huckster Carton and eccentric aristocrat Darnay. And, no doubt, Welles was also drawn to Carton's theatrical courtroom rescue of the restrained Darnay.

Welles's radio experimentation depended on merging public and private narratives, taking public performance into the home. What better source could he find for expressing this kind of ambivalence than Dickens's *Tale of Two Cities*, which Catherine Gallagher describes "as a nightmare of transparency, of publicly displaying what is hidden, intimate, secret" (Gallagher 1987: 76). Welles wanted to create a sense of intimacy through mass media, capturing individual experience through collective broadcast. In a *Newsweek* article (11 July 1938) he promised to avoid "cut-and-dried dramatic technique" in the radio scripts to focus instead on his own power as narrator, cultivating his ability to draw "his listeners into the charmed circle" of his storytelling ("First Person Singular" 1938: 25). Welles believed the "invisible audience should never be considered collectively, but individually" (Naremore 1989: 13). At the same time, however, he was profoundly aware of the breadth of his new audience. In fact, he became a master of manipulating individual experience within a mass-oriented performance, though he remained personally ambivalent about the tension between his sense of himself as isolated genius and the mass adulation that he craved.

Both the text of *A Tale of Two Cities* and the radio play depict a constant fear of exposure, particularly as related to narrative. Manette fears, and the reader fears for him, the discovery of his hidden jailhouse narrative, a narrative that ultimately threatens the security of his daughter's happiness and, in fact, her very life. Similarly, Darnay fears the exposure of the same story, but from a different narrative origin. Manette and Darnay share circumstances of past plot, but each conceals his perspective on the St. Evrémonde plot within very different narrative forms. Darnay's narrative exists as lived past, whereas Manette's exists as recorded memory. Darnay's past is therefore always mutable, open to reinterpretation whether by a jury or by the reader. When Carton intervenes in Darnay's story at his first trial, he alters "reality" by adding a layer of narrative – he transforms the story from treason to twins. But when Manette's story is "discovered" by Defarge, it is revealed as static "truth," clear evidence against Darnay. The two French trials are conflated in Welles's version, but in both versions, the courtroom provides a forum for the reinterpretation of Darnay's past, and there ensues an audible struggle over who can control textual meaning for the listener in Welles's production. The Defarges turn the public tide against Darnay by trumping Manette's spoken word with his written word, thus ultimately controlling meaning and destiny; Carton alone remains as the master-author, controlling the outcome of both trials, scripting his own death, and ensuring the legacy of its interpretation with his final vision.

Welles's production focuses upon these anxieties of writer and interpretation, juxtaposing Manette's narrative with Madame Defarge's knitting, which Harold Bloom calls "a metaphor for the storytelling of the novel itself" (1987: 7). The opening scene of Welles's broadcast reveals Manette in prison writing with charcoal dipped in blood the tale that he will hide, but that will resurface. This opening marks a shift from the original manuscript for the broadcast which opened with Welles as Jarvis Lorry stating, "This is a history of events that took place in London and across the Channel in France in the years immediately preceding and during the great French Revolution. My name is Jarvis Lorry." In the actual broadcast, Lorry's speech is moved to the end of scene 2, therefore shifting the focus onto Manette's narrative within Lorry's. The change in narrative progression effected a change in Welles's own roles: he was to play Lorry in the rehearsal script, but in the broadcast he plays Manette and Carton. He thereby shifts interest from the exterior observer to the writer-within-the-narrative, particularly exploring the struggle to control meaning in the courtroom and the individual fear of being "misread" by the masses, a fear mirrored in the radio series itself. Welles's notorious *War of the Worlds* broadcast only three months later would tangibly illustrate the danger of mass narrative misinterpretation.

But even as he presented himself as the quintessential first-person-singular *auteur*, Welles's work was heavily dependent on a complex negotiation with audiences, sponsors, and fellow actors. This emerges clearly during his final adaptation of Dickens in 1938, his radio production of *A Christmas Carol*. Already this performance differed in that Welles inherited it from his sponsors, Campbell Soup.

"First Person Singular" had now become "Campbell Playhouse," and this would be the fourth year of their popular presentation of *A Christmas Carol*. As Guerric DeBona argues, Dickens became enormously popular in the 1930s, and *Christmas Carol* in particular emerged as a cultural icon (2000: 109). The draft script for the show demonstrates a tight level of control anticipated by the sponsor, including the return of Lionel Barrymore as Ebenezer Scrooge. Lionel had been featured by Campbell's as Scrooge since 1934, although his brother John had to step in for him at the last minute in 1936 when Lionel's wife died (Norden 1995: 143). The show was popular with the company, the audience, and Lionel, and the sponsor wanted to integrate Welles into this mix smoothly. The "Suggested Carol Opening" scripts the introduction for Welles – a critical part of his vision of performance, the moment that he felt established or lost "intimacy" with the audience. The script suggests: "Introduction from Orson Welles in New York – planting fact that this is Campbell's Christmas present to the listener – that it's the fourth year of its presentation, etc. etc. (Welles – as Campbell's spokesman)" (all references taken from the script in the Lilly Library). The script further anticipates the opening exchange between Barrymore and Welles – no improvisation required: "In introducing Barrymore, Welles makes use of the phrase we have used for three years, in describing him: – 'America's grandest character actor.'" To which Barrymore would respond how happy he was to be there once again with " '... as much respect and admiration as *I* have for Orson Welles – whom I might describe as *Radio's* grandest actor.'"

One could anticipate that this particular stage might be too small to share, that Welles would not take pleasure in subordinating his performance concepts to a soup company and its commercial traditions. Barrymore, suffering from a sudden illness, never appeared. The actual performance concluded with a "Follow Script" announcement: "We are sorry that Lionel Barrymore, our Scrooge in past years, was not able to come to New York to be with us tonight but we hope that he will resume his pleasant habit next year." He did, in fact, and Welles would return from Hollywood to play narrator to Barrymore's Scrooge in 1939. But by then, radio seemed a mere source of easy money for Welles, rather than a forum for experimentation.

In 1938, as Welles moved the Mercury Theatre onto the airwaves, radio permitted him to experiment with conventions of spoken word and perspective that powerfully enhanced his dominant, *singular*, and *personal* voice. Although he would prefer film to radio experimentation a year later, he publicly lauded the possibilities of radio over theater in 1938, promising "to treat radio itself with the intelligence and respect such a beautiful and powerful medium deserves" (quoted in Leaming 1985: 152–3). Radio could do things that realistic theater could not, he argued in a draft manuscript of an article for *Radio Annual*: "A few words can conjure up a scene beyond the furthest extension of the powers of the boldest and most resourceful technicians" (Lilly); its central focus on the speaking voice offered the performance technology he craved, to convey his ongoing absorption with first-person perspective.

The allure of Hollywood

His enthusiasm for radio notwithstanding, Welles was already being seduced by the power of cinema. In a speech to the National Council of

Teachers of English in New York, he lambasted theater in favor of film, calling its entertainment value "vastly inferior to the movies" ("Welles Laments" 1938: 12). He knew that reinterpretation of the classics had a market in Hollywood. But he wanted to hold out for a contract that would give him artistic control over his works while securing the public perception of him as a genius *auteur*, a perception palpably increased by his *War of the Worlds* production on Halloween of 1938. Before the RKO offer in 1939, he rejected offers from MGM and David Selznick because they asked him to share power and creative license, to choose among his roles as showman, director, author, and promoter. Welles told Selznick he would prefer to focus on "planning the productions of plays in which I am myself to appear" (Lilly 19 May 1937). By the late 1930s, he was working hard to de-emphasize his creative reliance on John Houseman and others, to tap into the small circle of powerful Hollywood executives like Selznick, who had himself adapted Dickens's *David Copperfield* in 1935.

By 1939, Welles had landed his contract with RKO, a studio known for its focus on creativity and independence in design, and his contract stunned the media and Hollywood with its generous terms. However, the contract also demanded a pace of production that would become a severe problem for Welles. RKO clearly wanted Welles to reproduce the success of his radio reinventions of the classics, and to produce films at the rapid pace that had characterized his radio work.

In part, Welles's difficulty with the studio developed out of his interest in constructing narrative from a first-person-singular perspective. His aesthetic interest in modernist conceits like stream-of-consciousness, intersubjectivity, and deconstruction of reality equaled his self-promotion as a commercial lowbrow entertainer. This unusual combination of characteristics became a hallmark of Welles's performances. Michael Anderegg points out that Welles was part of a budding mass-marketing culture in America focused on selling the intellectual as a commodity, a movement marked by creating the Book-of-the-Month Club in 1921, marketing Great Books seminars, and using radio as a "movement to popularize culture" (1999: 11). Analyzing the ability of MGM's 1935 *David Copperfield* to bridge the span between "classic" and "popular," DeBona remarks, "Dickens-ness" appealed to "leaders of industry, the Arnoldian intellectuals, the respectable middle class, and even the anonymous masses" (2000: 110). Welles was not only a significant contributor to a culture that mingled the huckster with the intellectual, but also a product of it. In order to meet the demands of quick and yet quality production, Welles turned to the literary classics, as he had on stage and radio before.

For his first RKO film project Welles chose to adapt *Heart of Darkness* (adapted by Welles for radio in 1938) and to play both Marlow and Kurtz. In his study of this unmade film, James Naremore suggests that Welles's goal was to "fuse theatrical spectacle with the narrative potential of the novel . . . to substitute the eye of the camera for the 'I' of Conrad's narrator, the camera would become Marlow, whose voice, that of Welles himself, would be heard offscreen" (1989: 21). But with Welles playing Kurtz as well as Marlow, the narrative visually splits an aural narrative that is singular. This strategy clearly recalls his adaptation of *A Tale of Two Cities*, in which radio directly transmits the "I" to the listener, but also extends the first-person perspective to more than one central narrator (Manette, Carton, and Lorry). The use of the camera to evoke the aural, however, adds a layer of complexity to the structure itself, and to the act of filming. It turned out to be almost impossible to achieve the effects Welles wanted without shattering RKO's budget. Despite the fact that parts had already been cast and actors were already on salary, the project was shelved by RKO at a substantial loss. Welles was finding that his aesthetic concepts did not easily translate into the complex medium of film, a medium which offered tantalizing possibilities, but limitations as well.

Eventually, Welles was able to translate something of the first-person-singular concept into his first complete project for RKO, *Citizen Kane*. Yet even before the Hearst organization started its war against the film, RKO had discovered the deep flaw in their plan for Welles. RKO President George Schaefer brought Welles to RKO specifically because of his association with both quality and experimentation. Schaefer, a "prestige producer," was part of the RCA-Rockefeller group "who wanted a 'quality' image" (Naremore 1989: 18). Welles, known already as an "Innovator on Stage, [who] Experiments on the Air" ("First Person Singular" 1938: 25), and who had turned radio "to a New Art Form" ("The Shadow Talks" 1938: 10), seemed a natural fit for his ideal of a quality image that would also turn a profit. But RKO quickly discovered that classic quality did not necessarily translate into profit.

By the early spring of 1940, Welles and RKO were under pressure from a variety of fronts. *Citizen Kane* was proving controversial. Welles was involved in a costly divorce. Herman J. Mankiewicz was threatening a lawsuit over his billing as the author of *Kane*. And Welles had failed to fulfill the rapid-pace production that his RKO contract required and that would repay the large sums the studio had already invested in him. Both Welles and the studio realized that he had to start working immediately on a new idea that would rescue them both.

In this crisis, Welles returned to a familiar pattern. He looked toward the Mercury, Houseman, and adaptations of earlier radio projects for

RKO. Welles wired Houseman on November 28: "Hope to come east for a Christmas week or so and see much of you. How about a job on your Campbell Playhouse? Every means of income, as you possibly know, has been cut off and I have no prospects whatever" (Lilly 28 Nov. 1940). Sharing the stage with Barrymore for *A Christmas Carol* would have been welcome at this point. Welles's lawyer, Arnold Weissberger, grew increasingly worried about Welles's finances, and asked Richard Baer to "Please let me know what the plans are, if any, with respect to the second picture [in the RKO contract]...We cannot possibly approach RKO for re-allocation of the contract payments until the second picture is under way" (Lilly 13 Nov. 1940). Weissberger emphatically reminded Welles on 26 December 1940 that

we are in default for not having completed the picture [*Citizen Kane*] by October 1st, and for not having commenced the second picture by December 1st. If for any reason RKO should wish to take advantage of any breach on our part, it could readily use this. (Lilly 26 Dec. 1940)

Welles needed a story idea fast. If past patterns were a predictor, he would return to adapt one of his radio classics, an approach which would allow him to recycle a Mercury script and actors.

Welles and Houseman had brought up the idea for an adaptation of *Pickwick* to radio executives in New York at a 29 September 1939 meeting in which they assigned a grade to possible story adaptation ideas. This preliminary meeting focused sharply on adapting what they regarded as "classics," whether from present or past authors. They considered titles ranging from *The Great Gatsby* to *Trilby*. They would later be involved with many of these texts in film production. For example, Welles's successful 1938 radio performance as Rochester was reprised in the 1943 *Jane Eyre*. Welles also used the recording of the 1939 Mercury radio version of *The Magnificent Ambersons* to convince George Schaefer to produce it at RKO (Naremore 1989: 85). At the September 1939 meeting, Houseman and Welles both gave an "A" to *Pickwick*. Resistance seems to have come from the two executives, who had not read the novel, but promised to listen to the recording of the 1938 Mercury radio production, featuring Welles as Alfred Jingle (Lilly). The idea remained interesting enough for Welles to suggest to the *Saturday Evening Post*, six months after the meeting, that he "wanted to make Pickwick with W. C. Fields, but that great actor was under contract elsewhere" (Johnston and Smith 1940: 40). Certainly in this crisis *The Pickwick Papers* would have been a natural choice for Welles. It offered an already completed scenario coupled with the appeal of a major star who had already successfully adapted Dickens to screen as Micawber in MGM's *Copperfield*.

Why then didn't Welles use it? The answers are complex and several.

Between 1940 and 1941, Welles developed a greater interest in contemporary authors and experimental projects. He became particularly interested in south-of-the-border issues, stirred, in part at least, by his relationship with the Mexican actress Dolores Del Rio. As early as 1939, a month after the meeting on *Pickwick*, he was spotted carrying *The Conquest of Mexico* into a New York City film meeting, though he deflected the question of it as a possible film project (Crisler 1939: 5). Over the next two years Welles proposed several Latin American story ideas to RKO. In these projects Welles continued to explore the first-person-singular narrative that began with his radio *A Tale of Two Cities*, but carried his exploration back to the Americas.

When Welles moved to Hollywood, press releases and interviews stressed the image of a talented *auteur*, sole inheritor of the legacy of his earlier, controversial productions, like the notorious *War of the Worlds*. Reporting on his shift to Hollywood, Richard O'Brien raved over Welles's "courage to produce, write, cast, direct and play a leading part in a picture" (1939: 12). Thus, even before he had released his first film, Welles had become his own brand name – a brand RKO was, originally, more than happy to exploit, seeing Welles's personality and the public perception of him as *auteur* as keys to his box-office success.

The effort needed to maintain that image emerged in the controversy over the writing credit for *Kane*. When Mankiewicz reasserted his right to a screen credit in the fall of 1940, Welles's lawyer advised his client to handle this volatile situation with a combination of tact and threat: "...indicate that your allowing him to have credit is a matter of good will on your part" (Lilly 23 Sept. 1940). As the first major effort of the all-round genius, *Citizen Kane* needed to have Welles's name on it as writer, as director, and as star. In fact, Welles's *auteur* contract with RKO demanded his productions be written and directed solely by himself.

RKO found itself at odds with its own contract because it needed Welles to combine genius originality with commercial predictability. They wanted at least a film a year, based on material with a guaranteed public appeal. That is not what they were getting from Welles. His *auteur* approach sacrificed the quick quality adaptation method for which he was known to an emerging image as sole creator – first person singular of film. The *Kane* controversy seems to have strengthened Welles's belief that his best hope for both financial success and artistic freedom came through seeking artistic isolation and independence. Inevitably, then, *Pickwick Papers* became impossible. It would not feature him in the central role, and it would feature adaptation over original screenplay. Dickens in particular would interfere with Welles's growing image as *auteur* because his texts already contained a sense of theatricality and a love of performance. The picaresque Pickwick appealed to Welles's sense of irony and the flawed hero, but George Amberson offered similar anti-romantic complexity along with a chance to emphasize Welles's perspective on modern American decline.

Welles faced logistical hurdles in making *Pickwick*, but these obstacles seem comparatively minor. Although W. C. Fields was under contract to another studio, it seems unlikely that RKO could not have worked out this obstacle to producing *Pickwick Papers*. Fields had, after all, been loaned to MGM to play Micawber. The real impediment to this project seems to stem from Welles's growing ambivalence toward his own practice of adapting the classics, an ambivalence rooted in his need, and his bosses', to ensure his *auteur* persona. By 1941 Welles recognized the need to assert absolute creative control and emphasize his own role as a "classic" author. He emerged from the double debacle of *Citizen Kane* and *The Magnificent Ambersons* deeply disillusioned. But he also felt himself to be, in a significant sense, redeemed, with a clearer perception of his own ambitions and an enhanced sense of his own first-person singularity. As he wrote during 1940–1:

There has never been a picture of consequence that has not been the product for the most part of one man – the man who dominates the making of the picture. This man can be the producer, the director, the writer, the star or even the cameraman. Pictures invariably achieve the level of this dominant personality. (Lilly)

Welles effectively defines the aesthetic of the *auteur* in this passage. By seeking to place his creative stamp on his work, and thus to exclude the mingling of his own vision with that of others, his interest shifted away from adapting the classics toward creating a new, uniquely Wellesian view of American performance. In choosing *The Magnificent Ambersons* as his next project, Welles did return to his radio productions, and to a well-known author, but he also asserted a connection with modern American experimentation and separated himself from the British classics of Conrad and Dickens. Booth Tarkington, although critically acclaimed, did not hold the status of a "classic." Increasingly, Welles moved his work away from the first half of the Mercury's stated mission, to produce "plays of the past," toward the second part of its mission, to create productions "that have an emotional or factual bearing on contemporary life" (Welles and Houseman 1938: 1). At this stage of his career Welles chose contemporary critique as his production imprint. He rejected the overshadowing personality of Dickens in favor of a well-regarded contemporary, and traded the English Pickwick for the Midwestern Ambersons.

REFERENCES

I am thankful to the Orson Welles collection of the Lilly Library at Indiana University for their generous support of this article in the form of a Helm Research Fellowship, and for the invaluable assistance of the librarians and staff. Throughout the essay I cite items from this collection as Lilly.

"Welles Laments Wane of Theatre." 29 June 1938. *New York Times*. 12.

"First Person Singular: Welles Innovator on Stage, Experiments on the Air." 11 July 1938. *Newsweek*. 25.

"The Shadow Talks." 14 Aug. 1938. *New York Times*. Sec. 9: 10.

"Negotiates RKO Contract." 25 June 1941. *New York Times*. Sec. 17: 2.

Anderegg, Michael. 1999. *Orson Welles: Shakespeare and Popular Culture*. New York: Columbia University Press.

Bloom, Harold, ed. 1987. *Charles Dickens's A Tale of Two Cities*. New York: Chelsea House.

Crisler, B. R. 1939. "The Movies Come of Age Again, Etc." *New York Times* 20 Aug., sec. 9: 3.

DeBona, Guerric. 2000. "Dickens, the Depression, and MGM's *David Copperfield*." *Film Adaptation*. Ed. James Naremore. Piscataway, NJ: Rutgers UP. 106–28.

Gallagher, Catherine. "The Duplicity of Doubling." Bloom 1987: 73–94.

Johnston, A. and F. Smith. 1940. "How to Raise a Child." *The Saturday Evening Post*. 3 Feb.: 27+

Leaming, Barbara. 1985. *Orson Welles: A Biography*. New York: Penguin.

Lilly Library. Orson Welles Collection. Indiana University, Bloomington.

Naremore, James. 1989. 2nd edn. *The Magic World of Orson Welles*. Dallas, TX: SMU Press.

Norden, Martin. 1995. *John Barrymore: A Bio-Bibliography*. Westport, CT: Greenwood Press.

O'Brien, Richard B. 1939. "Unmasking a Hobgoblin of the Air." *New York Times*. 29 Oct.: sec. 9: 12.

Welles, Orson. Selected letters. Lilly Library, Indiana University, Bloomington.

Welles, Orson and John Houseman. 1938. "The Summing Up: The Directors of the Mercury Theatre Look Over Their First Year." *New York Times*. 12 June: sec. 10: 1–2.

Wood, Bret. 1990. *Orson Welles: A Bio-Bibliography*. New York: Greenwood Press.

14   *David Copperfield* (1935) and the
US curriculum

Steve J. Wurtzler

This chapter revisits the moment of *David Copperfield*'s release (MGM 1935) to show how US educators attempted to incorporate this particular film, and films in general, into school curricula. Examination of the rhetoric surrounding *David Copperfield* also illustrates the ways in which educators approached, or indeed selectively avoided, issues surrounding cinema's cultural value and its relationship to literature. Popular film's entrance into the US school curriculum involved both motion-picture appreciation and the cultivation of conventional notions of taste and discrimination. Advocates of film education were consistent in suggesting that properly educated children, that is those who had obtained some experience studying cinema in their schools, could and would make the "right" choices in selecting their screen entertainment. English teacher Clifford Bragdon, of the Hawken School in Cleveland, Ohio, argued that "The school, public or private, can help children to overcome the habit of indiscriminate movie attendance by supplying information, arousing attitudes, and thus helping to establish habits which will enable children to find more sources of interest in the movies than they found before" (Bragdon 1937: 378). By one account, more than a hundred thousand students of at least a thousand different teachers were, in 1934, studying motion-picture appreciation, and at least seven state departments of education had officially sanctioned teaching film appreciation in their schools (Dale 1936: 113). Not surprisingly, pedagogical efforts surrounding the popular US film most often focused on adaptations of the generally agreed-upon canon of great literary works, like *Copperfield*. Such an approach to film education was, of course, consistent with prevailing attempts to foster appropriately disciplined leisure readers willingly identifying and appreciating the works of canonical authors.

The US film industry actively supported this film-education movement. By providing schools and teachers with film posters, stills, pressbooks, and even free tickets for underprivileged children, the major film producing and distributing companies could use film-education efforts (if not outright coopt them) as an extension of a larger film-promotion apparatus. In fact, the US film industry's primary trade organization, the Motion Picture Producers and Distributors of America (MPPDA), provided partial financial support for published materials to be used when teaching film appreciation during 1933 and 1934 (Selby 1978: 80). Local theater owners actively collaborated with film education as well by offering reduced admission rates for students accompanied by a teacher, by organizing private preview screenings for teachers and administrators, or by hosting film-education efforts at the theater itself. The film-education movement in New Haven, Connecticut, for example, benefitted from all of these examples of collaboration with the film industry as well as theater-sponsored radio programs on film education, a visiting lecture by a representative of the MPPDA, and access to free copies of educational films (Eldridge 1937: 175–83). Such an informal partnership benefitted the film industry. Prestige garnered through producing a literary adaptation might be redoubled in those communities in which some temporary relationship could be developed between theater owner and local school system. MGM and the local theater brought Dickens's "masterpiece" *David Copperfield* to New Haven and New Haven's high schools sent their students to the local Bijou. The release of Hollywood adaptations of literary classics and the incorporation of filmgoing into the school curriculum thus represented a convergence of commercial and educational interests. Hollywood's entrance into the English curriculum during the mid-1930s also provided a culturally valorized rationale for movie attendance in the immediate aftermath of widely publicized critiques of the roles movies played in the lives of American children.

The publication of and publicity surrounding a series of scientific studies of filmgoing and children provided a crucial context for the development of a film-education movement in the US. Called the Payne Fund Studies, the twelve-volume series of works published in 1933 sought to qualitatively describe and quantifiably measure not only the scope and nature of children's movie attendance, but also the content of those films and, importantly, the emotional, psychological, and behavioral effects of movies on youth. The publication of the studies and particularly the sometimes exaggerated, popularized summary of results by Henry James Forman, *Our Movie Made Children*, provided ammunition for a variety of groups concerned with the roles played by film in American life. Popular discussion of the Payne Fund results often focused on their demonstration of the susceptibility of children to movie "inducements" to engage in criminal and sexually transgressive behavior, of film's disruption of children's sleep and dream patterns, and of the cinema's cultivation of unrealistically materialistic definitions of success.

In the mid-1930s, W. W. Charters, Director of the Bureau of Educational Research at Ohio State University, strategically invoked the Payne Fund Studies in which he was a participant, in arguing for the inclusion of films across the curriculum at all levels of instruction. Charters's survey of the educational-cinematography field in 1935, published in *The Educational Record*, emphasized the potential of well-designed educational films that combined sound pedagogical principles with the principles of film drama (Charters 1935: 312–20). But Charters also stressed the role that could be played by including popular, mainstream theatrical releases in classroom studies of cinema. Citing social-science research that demonstrated film's ability to aid knowledge retention and powerfully to influence students' attitudes, Charters emphasized the crucial role played by children's recreational filmgoing. Commercial filmgoing provided an important component of the "curriculum of childhood." Educators needed to recognize "that the motion pictures which children attend once a week and think about every day provide a very intense and powerful portion of the total curriculum by which children are affected" (313). The "factor of emotional possession in commercial pictures," the manner in which children "devoured the picture – watched with all their mental powers alertly focussed upon the film" (316) could be both a cause for concern about the movies' influence on young children's attitudes, or a tool through which the educator might intervene in the "total curriculum" of youth.

1930s educators conceptualized the "problem" of film as, in part, textual indeterminacy: the realization that no text, particularly not a popular film, could ultimately guarantee the way in which it was experienced. In the aftermath of the Payne Fund Studies, the issue facing educators was not simply a desire for "better" films, but also a desire to manage children's reception of *any* film. Film educators thus sought to intervene in that negotiated space between textual features and readers who encountered them. Film-appreciation curricula sought to inculcate certain ways of watching, ways of experiencing films, in addition to fostering a critical evaluative judgment that would predispose young audiences to "better" films. It was not enough to shape the tastes of young filmgoers. Film-education efforts sought further to influence the manner in which students experienced *all* films.

Central to the film-education movement was an attempt to, in part, demystify the film production process. Glimpses behind the scenes at the Hollywood production process had long been a staple of film-industry promotional practices. Within the film-education movement, such a demystification was mobilized to fulfill a pedagogical function and to foster shared standards for evaluation. "Better" films involved a more intensive preproduction labor and a highly specialized division of labor during production. Here, film educators closely followed rhetorical tropes common to Hollywood promotional practices. Some film educators advocated incorporating children's leisure reading of motion-picture magazines into the curriculum as part of the demystification of film technique. "It is good, too," Elizabeth Watson Pollard wrote, "to discuss how sounds and settings are faked in order to dull the fright and intense excitement which stir children too deeply...Let them discuss how a ship sinking at sea is photographed in a tub, and jungle scenes taken on the lot. Many children are suffering today under nervous excitement that lasts for days because they are unable to detach themselves from the reality of the thrilling scene" (1936: 22).

This demystification of film production also took the form of direct student encounters with the cinematographic apparatus. Film education often included trips inside the projection booth at the local theater and, sometimes in collaboration with science teachers, classroom demonstrations of both cameras and projectors. At many US schools, as the 1930s progressed, film-education efforts even included exercises in student film production, as described in articles such as Elias Katz's "Making Movies in the Classroom" (1936), Kerry Smith and Irene Lemon's "Learning Through Film-Making" (1937), and William G. Hart's "Possibilities in the Use of the School Newsreel" (1938). But, although filmmaking was increasingly incorporated into the curriculum, the primary site of educators' intervention was imagined as the orchestrated discussion, reading, research, and writing surrounding student moviegoing.

MGM's 1935 film adaptation of *David Copperfield* fulfilled many of the pedagogical needs and desires of film educators. It was a prestige production, free of the salacious content or criminal violence that provoked such concern from post-Payne Fund film reformers. It was also free of visual representations of extravagant lifestyles and commodity consumption that some credited with inculcating distorted values in children moviegoers. Its production history – or at least MGM's public presentation of that production history – bore traces of the historical research that educators linked to film quality. The literary source upon which the film was based carried the pedagogical cachet of an unquestioned canonical work of literature by an author already firmly ensconced within the curriculum. Yet *David Copperfield* could not directly and unproblematically be incorporated into the 1930s US curriculum. The nature of *David Copperfield* as a literary work required some careful rhetorical negotiation, a careful discursive management to incorporate both the literary work and the film, and particularly the process of adaptation, into the emerging film-study canon.

Timed to coincide with the film's theatrical release, The National Council of Teachers of English published a *Study Guide* for teachers and students to better foster a critical appreciation of the film. In the same year it also published *Study Guides* to accompany the films of *Little Women*, *Alice in Wonderland*, *The Emperor Jones*, *Treasure Island*, *Great Expectations*, and *The Little Minister*. In the following year, the *Study Guide* publishing project was continued by a new organization, Educational and Recreational Guides, Inc. In 1936 they released *Study Guides* for *Romeo and Juliet*, *Mutiny on the Bounty*, *A Tale of Two Cities*, *The Last Days of Pompeii*, *The Three Musketeers*, *Little Lord Fauntleroy*, *Les Miserables*, *Mary of Scotland*, *Scrooge (A Christmas Carol)*, *A Midsummer Night's Dream*, and H. G. Wells's *The Shape of Things to Come*. The 1936 *Study Guides* include pronounced evidence of film-industry cooperation. The number of film stills increased, and individual *Guides* included introductory remarks by producers (Irving Thalberg for *Romeo and Juliet*, Darryl Zanuck for *Les Miserables*), statements by directors and screenwriters (Richard Boleslawski and W. P. Lipscomb, the director and the screenwriter for *Les Miserables*), and set-design sketches for the films (Cedric Gibbons for *Romeo and Juliet*).

The *Copperfield* pamphlet, the fourth in the series of similar *Study Guides*, was explicitly intended to be used within the emerging photoplay-appreciation movement. While a studio like MGM could garner a certain public-relations cachet (in addition to any potential profit generated by the film itself) through the adaptation of Dickens for the screen, 1930s educators sought, through the use of theatrical motion pictures in the curricula, a different kind of social and educational cachet. Teaching Dickens's *David Copperfield* in relation to MGM's film adaptation offered educators, in the words of the *Study Guides* series editor Max Herzberg, the opportunity to foster "a better understanding not merely of photoplays in general but also of Dickens himself" (Abbott 1935: 3). Herzberg noted that the *Study Guide*'s author, Mary Allen Abbott, had aimed the pedagogical advice "at younger students and at those not particularly bookish" all of whom "can be made members of the great Dickens clan" (3). MGM's theatrical film thus offered educators the opportunity to inculcate not only greater appreciation of "better" films but also the reading loyalty of those who had yet to be assimilated into the clan of Dickens.

Ultimately, how teachers actually made use of an individual *Study Guide* or the series is beyond the scope of this article. Further, the type and degree of effect that the study of *David Copperfield* as a film adaptation had on schoolchildren, their reading habits, and tastes in films is largely lost to the contemporary historian. Instead, in what follows I explore the *Study Guide* as rhetoric that attempted to intervene in the cinemagoing of schoolchildren. The *Study Guide* as a text simultaneously addressed teachers and students and it articulated and had embedded within it a series of assumptions about literature and reading, as well as cinema and filmgoing. Those assumptions are crucial to understanding how educators sought during the height of Hollywood's studio-system era to recuperate commercial leisure as a socially redeeming activity.

At a distance of nearly seventy years, the goals of this attempt to incorporate Dickens and film into the school curriculum are rather transparent. Such a combination of traditional literary studies with the classical Hollywood film was intended not only to foster greater appreciation for "better" commercial films, but also to use the allure of the motion-picture show to convert to the clan of Dickens those "not particularly bookish." Teachers could ideally use the appeal of cinemagoing to shape students as readers even as the process of discussing and writing about the film sought to interpellate students to particular modes of critical film spectatorship.

The *Study Guide* was split into a series of sections and provided pedagogical suggestions for a variety of age groups or degrees of student interest. After general contextualizing information about the film's production framed as information for students prior to seeing the film, Abbott included highly selective and directive information about comparisons between MGM's film version and Dickens's book, a brief discussion of "camera technique" (emphasizing close-ups and the expressive potentials offered by shot scale), a classroom questionnaire designed to provoke discussion of the film, a list of research topics identified as "For Those Who Like Dickens," a series of research/writing ideas identified as questions for those more interested in film technique, and a list of resources for students interested in further study of either Dickens or motion pictures in general.

Abbott's *Study Guide* began with descriptive information about MGM's production designed to introduce students to the film. After identifying the locations and period for the film, Abbott noted the absence of some characters and events originally in Dickens's work that were omitted from the film. Such omissions were rhetorically framed in terms of the productive labor involved in bringing Dickens to the screen, as Abbott emphasized the contributions and previous careers of producer David Selznick, director George Cukor, screenwriter Howard Estabrook, and literary advisor Hugh Walpole. This account of the production of the film drew substantial attention to the efforts of MGM's "research department" and the lengths to which the studio went to ensure realism in costume, speech, and historical details of setting. Abbott's account of the "research work" behind the film collaborated with similar efforts by the publicity department of MGM, echoed in reviews of the film, that emphasized the "authenticity" of Selznick/Cukor's adaptation. Commentary and background information on both casting and the music of William Axt further highlighted issues of authenticity and the labor of production. Abbott sought to reinforce in young viewers and their teachers a common-sense definition of film quality hinging on both extensive specialized labor and an ill-defined appeal to the "authentic." In its emphasis on the film's "authenticity" and the "research" undertaken by MGM, the *Study Guide* functioned as an extension of and a complement to MGM's promotional efforts to foster a commercial identity for the film. "Authentic" details of Victorian England would, of course, be largely lost on film spectators of the 1930s unless those details were foregrounded rhetorically in the promotional apparatus that surrounded a film. Written, perhaps apocryphal, accounts like Abbott's of "material collected in England, old books, photographs, sketches, costumes – a vast amount of material, enough, one would judge, to fill a moving van – . . . shipped to the California studio, there to be catalogued and indexed for quick reference by scores of workers" served as implicit arguments about film quality, both valorizing the production of *David Copperfield* and implicitly critiquing those competing films for which such inordinate labor was either unnecessary or unremarked upon (6).

Abbott introduced the relationship of the film to Dickens's novel by instructing students to read the book in preparation for viewing the film, but she insisted that they "read as rapidly as possible" (4). Repeated only three sentences later, this insistence that students read quickly and attend only to character and story prepared them for a particular experience of both the literary work and the film. Contemporary reviews for *David Copperfield* sometimes stressed that the true indication of a member of the "Dickens clan" involved the capacity to quote unaided long passages of text. Thus a reviewer of the film in *Commonweal* confessed to "that passionate addiction to Dickens the test of which is set by Mr. [G.K.] Chesterton (leader of all contemporary addicts) as the uncontrollable reeling off of long paragraphs verbatim in any Dickensian argument" (22 Feb. 1935: 470). But Abbott's attempt to incorporate the film version of Dickens into the curriculum hinged on reading of a different sort. Although her self-professed goal was "a revival of those days when everybody knew Dickens's characters," such knowledge of character was to be the product of a particular kind of reading that eschewed attention to any nuances of literary presentation or descriptive detail (7). Students were to read so as to become familiar with plot events and characters, precisely those elements most obviously in common with the film version of a novel.

PART I: STUDENTS' GUIDE
BEFORE SEEING DAVID COPPERFIELD

If possible, before seeing the motion picture, read the book. Read as rapidly as possible. Do not read the footnotes. After seeing the film, however, you may want to use them in a more leisurely reading. As preparation for the film, read as rapidly as possible. Read for the story (or rather for the stories, since in Dickens' novels there are always several stories) and read for what you can learn about the characters. Read attentively what they say. If you have time, read carefully Dickens' descriptions of people and places. Read for enjoyment, not because you fear you are going to be questioned.

FACTS TO KNOW BEFORE SEEING THE PICTURE

The Locale:

England—Blunderstone, near the seacoast
Yarmouth, on the seacoast
London and vicinity
The Dover Road
Dover, on the seacoast
Canterbury

The Period:

Early Victorian, covering about twenty-five years.

The Costumes:

Costumes follow the original "Phiz" drawings and represent a treatment of the styles of 1835-45.

The Characters:

It was impossible, of course, to show all the characters of the book. Writing his story in monthly installments, Dickens was free to introduce a new character or a new story-interest whenever he felt inclined. Each character may be said to live in a little world of his own. It was Dickens' task to bring these characters, these story-interests together. Sometimes he made use of a long-lost relative, husband or friend who "turns up" at a convenient moment—or rather an inconvenient moment as far as somebody in the story is concerned. In *David Copperfield*, it is Aunt Betsy's husband, believed dead, who "turns up" rather unconvincingly.

Fortunately Aunt Betsy's husband does not turn up in the film. Other characters omitted, a host of them, are various relatives or friends of the main characters, important persons in their own little world and

[4]

Fig. 14.1. Page from *A Study Guide to Dickens' David Copperfield*, Mary Allen Abbott, 1935

TO HIGH-SCHOOL SENIORS

Scenes in the Screen Continuity Compared with the Book

You may be interested, after seeing the film, to analyze some scene which you noticed particularly (perhaps because you liked it?) and find its original in the book. You may discover that you do not find it—not exactly as in the book. The dialogue may be cut, for long speeches are impossible on the screen where the tempo is of course faster than in a novel or even than on the stage. (Also more expensive! See interview with Hugh Walpole in *New York Times,* Sunday, December 9, 1934.) Some bit of added invention you may find. (Did Dora and David meet for the first time at the theatre?) You may find in some scene a massing of dialogue and action which occurred in different parts of the book; for instance, the scene of Dora's failure of a dinner-party followed by the scene when she "held the pens" for David—all that came from widely separated pages of the book. The guests are not the same as in the book, and the leg-of-mutton—that ill-fated leg-of-mutton which was grey with ashes and was both burnt and raw—was transplanted boldly from the original scene where David entertained the Micawbers. The various incidents and dialogue used in this excellent scene sequence, as far as can be discovered, came from Chapter XII and Chapter XV, and the leg-of-mutton from Chapter V!

A dramatist would say this massing of material was necessary; one could not make a good scene (which must be a step in a dramatic progression) out of a scrap of talk or a scrap of description in a book. Perhaps you will learn more about the differences between novel and drama by analyzing a single scene from *David Copperfield* than by hours of studying abstract principles of dramatic construction.

CAMERA TECHNIQUE

Close-ups:

Close-up is a familiar term and sometimes a too-familiar experience in seeing motion pictures. When you see *David Copperfield,* notice how the director, Mr. Cukor, uses close-ups. With restraint? Or does he exploit the features and emotion of some star player? Sometimes in motion pictures we have seen close-ups so huge that the eyelashes seemed a foot long and tears as big as snowballs were rolling from the eyes of "the star." Was Mr. Cukor guilty of such close-ups?

[8]

Fig. 14.2. Page from *A Study Guide to Dickens'* David Copperfield, Mary Allen Abbott, 1935

In a section addressed to high-school seniors, Abbott directly took on the issue of adaptation. However, she carefully framed the appropriate methods for such comparative work, thereby policing the possible results. The work of comparative criticism was about demystifying the process of adaptation, not about evaluative judgment of the end result of that adaptation. Close comparative analysis of a film version with its literary source could provide insight into principles of dramatic construction, but the goal of such critical activity was clearly not to find either work ultimately lacking.

Overt calls for evaluative critique did appear in the *Study Guide*'s subsequent section on "camera technique," where students were asked to judge *David Copperfield*'s use of film techniques. Abbott instructed students to consider whether Cukor used close-ups with "restraint" or to "exploit the features and emotion of some star player" (8). She further encouraged students to consider issues of shot scale in general – noting the different functions that image composition might fulfill as well as the different functions of mise-en-scène, including any contribution it made to narration. Like the *Study Guide*'s earlier section on film music, her approach insisted students attend not just to the story and the characters but to the manner in which such characters were rendered and such a story told. Here the *Study Guide* departed dramatically from its initial approach to the novel: "read as rapidly as possible." Close textual analysis and evaluative critique were appropriate, the *Study Guide* allowed, but only for the critical appraisal of a film as a film, not for the appraisal of a film as an adaptation, nor for analysis of the original work of literature.

Abbott's study questions for writing and discussion after viewing the film cultivated a series of skills, encouraging students to adopt ways of watching and thinking about the film. The majority of questions simply asked students to recall the film. "Can you quote what Aunt Betsy [*sic*] said as a parting word of advice when David went off to school?" "What was the very first picture in the photoplay?" The pedagogical principle here involved fostering in students a greater attention in viewing, a more focused mode of reception. While a few questions invited students to compare the film with its literary source, these questions were never framed in such a way as to invoke an evaluation. Instead such evaluative judgments, when they were encouraged, focused internally to the film, asking students to exercise critical judgment in terms such as "What was the most picturesque scene?" or "Which player or players do you think acted the best?" Finally a few of the discussion questions asked students to use the film as a starting point for larger reflections about community standards or moral judgments. "Would you recommend *David Copperfield* for younger children?" "Was Uriah Heep sufficiently punished in the film?" (14).

Fig. 14.3. Photograph (from the David O. Selznick version of *David Copperfield*) from *A Study Guide to Dickens'* David Copperfield, Mary Allen Abbott, 1935

Students' critical skills were most overtly invoked only in the culminating section of the *Study Guide*, but even here they were tellingly split
into two categories of research identified with two distinct types of practi-
tioner: students interested in Dickens and those interested in film. Literary research was to be the domain of "those who liked Dickens." Motion-
picture research was to be practiced by those "especially interested in
technical problems." This culminating section literalized the distinction
implicit elsewhere in the *Study Guide* (and indeed elsewhere in the film-
appreciation movement) that ultimately, overt, evaluative judgments of
the relationship between a literary source and a film adaptation were
properly the domain only of those already interpellated into the "clan of
Dickens" or its equivalent. Students self-identified as Dickensians were
encouraged to "see if the director left anything out," or to "try to catch
the Peggottys not talking in character." Other questions included: "What
bits did you notice in the film that were not in the book?" or "Look
up quotations from *David Copperfield* in Bartlett's Familiar Quotations.
Who said them? Did the motion picture use them?" (15–16). Admittedly,
those who had only read the novel "as rapidly as possible" would be ill-
equipped to answer such questions. But importantly here, Abbott split
the study of Dickens and the study of adaptation into a kind of academic
division of labor; only the properly interpellated were suited to the task
of evaluative judgments that involved comparisons between the two types
of textuality.

Meanwhile, for the technical-minded motion-picture fans, the *Study
Guide* encouraged critical attention to transitions (cuts, dissolves, fades),
to double exposures, or to mise-en-scene. Students in this latter group
were asked to evaluate the film with a critical eye. Were interiors too
cluttered? Were the lighting effects too bright for England? Were details of costume, hairstyle, and make-up consistent with early-Victorian
England? "Did you see any pepper trees or any other evidence that the
actual filming was done in California?" (17). Here, students were to evaluate the film based on standards of realism – although one must wonder
from where such standards would come.

In general, Abbott's *Study Guide* implied that the goal of close, comparative analysis involved not evaluating an adaptation's success in relation to
its source but instead understanding adaptation as a process and learning
principles of dramatic construction. This emphasis and careful location
of the site of evaluative judgment echoed the rhetorical framing of the
film as the product of labor designed to guarantee authenticity. The process involved a partial demystification of film production in a way that
foregrounded what MGM promoted: the value of exhaustive historical
research in the realization of the film. A student's critical judgment was

Fig. 14.4. Frank Lawton as David and Madge Evans as Agnes in *David Copperfield* (1935)

relocated through the rhetoric of the *Study Guide* to the realm of film technique or to identifying evidence of "inauthenticity." This process could be
generalized to virtually all films and consequently intervene in the "whole
curriculum of childhood" by critically arming students against whatever
salacious or otherwise inappropriate content Hollywood might muster.
But students were not encouraged to bring their evaluative talents to bear
on Dickens's text in light of what they had learned about the principles
of a "good story." The *Study Guide*, not surprisingly, took the value of
Dickens as a given. Students' evaluative critical skills could and should
be easily applied to other films, to any film, but not to the film's original
literary source.

   In one passage within the *Study Guide*, Abbott acknowledged the indeterminacy of film reception (or perhaps even of reading), noting that
"Each one in the audience will have some special interest which will
run along with the picture he is looking at and will partly determine his
reaction to the play." She went on to list as examples of such "special
interests" comparisons with Dickens's original text, camera work, actors
and actresses, music, costumes, "the art qualities" of the film, or even,

for specialists in speech, "the voices and the inflections and the pronunciation" of the actors" (6). For film educators, such indeterminacy was
the crux of the cinema problem. As the Payne Fund Studies indicated,
students not only attended films of which social reformers, concerned
parents, and teachers disapproved, but all children were susceptible to
responding to even relatively innocuous films in uncontrolled or even
deleterious ways. Despite this tendency for audience members to experience the same film differently, Abbott, and indeed the *Study Guide* and
the larger film-education movement, believed that all audiences might be
united in their shared attention to a film's story. "One interest, however,"
Abbott wrote, "everyone in the audience has in common, and that is the
interest in a good story" (6). The *Photoplay Study Guide* series shared
with the conventional wisdom of the Hollywood film an implicit, at times
explicit, sense of what qualities constituted a "good" film story: "In a good
screen story, the events must flow along smoothly leading your interest
up to some high point in the story and to a satisfactory or to a logical outcome. The characters must be believable and some of them likable; they
must appear in probable situations and, since this is a dramatic version
of the novel, they must be sharply confronted with moments of decision
or conflict" (6). Film educators sought to cultivate in their students this
definition of a "good story" as a shared critical standard to be applied to
all films.

But with such a standard established, Dickens's *David Copperfield* had
to be framed as a special case. In Abbott's words, "Since this is Dickens
we are seeing, there will be more than one story and we may find several
high points of interest" (6). While audiences could agree on the qualities
of a good screen story, educators had to be careful that students did not
generalize from that shared definition of narrative and apply it to literary works. Any comparisons between novels and films as narrative forms
had to be carefully framed in terms of the difference between these two
expressive forms. Abbott, in fact, even sounded apologetic at times, in
recognizing that no film could essentially recreate the narrative richness
of a Dickens novel. In this assessment she echoed one of the dominant
notes of contemporary reviews of the film, almost all of which stressed
the inherent impossibility of fully adapting Dickens to the screen. Thus,
Grenville Vernon could admit in *Commonweal* that "it is of course impossible to put the great panorama of a Dickens novel in its full richness into
a bare two hours...and in a work of the length and richness of 'David
Copperfield' this is particularly true" (1935: 403). While in other hands
such a contrast would provide the basis for arguments that the Hollywood
film could only ever provide degraded versions of literary masterpieces,
the rhetorical frame imposed on spectatorship by the goal of incorporating

Fig. 14.5. Lennox Pawle as Mr. Dick in *David Copperfield* (1935)

film into the curriculum necessitated that film and novel be viewed as two distinct narrative forms, thereby limiting the extent to which teachers and students might compare the two and find one lacking.

The *Study Guide* for *David Copperfield* exposes the convergence of distinct institutional interests surrounding film and filmgoing during the height of the US studio system. A literary source like Dickens's novel offered not only a recognizable narrative commodity that could provide the basis for a film, but also the novel's status offered MGM an opportunity to elevate the prestige of the studio through producing the adaptation.

Further, producing and distributing *David Copperfield* allowed the studio to present itself publicly as responsive to the calls of concerned citizens for "better" films. From an educator's point of view, the film adaptation facilitated the incorporation of film study into the US curriculum by offering a text bearing traces, at least, of the pedagogical cachet of the original. Here, the decision to adapt from one medium to another provided the opportunity to incorporate not only a text, but also the medium itself into pre-existing curricular standards. Not surprisingly, the film industry provided various degrees of cooperation with the emerging film-education movement. Because film educators clearly sought to use children's filmgoing as a point of intervention in the "whole curriculum of childhood" rather than to seek, for example, to substitute leisure reading for filmgoing, the movement itself offered Hollywood opportunities rather than a threat. Ultimately film-education efforts might have cultivated different ways of consuming films, but they did not seriously seek to challenge children's movie habit. These efforts thus provided the film industry with an additional site through which to promote commercial identities for their products.

REFERENCES

Anon. 22 Feb. 1935. "Filming the Classics." *Commonweal* 21: 470.
Abbott, Mary Allen. 1935. *A Study Guide to the Critical Appreciation of the Photoplay Version of Charles Dickens' Novel David Copperfield*. Chicago: National Council of Teachers of English.
Bragdon, Clifford. 1937. "The Movies in High School." *English Journal* 26: 374–81.
Charters, W. W. 1935. "The Motion Picture in Education." *Educational Record* 16: 312–20.
Dale, Edgar. 1936. "Teaching Motion Picture Appreciation." *English Journal* 25: 113–20.
Eldridge, Donald A. 1937. "Motion-Picture Appreciation in the New Haven Schools." *Sociology of Education* 11 (Nov.): 175–83.
Forman, Henry James. 1933. *Our Movie Made Children*. New York: Macmillan.
Hart, William G. 1938. "Possibilities in the Use of the School Newsreel." *Educational Screen* 17: 184–5.
Katz, Elias. 1936. "Making Movies in the Classroom." *Clearing House* 11: 153–6.
Pollard, Elizabeth Watson. 1936. "Increasing Motion Picture Appreciation Among Youth." *International Journal of Religious Education* 12: 22–3, 34.
Selby, Stuart Alan. 1978. *The Study of Film as an Art Form in American Secondary Schools* (1964). New York: Arno.
Smith, Kerry and Irene Lemon. 1937. "Learning Through Film-making." *Teachers College Record* 39: 207–17.
Vernon, Grenville. 1935. "The Play and Screen." *Commonweal* 21: 403.

15   Dickens, Selznick, and *Southpark*

Jeffrey Sconce

"Oh my God, they've killed Dickens . . . you bastards!"

Hollywood has long been the premier battlefield in mass culture's ongoing war between art and commerce. Diplomats from both sides of this campaign worked out a temporary truce, of sorts, during a meeting at London's Savoy Hotel on 16 May 1934. In a heavily publicized conference sponsored by the *News Chronicle*, Hollywood emissaries David O. Selznick and George Cukor (along with representatives of the British film industry) met with the distinguished board of the Dickens Fellowship, a group of writers and intellectuals serving as the cultural custodians of England's most celebrated nineteenth-century novelist. Their common goal that day was to select the ideal cast for the upcoming MGM production of Dickens's *David Copperfield*. As the sponsor of the event, the *News Chronicle* reported that "the Dickensians, headed by their President, Mr. Alfred Noyes, will analyze the main characteristics of the characters in *David Copperfield*. And the film experts will name the actors they consider could best represent those characters" (14 May 1934). A photo of the event shows Selznick and Cukor squaring off with Noyes and J. B. Priestley, debating the "authentic" essence of Copperfield, Micawber, Uriah Heep, and the other most remembered characters from the novel. Sponsored by the *Chronicle* as a contest for its readers, the entries that most closely matched those of the expert panel vied for a prize of £500. The winning cast included Leslie Howard as David Copperfield, Sir Cedric Hardwicke as Micawber, David Calthrop as Uriah Heep, May Robson as Aunt Betsey, Gordon Harker as Barkis, Elizabeth Allan as Dora, Diana Wynyard as Agnes, Victoria Hopper as Little Em'ly, Mrs. Patrick Campbell as Mrs. Micawber, Frederic March as Steerforth, and Edmund Gwenn as Mr. Peggotty (*News Chronicle* 17 May 1934).

Selznick's trip to England took place at a moment in Hollywood history when "prestige productions," movies made from celebrated and respected literary properties, were becoming increasingly important to the industry. While Selznick and Cukor's trip may have had limited value in terms of "practical" preproduction concerns (tellingly, none of the eleven principals chosen as the "ideal cast" for Copperfield actually appeared in the final production), the trip was of major marketing importance in bringing visibility to the coming feature film. It was a vital step toward imbuing the production with a sense of credibility, a quality essential to the successful economic and artistic adaptation of the literary property. Indeed, when the two men left on their trek to mine England's cultural capital, the *Los Angeles Times* described their trip as nothing less than "a search for authenticity" (4 February 1934).

Compare this to almost seventy years later, when the animated television series *Southpark* embarked on its own adaptation of Dickens, in this case a version of *Great Expectations.* In most episodes *Southpark* followed the exploits of four foul-mouthed children, Stan, Kyle, Eric, and Kenny, as they pursued satirical and surreal adventures in their small town in Colorado. In November 2000, however, the series took the time to explore the background of one of the show's many incidental characters, a schoolmate of the children named Pip. As the foreign transfer student in town, Pip presented a target for endless abuse from his cruel and xenophobic classmates. Outfitted in antiquated British garb, Pip repeatedly attempted to befriend his American school chums only to be rebuffed with vulgarities and insults, all of which Pip endured with pathetic politeness and eternal optimism ("Screw you Pip!" "Right-ee-oo!").

Pip's special episode (entitled simply "Pip") begins with a non-animated sequence of esteemed British actor Malcolm McDowell seated in his study leafing through a book: "Ah, Dickens, the imagery of cobblestone streets, craggy London buildings, and nutmeg filled Yorkshire pudding." Closing his book, McDowell looks directly into the camera and introduces himself. "Hello, I'm a British person." At the turn of the twenty-first century, apparently, the truce of authenticity negotiated by Selznick decades earlier has devolved into hollow absurdity. The cultural authority of the British, so long courted by the American culture industries, serves in this context as little more than fodder for a joke about America's (or more specifically, the typical PBS subscriber's) haughty search for cultural enrichment in the English classics.

Continuing in this vein, McDowell resumes his broadside of countryman Alistair Cooke:

For years now the character Pip has been featured prominently in the American show *Southpark*. However, many Americans don't realize where Pip came from. He's the prowling, adorable little Englishman from Charles Dickens's timeless classic, "Great Expectations." And so tonight, the makers of *Southpark* have agreed to take a break from their regular show, and instead present the prestigious

Dickens tale in its entirety, from beginning to end. Indeed, after watching this show, you will know the timeless classic as if you had read the Cliff's Notes themselves.

We then cut to Pip back in England on his way to the graveyard to visit his parents, where he quickly meets Magwitch and initiates a whirlwind, twenty-two-minute cartoon version of the novel.

Sharing only Dickens as a common denominator, these two adaptations are divided by history, medium, and genre. Examining Selznick's and *Southpark*'s attempts to capture the "Dickensian" allows us to interrogate the specific textual strategies of these two media in quite different historical moments and, in the process, explore the textual influence of the "Dickensian" on both film and television. I am especially interested in how these two adaptations foreground the politics of taste and literary prestige informing each medium in its own historical moment. Which is the better adaptation of Dickens – a two-and-a-half-hour motion picture based on painstaking research or a twenty-two-minute cartoon? The answer would have been obvious to American studio heads in the 1930s. It would be irrelevant to American television producers in the 1990s.

A most pretentious production

The Selznick adaptation of *Copperfield* took place in a time when many still held great hope that the movies might enlighten and edify the masses, however they might be conceived. While modernism and progressivism may have given up on the medium by the 1930s (for different reasons), many critics still believed that movies could bring great literature to the screen relatively "intact" and thus provide a useful service to the viewing and (one hoped) reading public. Like Shakespeare, Dickens embodied (particularly for American audiences) the perfect balance of familiar entertainment value and "classic" cultural capital. Appropriately, a teacher's manual and study guide issued to coincide with the release of *David Copperfield* introduces its subject with a meditation on Dickens's place in "great literature." The manual begins by quoting Ashley H. Thorndike's *Literature in a Changing Age* in detail:

Among men of creative genius Dickens is the great democrat. He had more readers than anyone else during his lifetime, he has probably had more readers than any other English writer during the century. The art of Dickens bears the marks of his popularity. He is writing for those who had never read any good novels before and not primarily for those who are acquainted with the best that has been known and said. He is not worried about the connoisseur, he tells his stories for the millions. (1935: 4)

Such a tribute would not be out of place in introducing Hollywood cinema or network television. In short, Dickens possessed the perfect balance of popularity and prestige for maximum exploitation by Hollywood. A bona fide "creative genius," Dickens could also be appreciated by the middle-brow "millions" who filled theater seats week in and week out across the country. Moreover, for studios and audiences looking for a prestigious brush with "culture," Dickens and, perhaps more importantly, the "Dickensian," stood as the most familiar and accessible pathway into a semiotic state of "Britishness," a culture regarded (then as now) as inherently more cultivated, civilized, and refined.

However, like most decisions in Hollywood, the industry's move in the 1930s toward prestige production and literary adaptations like *David Copperfield* was less a function of artistic ambition than of economic opportunity. On a public-relations front, prestige films did help to mollify the censorship cries of the Legion of Decency and other public-interest groups outraged by Hollywood's increasing forays into more explicit sex and violence (a trend most famously embodied in the popular gangster cycle of the early 1930s). But in the end, the move toward prestige production at mid-decade simply continued a trend temporarily interrupted by the Depression. As Tino Balio notes, "The ability of prestige pictures to attract audiences was well understood by Hollywood. However, the heavy investments required to make these pictures placed them out of the reach of most companies until general economic conditions improved and operations stabilized" (1993: 189). Productions like *David Copperfield*, a film that cost MGM just over one million dollars to make, represented a significant financial commitment on the part of the studios. Depending on their financial health, studios could only mount between one and six such productions each year, filling out the rest of their schedule with programmers and B-films. Prestige films held the potential for major profits: despite MGM's initial reservations, *Copperfield* made just under three million in its initial release. But they also required carefully planned promotional campaigns to maximize their status as cinematic events.

Within this general trend back toward prestige production, the work of Charles Dickens became a valuable property. "The studio favourite at the moment is Dickens, who has suddenly come into prominence after ten odd years of neglect," reported the *Observer*. "The American library demands for the Dickens novels, I am told, are heavier this year than at any time in recent history, and the film chiefs, never slow to neglect these box-office indications, have announced at least four, and possibly five, impending Dickens adaptations on their new schedules" (12 May 1934). Making it to the screen in the wake of *Copperfield* were Universal's version of *Edwin Drood* (1935) and MGM's adaptations of *A Tale of Two Cities* (1935) and *A Christmas Carol* (1938). Preceding MGM's high-gloss treatment of *Copperfield*, Hollywood had staged two previous Dickens adaptations in the sound era, *Oliver Twist* (Universal, 1933) and *Great Expectations* (Universal, 1934). Neither was particularly well received, particularly by the British. One English source labeled Universal's *Oliver Twist* an "unfortunate adaptation" featuring "a nice little American boy, much too babyish for the character, and a Fagin who could scarcely be recognized through the white-wash" (*Birmingham Post*, 24 May 1934).

Predictably, writers aligned more closely with the interests of "high" culture over Hollywood staged a backlash against the prestige trend almost from its inception. "The rush to put Dickens on the screen seems to us a momentary form of madness from which it is to be hoped the producers affected will recover before they have completely lost their senses," complained *Film Weekly* on 1 June 1934.

> But it has still to be proved whether even *Copperfield* can be satisfactorily brought to life on the screen. The difficulties to be overcome are by no means inconsiderable, and the reception which the completed picture will receive must remain a matter for conjecture until it has actually been shown and approved by the millions of Dickens-lovers throughout the world – and especially in this country.
>
> Have the producers who are now so anxious to film *The Pickwick Papers*, *Great Expectations*, *Edwin Drood* and other Dickens novels of problematic screen value stopped to consider the nature of their undertaking?
>
> Or are they simply rushing blindly into it, caught up by the temporary fascination of the "new" field suddenly opened to them?

Yet, despite its general disdain for Hollywood, *Film Weekly* concluded by applauding the Selznick project. "By all means, let us have an occasional Dickens film, such as *David Copperfield*, the production of which was undertaken before the present 'boom' developed, and is being pursued with a keen sense of the responsibility incurred."

Whether regarded as a burden of "the responsibility incurred" or a mere publicity junket, Selznick and Cukor's trip was in and of itself an important step in the process of adapting *Copperfield* to the screen. In order to exploit fully the prestige value of the novel, MGM's creative team had to go beyond simply tinkering with the plot mechanics of Dickens's story. They also had to signify through a variety of extratextual venues the proper air of respect and reverence, necessary prerequisites to deriving an authority of adaptation that would contribute to the film's ultimate success when marketed. Throughout their tour of England, Selznick reiterated in almost every interview the impossibility of filming *David Copperfield* with an American cast. "This shows a laudable intention on the part of Mr. Selznick and his collaborators," noted the *Birmingham Post*, demonstrating the pre-release goodwill generated by the producer's visit. When asked about the possibility of an American Micawber, Selznick is reported to have replied, "we intend our casting to be true to the Dickens interpretation of the originals, and we have come here to find English actors and actresses for important parts" (*News Chronicle* 12 May 1934).

Before leaving on his trip, Selznick had promised to the *Los Angeles Times* that he would "adhere rigidly to the spirit and color of the book; it will not be 'modernized,'" prompting the paper to observe, "Dickens would appear to be in reasonably safe hands" (4 Feb. 1934). Selznick even hinted during his trip that the entire production might take place in England, but also assured "we shall . . . take back to Hollywood (assuming the picture is made there) a leading authority on Dickens and his time to advise on atmosphere and other technical details" (*Daily Telegraph* 12 May 1934). That leading authority proved to be novelist Hugh Walpole, who besides aiding Howard Estabrook in adapting the screenplay, also took a bit part in the finished production. Beyond the esteemed Dickens Fellowship, finally, Selznick was also advised "to consult original manuscripts in the British Museum, and possibly to confer with various members of the Dickens family" (*Observer* 12 May 1934). Asked if he would need to alter the book significantly, Selznick told a reporter, "Hollywood would never dream of altering Dickens at all." Whether the reporter was being sincere or icily ironic, his response to Selznick was to write, "it is pleasant to know that somewhere art is reverenced" (*Daily Telegraph* 12 May 1934).

Like many other prestige projects of the era, MGM's *Copperfield* followed a very public process of adaptation. As the *Los Angeles Times* reported, "Letters have been pouring into the MGM offices . . . from Dickens readers the world over – expressions of enthusiasm, suggestions for casting and treatment, and dire warnings against perverting or distorting the original" (4 Feb. 1934). Such widespread interest in the project testifies to the unrivaled centrality of Hollywood in 1930s popular culture, the still monumental place of Dickens in popular memory, and the ingenuity of the MGM publicity department (for planting this item in the *Los Angeles Times*). As preproduction continued, there was no shortage of Dickens experts ready to contribute advice from both sides of the Atlantic. Beyond the concerns for casting and authenticity of detail described above, critics of both Dickens and Hollywood wrote more generally about the challenges, strategies, and efficacy of adapting novels into film, a popular topic repeatedly addressed in the pages of *Publishers Weekly*, *The Saturday Review of Literature*, and *Film Weekly* throughout the 1930s.

MGM further cultivated this sense of authenticity in adaptation by publicizing the extreme efforts made to find the proper child actor to play the boy David. One source claimed that ten thousand young boys had been interviewed for the role. Another pool of three hundred children led to only six that could speak with a proper British accent. The role finally went to British newcomer Freddie Bartholomew. This mania for the perfect performer went beyond the title role. Over the course of the production, fifteen thousand actors were interviewed for various parts, resulting in over two thousand actual screen tests. The studio, of course, made sure this heroic effort was reported in the pages of *Hollywood Reporter*, *Daily Variety*, and a number of popular film periodicals, all of which helped to build credibility and anticipation of the film. The extraordinarily large cast of the film, moreover, became a central focus in its eventual marketing. Upon release, every print ad for *David Copperfield* emphasized that sixty-five players appeared in the cast, thereby testifying to the studio's fidelity to Dickens's notoriously Byzantine vision.

As the promotion of its gigantic cast suggests, producers and audiences recognized that the major challenge facing any Dickens adaptation was one of length. "All of Dickens' novels are so diffuse and scattering that the difficulty of reducing one to form and order for a running film is a serious matter," began Marguerite G. Ortman in her account of *Copperfield*, adding, "Any edition of it in fairly readable type printed on a page not too badly crowded can hardly require less than eight hundred pages" (1935: 115). In fact, estimating the length of one's own personal copy of *David Copperfield* seems to have been a starting point for debate in such articles. The novel, noted another writer, "unless it is in very small type, must run to six or seven hundred pages, which will have to be compressed into an hour and a half's entertainment" (*Birmingham Post* 24 May 1934). Even Howard Estabrook himself, the author of the screenplay, fell back on this device in his *Film Weekly* account of the adaptation process. "My copy of *David Copperfield*, from which I am making the adaptation, contains nine hundred and sixty-one pages; obviously enough material to provide a screen entertainment almost as long as Wagner's 'Ring' cycle" (*Film Weekly* 8 June 1934). "Nearly 1000 pages!" proclaimed a headline in the piece.

At one point, Selznick considered shooting and releasing the film in two installments, hoping to minimize the amount of plot material excised from the source. Another plan, also discarded, involved ending the film with David still a child. Commenting on his source material, Estabrook made note of Dickens's often desultory manner of writing, and claimed to have talked to several readers about which parts of the novel "impressed them most deeply" (8). Estabrook's rather logical conclusion was that at the core of the novel were the characters that touched Copperfield's life most closely, which proved to be his framework in the adaptation. As in many Hollywood productions, however, the process of editing the source material did not end with the final script or even after completion of principal photography. After a less than successful preview screening in Bakersfield, California, Louis B. Mayer ordered Selznick to cut the film from its 133-minute running time, a task Selznick accomplished by eliminating Lionel Barrymore's Dan Peggotty. At a later screening in Santa Ana, however, Selznick decided to reinstate the missing footage after speaking with four schoolteachers who objected to the excision. Thus did Dickens's characters and plot remain subject to negotiation even up to the film's premiere in January of 1935.

One might think that MGM would prefer its potential audience not to discover this elaborate process of editing and selection, that the film be seen instead as a divine and unmediated creation appearing magically on the screen. Rather than hide this information, however, MGM proudly included it in its promotional campaign. In the pressbook for *David Copperfield*, nestled among the stories of the worldwide search for a young David and the fidelity to the drawings of Phiz, appeared the banner headline, "Seven Scenarios Discarded Before Final Selection was Made." This did not communicate uncertainty, ineptitude, or excess. On the contrary, MGM was once again trumpeting the utmost care taken in realizing the "perfect" adaptation of the beloved novel.

For contemporary critics of Hollywood it would be easy to dismiss Selznick's pledges of fidelity and the epic search for a proper *David Copperfield* as mere publicity stunts. Such a judgment, however, dismisses the complexities of Hollywood's relationship to "great literature" and "popular narrative" in the mid-1930s. While the industry certainly had no shortage of critics bemoaning the cinema's seeming deterioration in the sound era under the venal command of the studio bosses, there remained a general enthusiasm for the social responsibilities and artistic potentials of film as a narrative medium. There is little doubt that Selznick himself, for example, possessed a genuine passion for "classic" literature, or that he sought to realize them as "faithfully" as possible on the screen. He had previously worked with Cukor on a critically acclaimed adaptation of *Little Women* (1933), and would go on to mount celebrated screen versions of *A Tale of Two Cities* (1935), *Jane Eyre* (1943), and of course, *Gone With the Wind* (1939). Schatz writes "Selznick acknowledged... there were 'very few producers with sufficient understanding' of the classics and 'very few directors with sufficient taste and talent to transcribe them with an accuracy of spirit and mood.'" And yet, Selznick also believed "there were 'millions of fans' who knew movies better than the average producer, and thus were 'even more familiar with the hackneyed situations than the makers of the films who have been grinding them out with machinelike efficiency and standardization'" (1988: 168). Reporting on Selznick's trip to England, one paper quoted Selznick as predicting "a flood of period pictures dealing with classics and history" (*Today's Cinema* 12 May 1934). Perhaps recalling his battles with MGM head Louis B. Mayer to get the picture made, Selznick also predicted the trend's ultimate demise. "The inevitable reaction will set in, for so many of them will be badly done. It is much more costly to make a period picture, but we had got as far as we could with modern stories."

Mayer and Selznick may have had conflicting visions on the merits and utility of *David Copperfield* as a project (Mayer, reportedly, had at one point wanted MGM's child star Jackie Cooper to play David!), but once the production was under way as a prestige picture, it commanded the full resources of its parent studio, a business entity that understood that successful execution, promotion, and exploitation of this literary classic demanded strict attention to authenticating detail. Toward that end, MGM spared no expense to construct a Victorian soundstage. The studio hired Dr. William Axt to research authentic period English music for the production, while L. and H. Nathan, a London company that had worked under Dickens's personal supervision one hundred years earlier, was contracted for the costuming. Filming the novel involved constructing seventy-three different sets, a number far exceeding that of a typical programmer. Set designers are reported to have placed the original Phiz illustrations for the novel under a microscope so that they could be minutely copied for art direction and wardrobe. MGM's head of research, Nathalie Bucknall, worked with ten researchers stationed in England as well as numerous photographers assigned to capture the essence of certain British locations. As a culturally ambitious producer, Selznick no doubt felt such detail was necessary to be true to Dickens's vision of *David Copperfield*. At another level of signification, however, the studio was in the business of transporting its audience to commodified worlds of fantasy. The studio certainly did not want to alienate audiences with the threat of a dry and boring "classic," but it did hope to thoroughly exploit the various currencies of cultural capital (literary, industrial, artistic) to be had in producing the *definitive* adaptation of a Dickens novel, an honor that would translate into pure economic capital. Importantly, signifying the "definitive" was as important a project for the production as actually capturing the "definitive." While the movie might be expected at best to only placate the diehard Dickensians, its more important function was to signify a promised "Dickensian-ness" to its much larger target audience of American filmgoers.

The MGM version of *Copperfield* presented an ambitious bid to render a once extremely popular entertainer turned canonized author into the language of a once reviled popular medium still searching for artistic legitimacy. As Guerric DeBona notes, "Like Matthew Arnold, Charles Dickens visited America twice, and no less than Arnold he shaped the nation's ideas about culture, ameliorating tensions between the barbarians, the philistines, and the populace" (2000: 106). Given such a volatile terrain of "high" and "low," small wonder that Selznick and Cukor felt they needed to travel to England to negotiate personally a pre-emptive truce, or at the very least to help exorcise the personal demons of perceived inferiority felt by both Hollywood and America at large. Sixty years after his death, Dickens had already been discussed as the distant father of Hollywood narration. And yet, if anything, the MGM/Selznick production of *Copperfield* sought to renounce such lineage, its obsession with cultural pilgrimages and authenticating detail standing as tribute, not to Dickens the narrative populist, but to Dickens the literary legend. This tension between popular medium and prestige production, Dickens the entertainer and Dickens the authorial signature, found concise expression in MGM's publicity for the film. Hoping to lure audiences with the promise of movie entertainment and literary education, MGM assured viewers that the studio had given this "spectacular romance its most pretentious production" (Pressbook: n.p.).

Pip versus the robotic monkeys

Few producers today would set out to create a "most pretentious production." The mandate in Selznick's day, obviously, was to both entertain and enlighten the masses, a strategy that had been central to the cinema's overall bid for middle-class legitimacy since its early history. Unburdened by poststructural or multicultural theory, adaptation in the studio system was guided by the principle that, even if producers had to somewhat modify material to meet cinematic narrative demands, the "spirit" of a work could be successfully retained. For Selznick, clearly, the Dickens was in the details, where attention to narrative and period fidelity would make his definitive adaptation exactly that – a cinematic version of the novel whose authority could not be challenged.

Before the massive fragmentation of its audience in the age of cable, network television in the United States operated much like the Hollywood studio system that preceded, informed, and supplied its cathode cousin. No such illusions of authority or consensus guide contemporary entertainment, however, especially in television and even more so in the post-network era. Such an environment has made a series like *Southpark* possible, a program that, like many other contemporary comedies, would be far too offensive and divisive for the old network system. Such fragmentation has made contemporary television a far more diverse and sophisticated textual arena than that of classical Hollywood. Though studio product was greatly diversified by genre and quality, it was far more restricted in terms of tone, morality, and formal design. In the new environment of TV "narrowcasting," on the other hand, it is now acceptable not only to target but to insult entire populations of the country, the latter a provocation unthinkable in either the studio or network ages of (false) consensus. Mormons, Southerners, Dickensians, and any other group seen outside a program's key demographic are now fair game. One episode of *Southpark*, for example, featured a spoof commercial for a new kid's action figure, "Alabama Man," a superhero whose main "power" consisted of coming home drunk from bowling and beating his wife (sold separately).

When Malcolm McDowell opens *Southpark*'s "Pip" with the salutation, "Hello, I'm a British person," it demonstrates that the English (and American Anglophiles) no longer speak from the position of absolute cultural authority evident in Selznick's day. If MGM harnessed its vast resources to produce a "most pretentious production," this particular episode of *Southpark* opens by explicitly puncturing such "pretension." Like "Alabama Man," the literati and intelligentsia are also now mere fodder for the satirical omnivore that is television. Their previous authority rested on the legacy of a "literate" culture inherited from the British that has of course almost completely dissipated in our "post-literate" (but not necessarily "illiterate") moment. Television has obviously been a key agent (or culprit) in this transition, not simply in the bromidic (and wrong) judgment that people have quit reading in the age of TV, but through television's almost acidic ability to erode a variety of cultural boundaries and hierarchies. At the very basic level of televisual intertextuality, it is very difficult to invest the same authority in nineteenth-century British literature now that television has brought us Monty Python, Beatlemania, lager lads at British soccer riots, Ziggy Stardust, Benny Hill, Tinky Winky, and the melodramatic intrigues of a pot-smoking prince. (For another account of American attempts to come to terms with "Britishness," see Luckett 1997.)

McDowell's comical attempt to invoke the cultural power of the Brits shows that "Britishness" is no longer the stable signifier it was in 1935. More than a joke at the expense of the Empire's collapse, however, this joke is also targeted at the "wine and brie" demographic of American Anglophiles who still cling to PBS and its co-dependent relationship with the BBC as the exclusive source of their "television culture," an audience that for the most part does not realize the BBC and ITV productions packaged for the USA by Masterpiece Theater play in their native country as little more than potboiler melodrama. (For every Dickens adaptation, after all, there is a *Danger UXB* or R. L. Delderfield novel to endure.) Although a twenty-minute version of *Great Expectations* could seem an insult to Dickens, *Southpark* (and television in general) may ultimately prove more "true" to Dickens than his mummification at the hands of 1930s Hollywood. Like all commercial artists working in popular media, Dickens was not above a few populist broadsides against the hypocrisy of aristocratic taste and refinement, even as he may have unwittingly contributed to the very ideology that maintained such class relations (an indictment that depends on how one feels about the "evils" of bourgeois realism).

What most links Dickens to television, however, is not the penchant for class satire, but the incredible variety of colliding and conflicting discourses woven together to create his prose. This of course is precisely the form of "heteroglossia" so celebrated in Dickens by Bakhtin, who notes of Dickens and his literary comrades, "in the English comic novel we find a comic-parodic re-processing of almost all levels of literary language, both conversational and written" (1981: 302). Despite frequent dismissals of *Southpark* as merely a series of expletives and fart jokes, the series (like Dickens) is actually quite rich in its orchestration and "reprocessing" of a variety of "languages" (including, on this occasion at least, the Dickensian itself). One week *Southpark* can invoke the iconography and animated puffery of the kids' action-figure commercial to satirize (or confirm?) larger stereotypes of Southern rubes (as a thirty-second segment nestled in a larger story of a Japanese toy company's plans for world domination through a cousin of Pokémon). The next week the show presents Dickens in a metajoke about the impossibility of contemporary literary adaptation. All of this discursive play, finally, contributes to the overarching diegetic reality that is the mythical (and yet strangely real) world of four young boys in Colorado. It is just such textual "promiscuity" that has made variations of the "heteroglossic" so central to theoretical conceptions of television, ranging from John Fiske and John Hartley's model of "bardic television" (1978) to Horace Newcomb and Paul Hirsch's analysis of television as a multi-voiced "cultural forum" (1983). In his later work, Fiske argued that the incredible popularity of certain programs could only be explained through semiotic instability and polysemy; that is, successful popular narrative must accommodate the interests and pleasures of a socially diverse audience who may actualize the text according to very different agendas. While one hesitates to make sweeping transnational and transhistorical comparisons, it is probably reasonable to assume that a similar process took place in a time when, as Jennifer Hayward assures us, Dickens's novels "became phenomena on the level of the O. J. Simpson trial or the first heady season of *Twin Peaks*" (1997: 21).

For all of Selznick's efforts at a "definitive" production, then, it may well be that classical Hollywood narrative was but a detour in the textual modes established in the serialized nineteenth-century novel and resumed by television, albeit in a wholly different historical moment of production and reception (see also Hughes and Lund 1991). In opposition to the rather Dickensian penchant for plot digressions and proliferation of details, classical Hollywood sought to constrain narrative diffusion (perceived as "incoherence" or "loose ends") as much as possible. The typical Dickens novel, receding through innumerable London alleyways, hinted at the thousands of stories that intersected with the five or six Dickens chose to isolate in any given novel. But the goal of the Hollywood producer in the studio system was to put up as many roadblocks as possible, to "correct" all those distractions that might detract from a well-made three-act play. How else can we explain the 1939 adaptation of *Wuthering Heights* ending with the death of Catherine Linton? While most literature on Dickens's legacy in the twentieth century has focused on his role in influencing Hollywood's focus on "bourgeois realism," it is in fact Dickens's (and the nineteenth-century novel's) emphasis on serial narrative and episodic emplotment that has proven a more lasting influence on the more lasting narrative technology of our past century – television. Hollywood certainly adapted certain aspects of nineteenth-century realism, but in its artistic and economic imperative to emphasize textual autonomy, unity, and comprehensibility (all organized around clear character causality), Hollywood sacrificed the narrative pleasures of serialized delay, diegetic expansion, and heteroglossic play (at least in its feature-film output). (For a more detailed analysis of this argument, see David Bordwell's "classic" discussion of "classical narration," *The Classical Hollywood Cinema* [1985], and his even more detailed study in *Narration in the Fiction Film* [1985].)

Television's "rediscovery" of these narrative strategies has led to reconceptualization of narration, diegetic space, and in the case of *Southpark*'s "Pip," the status of adaptation itself. For example, if Selznick's primary headache was to trim *David Copperfield* into a two- to three-hour film, one that did justice to the novel while also capturing the pace of a well-crafted Hollywood film, the producers of *Southpark*, like most creative teams in television, face the exact opposite problem. A twenty-two-minute version of *Great Expectations* might seem like an even greater challenge in terms of editing, but this misunderstands the nature of series television. Long-running television series instead face the problem of *filling* time (or even killing time) – often hours, days, and even months of diegetic time and space. In this respect, *Southpark*'s "Pip" should not be seen as a forum for presenting Dickens so much as Dickens's *Great Expectations* should be seen as a footnote to *Southpark*.

Series television is structured by what various critics have described (in their own terms) as a tension between repetition and difference. All popular series in any medium, it might be argued, must balance repetition of successful (i.e. commercial) story elements with a search for forms of difference that will provide novel variation and interest. Such balance, crucial in all popular genres, is especially important in television where a series may run for hundreds of episodes and depends on predictable, cyclical consumption. If Dickens wanted his audience to buy *All the Year Round*, television producers want their audience to watch "all the year round." Achieving both goals requires striking the proper balance between tried and true foundational formulas and moments of alternately inspired, gratuitous, and at times failed improvisation.

By "taking a break from their regular show" (as McDowell puts it) and following Pip back to nineteenth-century England for *Great Expectations*, the producers temporarily jettisoned the show's most popular story elements (the four leads and their usually less novelistic adventures). In devoting an entire episode to Pip and *Great Expectations*, the series was actually engaging in a form of "improvisational" self-indulgence rather unique to series television. The sheer textual volume of television production allows producers occasionally to shepherd personal and/or throwaway projects, episodes with only tangential or strained relations to the overall series architecture. Such episodes include "clip-shows" (employed to recycle previous scenes and save money), "message-shows" (influential creative teams using an episode to soapbox on a pet issue), or even "anti-shows." *Southpark*'s producers, for example, once heavily promoted the resolution of a highly anticipated "cliffhanger" only to thwart viewers with an entire episode devoted to wholly unrelated fart jokes – a juvenile retort to the program's critics. In each example, television's episodic seriality and textual density allows for a narrative elasticity unavailable to Hollywood cinema (then or now). The penchant to "digress" was of course not unknown to Dickens himself (or any other writer burdened with the routinized production of narrative), and while it may seem a sacrilege to discuss Dickens as digressive fodder, this was in essence his function in this particular episode. In the end, however, "Pip" proved a rather self-indulgent and failed effort on the part of the series to meet the obligations of its twelve-episode season contract. I label this episode "failed" only in terms of viewer response and ratings. Informal surveys of *Southpark* fan websites reveal "Pip" to be the single most unpopular episode of the series ever to air, a fact confirmed by the parent network's decision not to rerun this apparently *too* digressive episode later in the season.

But what of the program's merits as an adaptation of *Great Expectations*? Strangely, beneath the satire, sarcasm, calculated anachronisms, and random potshots at the Brits, there is in "Pip" a rather sincere attempt to come to terms with the "spirit" of the novel, although certainly not in the accumulation of authenticating "details" present in MGM's version of *Copperfield*. In their adaptation, writers Stone and Parker attempt to make Dickens relevant to *Southpark*'s primary audience – males aged twelve to twenty-four – while simultaneously satirizing that very audience's (perceived) inability to endure any form of narrative complexity (no small challenge). Thus, faced with the challenge of capturing the first uneasy and unequal exchanges between Pip and Estella, the episode resorts to vulgar retorts typical of the series, this time employed in the service of Dickens. As Estella leads Pip to meet Miss Havisham, she directs him though the house with such condescending insults as "This way, you pathetic squirt of vaginal discharge" and "Up here, you beef-witted, shriveled-up monkey's penis." The exchanges serve the scatological vulgarity so loved and expected by the series's main audience while also providing the necessary extremities of narrative economy demanded in a twenty-two-minute adaptation. Even the most untutored student of Dickens will realize after this "Cliff's Notes" dialogue that Pip and Estella have quite different social status in their first meeting. Later, when Estella breaks Pip's heart, she does so in terms any modern teenager might understand. Pip hopes to reunite with Estella at a magnificent formal dance, replete with Victorian finery and music, only to find that she has dumped him for a guy named "Steve." Why? "He's seventeen and has a car," she says impatiently, as if stating the obvious.

In the end, the "Pip" episode finally becomes a larger joke about literary adaptation and the very "non-literate" audience *Southpark* seeks to court, much in the way Beavis and Butthead used to insult the MTV audience that sat watching them from the couch on the other side of the screen. Midway through the episode's broad and yet relatively faithful adaptation of the novel, the viewer discovers that Miss Havisham exacts her vengeance, not only through manipulation of young Pip, but through a mad plan to harvest the tears of broken-hearted men to power her "Genesis Device." "You see, my foolish child," she tells Pip, "I am growing very old. But tonight, I will fuse my soul into Estella's once and for all. And then I can go on breaking men's hearts for another entire generation."

When "Steve with the car" tries to defend his girlfriend, Havisham opens a compartment full of high-tech controls on her rocking chair and has him captured. "And as for you, Pip, my robot monkeys should take care of you!!" Havisham flips a switch and a dozen robotic monkeys fall from the ceiling.

Miss Havisham's "revenge" may seem like the final nightmare for Allan Bloom, Neil Postman, William Bennett, and the innumerable other critics who have made a name for themselves bemoaning the loss of cultural literacy in the TV age. And yet, this profoundly heteroglossic moment where Dickens meets Jerry Bruckheimer is, like much television, as clever a joke as one cares to make it. I would hazard to guess that even the most dimwitted teens realize that there are probably no robotic monkeys to be had in Dickens. More likely, they recognize that this final sequence is actually a joke about contemporary Hollywood's inability to produce entertainment that does not depend on idiotic spectacle. According to such logic, then, Miss Havisham must become the "heavy," a super-villain equipped not only with the desire to inflict emotional damage, but also with sinister technology and a mad scheme to live for ever. As the robotic monkeys imply, she is an updated version of the "Wicked Witch of the West," who exists, not as the tragic and nuanced character created by Dickens, but as the one-dimensional emblem of absolute evil so favored in Hollywood's sophomoric action spectacles. After a commercial, Malcolm McDowell as "British person" returns in his over-stuffed library. "Ms. Havisham's robot monkeys prove a formidable foe," he observes, "but Pip is not about to let Estella's soul be forever consumed by the Genesis Device...And now, the thrilling conclusion of *Great Expectations*!" Pip, Joe, and Magwitch break into Havisham's lab where she is about to engage the Genesis Device. "Not so fast you ugly, ancient BITCH!!" yells Pip, playing the role of Bruce Willis. Together they kill Havisham and save Estella, but not before Joe dies in a shower of corrosive acid spat from Havisham's reptilian mouth. The joke (if it actually needs explaining) is in the irreversible confusion and collapse of all cultural hierarchies in post-studio, post-network (and yes) postmodern entertainment, a finale that even as it takes great liberties with Dickens's plot, echoes the Dickensian aesthetic in its satiric collision of the multivalent and polysemic languages of high and low. Idiots may thumb through Dickens looking for the robotic monkeys; average viewers, even if they have not read a word of Dickens, can appreciate the humor about the "Hollywood process," while Dickensians themselves, depending on their temperament within postmodernity itself, can ponder what has been gained, lost, and retained over the past 150 years.

REFERENCES

I would like to thank Emily Morrison for her assistance researching this article.

Books and Journals

Abbott, Mary Allen. 1935. *A Study Guide to the Critical Appreciation of the Photoplay Version of Charles Dickens' Novel David Copperfield*. Chicago: National Council of Teachers of English.

Bakhtin, M. M. *The Dialogic Imagination*. Ed. Michael Holquist. Trans. Caryl Emerson and Michael Holquist. Austin: University of Texas Press, 1981.

Balio, Tino. 1993. *Grand Design: Hollywood as a Modern Business Enterprise, 1930–1939*. Berkeley: University of California Press.

Bordwell, David, Janet Staiger, and Kristin Thompson. 1985. *The Classical Hollywood Cinema: Film Style and Mode of Production to 1960*. New York: Columbia University Press.

Bordwell, David. 1985. *Narration in the Fiction Film*. Madison: University of Wisconsin Press.

DeBona, Guerric O. S. B. 1935. "Dickens, the Depression, and MGM's *David Copperfield*." In *Film Adaptation*, ed. James Naremore. New Brunswick: Rutgers University Press, 2000. 106–28.

Fiske, John and John Hartley. 1978. *Reading Television*. New York: Methuen.

Hayward, Jennifer Poole. 1997. *Consuming Pleasures: Active Audiences and Serial Fictions from Dickens to Soap Opera*. Lexington: University of Kentucky Press.

Hughes, Linda and Michael Lund. 1991. *The Victorian Serial*. Charlottesville: University of Virginia Press.

Luckett, Moya. 1997. "Girl Watchers: Patty Duke and Teen TV." In *The Revolution Wasn't Televised: Sixties Television and Social Conflict*. Ed. Lynn Spigel and Michael Curtin. New York: Routledge. 95–116.

Newcomb, Horace and Paul Hirsch. 1983. "Television as a Cultural Forum." *Quarterly Review of Film Studies*. 8. 45–55.

Ortman, Marguerite G. 1935. *Fiction and the Screen*. Boston: Marshall Jones Co.

Schatz, Thomas. 1988. *The Genius of the System: Hollywood Filmmaking in the Studio Era*. New York: Pantheon.

Sconce, Jeffrey. "What IF? Conjectural Narrative and Recent American Television." In *The Persistence of Television*. Ed. Lynn Spigel and Jan Olsson. Durham, NC: Duke UP, forthcoming.

Newspapers

"A Town Called Hollywood." 4 February 1934. *Los Angeles Times*.

"Hollywood Takes Up Dickens." 12 May 1934. *Observer*.

"Film of 'David Copperfield.'" 12 May 1934. *Daily Telegraph*.

"Mr. Micawber on the Screen." 12 May 1934. *News Chronicle*.

"MGM to Produce in England." 12 May 1934. *Today's Cinema*.

"*David Copperfield* Contest." 14 May 1934. *News Chronicle*.

"Ideal Cast for *David Copperfield*." 17 May 1934. *News Chronicle*.

"Dickens and the Screen." 24 May 1934. *Los Angeles Times*.

"The Dickens Boom." 1 June 1934. *Film Weekly*.

"Bringing *David Copperfield* to the Screen." 8 June 1934. *Film Weekly*.

16   Tiny Tim on screen: a disability studies perspective

Martin F. Norden

A rail-thin boy with a sugarbowl haircut sweetly sings "Hark! The Herald Angels Sing" as his adoring family listens. Another lad declines an impromptu sliding contest on an icy London street, cheerfully noting that "I'm not very good at running." A boy suffering from a generic malady assures his father during a transatlantic telephone call that "I'll be okay; I'm just tired." Another father asks his son to name his favorite toy in a storefront window display, and the boy good-naturedly responds, "You said I can't have none of 'em, so I might as well like 'em all." A mute boy, the only African-American in the group, allows his siblings to decorate him as a Christmas tree. A cartoon mouse and a puppet frog hobble about on crutches.

As the astute reader has already discerned, I have based the above pastiche of word-images on moments from several screen adaptations of Charles Dickens's *A Christmas Carol*: in order, *Scrooge* (1935), *A Christmas Carol* (1938), *A Diva's Christmas Carol* (2000), *Scrooge* (1970), *Scrooged* (1988), *Mickey's Christmas Carol* (1983), and *The Muppet Christmas Carol* (1992). It centers, furthermore, on one of the most famous disabled fictional characters of all time: that crutch-bearing Cratchit urchin, Tiny Tim. One of many Dickensian characters with impairments or chronic illnesses (others include the villainous amputee Silas Wegg, the "invalid" Jenny Wren of *Our Mutual Friend*, and Bertha Plummer, a.k.a. the "Blind Girl," of *The Cricket on the Hearth*), Tim towers above them all in terms of fame if not notoriety. The reasons for Tim's durability are among the main concerns of this essay. As we plunge more deeply into post-literate times, it seems fair to state that his renown is based not so much on the Dickens book per se but on its myriad spin-off texts. This body of work, which Paul Davis has usefully labeled the *Carol*'s "culture-text" (Davis 1990: 4), is a formidable assemblage of popular-culture artifacts that includes numerous film/TV adaptations. According to a late-2000 estimate, more than twenty films and a hundred and forty television productions have been based on Dickens's tale. There is then a certain ring of truth to Fred Guida's assertion that "most of us know Ebenezer Scrooge and

Tiny Tim and Jacob Marley not from the printed page but from TV and film" (2000: 31).

If it is true that we "know" Tim primarily from the large and small screens, what exactly have we been presented with? In other words, what kinds of representations have filmmakers and TV producers devised for us, and why? These media practitioners, to say nothing of their audiences, have inflated the character's prominence well beyond Dickens's literary representation of him. It may be hard to remember, but Tim is a relatively minor character in the book. And it is worth asking how and why.

As a step toward answering these questions, I propose to examine the general film/TV construction of Tim from a disability studies perspective. A relative newcomer to the humanities/social sciences scene, disability studies is related to such emergent fields as feminist studies and queer studies, particularly in its focus on the body as the site of often conflicting discourses. Among its concerns is a desire to interrogate representations of disability to uncover the underlying attitudes, assumptions, and agendas that informed them. It draws an important distinction between the terms impairment and disability. As Rosemarie Garland-Thomson, a leading disability scholar, has noted:

"Impairment" . . . is a term that disability scholars and activists use to denote functional limitation. "Disability," on the other hand, is a term we use to describe the system of representation that produces discriminatory attitudes and barriers to full integration. In essence, "impairment" and "illness" are about bodily differences, whereas "disability" is about the social and political context in which our bodies operate. The distinction is much the same as the one that scholars often draw between "sex" and "gender." (Garland-Thomson 2001: B11)

The vast majority of disability scholars repudiate the two paradigms that have long structured the thinking on disability: the centuries-old moral model, which framed disability as punishment from God or symbolic of evil; and the medical model, which since the latter part of the nineteenth century has contextualized disability in terms of individualized "problems" to be overcome while privileging medical and rehabilitational authorities. Disability scholars have instead embraced the social model, which takes the view that "Otherness," such as a person's disabled status, is a social and cultural construction. As Kaoru Yamamoto, one of the earliest of such thinkers, observed in 1971 (and, ironically, in an old-paradigm rehabilitation journal): "Society determines whether some individuals should be regarded as different by selecting certain facets of their being and then attaching to these facets degrading labels and interpretations" (1971: 182). These scholars regard people with disabilities (now usually referred to as PWDs: Persons With Disabilities) not as a group of hard-luck individuals forever bitter about their misfortune – incidentally, one of the most deeply ingrained stereotypes of Persons With Disabilities – but as a political minority subject to the bigotry, paternalism, and indifference similarly experienced by other minorities and women.

As I have argued elsewhere, a mainstream society will maintain its authority by using various avenues of discourse such as films and television programming to define the issues, and those issues include the need to "Otherize" Persons With Disabilities as either demons or pitiable objects to assuage its fears and guilt and ensure its cohesion (Norden 1994: 1–6). Using the core group of moving-image texts represented in this essay's opening "pastiche," I hope to show that the film/TV practitioners who have labored in the *Carol* precincts have transformed Tim into an objectification of pity that goes well beyond the figure that Dickens had originally designed.

Dickens's Tim

In Dickens's 1843 text Tim is mostly a background figure. He occupies only the corners of *A Christmas Carol*. Dickens does not present him until about halfway into the book (in the third chapter or "stave" of the five-chapter text, to be precise), and then only as a part of a dream/fantasy concocted for Scrooge by the Ghost of Christmas Present. His other appearances are minimal. His family laments his recent passing in the possible future described in the fourth chapter. And he is noted briefly three times in the final stave.

The text reveals scant information about Tim's physicality other than his relatively small size, reinforced through scattered descriptors such as his "withered little hand" (124), "plaintive little voice" (126), and his father Bob's repeated characterization of him as a "little, little child" (156, 158). Indeed, his size has defined his very identity, with the term "Tiny" having long since migrated from simple adjective to form half of one of the world's most famous nominal alliterations. No one knows Timothy Cratchit, but everyone knows Tiny Tim. We also learn that an "iron frame" supports Tim's limbs (121), but Dickens seems rather unconcerned about the details of the boy's likely impairment: a failing kidney, or what Donald Lewis, a pediatric neurologist, diagnosed in 1992 as distal renal tubular acidosis ("What Ailed" 1992: 19). Dickens prefers instead to create the impression that Tim is not simply a child, but a child in fragile, miniature form: a child's child, in effect.

Partially as a result of the vagueness surrounding Tim's corporeality, his crutch looms large in the narrative. For example, the narrator refers to the sound of the boy's "active little crutch" (121), and the Ghost of Christmas Present warns Scrooge about "a crutch without an owner, carefully preserved" if nothing happens to change the course of the Cratchits' lives (124). The crutch becomes emblematic not only of Tim's unnamed impairment but of the boy himself: a *pars pro toto* on several levels.

Tim the person, as opposed to Tim the symptomatic and appliance-wielding body, is only slightly more detailed. The text presents the child (filtered through Scrooge's dream/fantasy, of course) as exceptionally well behaved. Bob reports to his wife that Tim was "as good as gold...and better" in church (121), and Dickens suggests that Tim's rapping "on the table with the handle of his knife" while awaiting the Christmas goose was unusual (122). Tim's manners do have their limits, however; he refuses to join in Bob's Christmas toast to Scrooge until the very end. "Tiny Tim drank it last of all, but he didn't care twopence for it" (125).

Though Tim is hardly magnanimous when it comes to his father's employer, Dickens nevertheless designed him as a deeply spiritual and caring child. As the boy has told his mystified father, he hopes that the people who saw him in church were reminded of Jesus Christ (121). In addition, he is the character who utters the *Carol*'s most famous line, "God bless us every one" (124, 172). And the narrator, speaking on behalf of Scrooge, proclaims to the spirit of Tiny Tim that "thy childish essence was from God!" (158). Little else is known of Tim, however, and even his spirituality and selflessness are open to debate; indeed, one disability activist has implied that such qualities mask a "crafty little con artist" and "stone-cold manipulator" (Lathrop 1997–8: 32).

Perhaps because of Tim's sketchiness, the earliest *Carol* readers had notably different interpretations of the character. As Paul Davis has observed, the immediate (i.e., mid-1840s) response to the book was to underscore the authenticity of its representation of the working poor, particularly those families with disabled children (1990: 78). By the 1870s, however, readers had moved beyond the book's reportage to interpret the Cratchits as the "Holy Family" with Tim as the Christ Child and Scrooge as a Wise Man en route to an epiphany. At the turn of the century, a modernist view of the boy began emerging. In a move away from the Victorian emphasis on Tim's relationship to the patriarchal figures of Bob, Scrooge, and God, readers now regarded Tim not so much as the Christ Child but as a representation of "the golden world of childhood," in Davis's words (101). It was a return to the 1840s social-realist view with its focus on Tim's mortality, but with a twist: Tim was now a sentimentally viewed Golden (or Beautiful) Child who did eventually die. As George Gissing wrote in 1898, "Tiny Tim serves his admirable purpose in a book which no one can bear to criticize; we know that he did die, but in his little lifetime he has softened many a heart" (quoted in Davis 1990: 102).

Film's Tim

We will never know the precise extent to which these early readerly "takes" on Tim have influenced filmmakers and TV producers, but, as I hope will be clear, major elements of them have found their way into the numerous moving-image productions of the *Carol* beginning in 1901 with W. R. Booth's fragmentary British film. (For a list of *Carol* adaptations during the early twentieth century, see Norden 1994: 33–4.) It is possible to discern a number of general characteristics of Tim's representation, all of which use Dickens's literary construction as their point of departure:

1. *Tim as an embodiment of absolute goodness and worthiness.* Though Tim is a religious child, his spirituality, beyond the actions and utterances noted above, is not particularly developed in the Dickens text. The *Carol* filmmakers and TV producers, on the other hand, have accentuated it at virtually every turn. He is almost invariably visualized as cute and angelic: pure of spirit, the beloved "runt of the litter," often possessing a singing voice worthy of the Vienna Boys' Choir, perfect in every way except for his impairment. (Intriguingly, the makers of the 1935 British film *Scrooge* attributed the famous "God bless us every one" line to its titular character, presumably to underscore his recent conversion.) Unlike the Tim of the Dickens text who is quite reluctant to join in the toast to Scrooge, the moving-image Tims harbor no resentment toward anyone. Indeed, the Tim of *Mickey's Christmas Carol* looks at the hopelessly meager Christmas dinner offerings and says without a shred of sarcasm or irony, "Oh, my. Look at all the wonderful things to eat! We must thank Mr. Scrooge." Instead of singing a sad song about a boy lost in the snow (as Tim does in the book), he sings such uplifting hymns as – in the 1935 *Scrooge* – "Hark! The Herald Angels Sing" and – in the 1938 *A Christmas Carol* – "Oh Come, All Ye Faithful." Looking as if he just stepped out of a shampoo commercial, the boy sings about "a beautiful day that I dream about, in a world I would love to see" in the musical *Scrooge* (1970), and, in *The Muppet Christmas Carol* (1992), the frog-puppet version of Tim cheerily warbles a tune inspired by the "God bless us every one" line.

2. *Objectification issues.* As is the case with the vast majority of disabled characters represented on the large and small screens, Tim is revealed to the audience from someone else's perspective. In other words, we are seldom allowed inside Tim's mind or experience anything from his point of view; instead, he is essentially an object to be looked at, discussed, and analyzed by others. The film/TV makers have again followed Dickens's lead, in that much of what we know about Tim in the book is conveyed by other characters or the narrator (e.g., the descriptions of the boy's behavior in church noted above, Bob's observation of "how patient and

how mild" he was [158]). Tim is also the primary object of Scrooge's look, a point that Dickens emphasized: "Scrooge had his eye upon [the Cratchits], and especially on Tiny Tim, until the last" (126).

The film/TV practitioners have taken this view of Tim and expanded it to new levels, often employing the standard film technique of objective-subjective crosscutting in the process. In *A Christmas Carol* (1938), for example, director Edwin Marin and screenwriter Hugo Butler invented a scene (suggested in the "pastiche" that begins this essay) in which Scrooge's nephew Fred slides down a long icy patch on a busy London street and then challenges Tim, whom he has just met, to do the same. When Tim says that he is "not very good at running," the film cuts from a close-up of Fred's smiling face to a shot of Tim's braced right foot. Similarly, the 1970 *Scrooge* shows Bob walking briskly toward the camera and then slowing down and smiling as he looks off to the left. This shot is immediately followed by a shot of Tim and his sister by a toy-store window. The children are filmed from the rear, and the movie's cinematographer made sure to accentuate Tim's disabled status by illuminating the boy's braced leg and crutch with an off-camera lighting source positioned low to the ground. The 1988 film *Scrooged* contains several close-ups of its "Scrooge" – a heartless TV network executive named Frank Cross – as he looks at his assistant's son, under lock and key in a padded cell: a mute African-American boy named Calvin Cooley (a rather dubious reference to "Silent Cal" Coolidge), represented in a series of shots that reflect Frank's point of view. During these moments, Fred, Bob, and Frank are acting as surrogates for the audience. We share their perspectives as they look at the Tims, but seldom if ever do we see things from the boys' point of view.

Tim's infamous crutch – a virtual appendage – is a highly conspicuous element of his objectification. Once again the moving-image practitioners have taken up where Dickens left off. The image of a crutch-toting Tim astride his father's shoulders, initially developed for an 1867 edition of the *Carol* (Davis 1990: 83), has passed into iconic status, undoubtedly with the help of the moving-image productions. In adaptations set in more recent times, such as *A Diva's Christmas Carol* (2000), something else – a wheelchair, perhaps – may take the place of the crutch, but the crutch-holding boy atop his father's shoulders remains the dominant image. Even in *Scrooged*, which endows its Tim with an impairment that does not require a mobility appliance, the visual motif appears several times: in a humanitarian society's logo, and in a painting that adorns the wall of a TV studio set.

3. Tim's return to able-bodiedness. Dickens was not only vague about Tim's impairment but also famously ambivalent on the boy's fate. An examination of the text reveals that Dickens never actually described Tim as having undergone a cure. He merely implied it while describing Scrooge's newfound benevolence and paternalism: "to Tiny Tim, who did NOT die, he was a second father" (171–2). The problematic "who did NOT die" does little to clear up Dickens's perspective on Tim's future. As is widely known, he did not include the line in the original manuscript but added it as an afterthought, presumably to reassure his readers (Davis 1990: 133; Hearn in Dickens 1989: 171). He also had second thoughts about the Ghost of Christmas Present's harsh line, "the child will die," and blunted it with the added phrase, "if these shadows remain unaltered by the Future" (124), again to give his readers hope that Tim might live (Hearn in Dickens 1989: 124). It is quite possible that Dickens initially believed Tim would soon die – he had named Tim "little Fred" in the original manuscript, a likely reference to his brother Alfred who had died in childhood – but thought better of it late in the writing process.

The moving-image adaptations often maintain the ambiguity of Tim's disabling circumstances. For example, when the Scrooge of *Mickey's Christmas Carol* asks the Ghost of Christmas Present what is wrong with Tim, the spirit merely replies "Much, I'm afraid" with no further elaboration. In *A Diva's Christmas Carol*, the doctors are unable to diagnose the cause of Tim's lethargy, weakness, and appetite loss. Seldom, however, do these productions reach Dickens's level of ambivalence on Tim's fate; virtually all imply that he will not only survive but also return to the ranks of the able-bodied. In *Scrooge* (1970), for instance, the title character, dressed as Father Christmas, proclaims to Bob in no uncertain terms that "We'll find the right doctors to get Tiny Tim well, and we will get him well." *Scrooged* pushes the idea to its absurd limits when Frank Cross, the Scrooge-like network executive, oversees a live television production of *A Christmas Carol*. He hires Olympics gymnastics star Mary Lou Retton to play Tim to show that the boy not only made a full recovery but also became proficient at executing back flips.

These characterizations are admittedly sweeping and do not reflect the full range of the many *Carol* adaptations, but I do believe they cut to the heart of the moving-image persona of Tiny Tim. What are we to make of them and the motivations behind them? Are they simply extensions or embellishments of Dickens's original conception of the character, or is something else at work?

Dickens and the *Carol* adapters followed considerably different agendas as they constructed their texts. Dickens, it is fair to say, was quite concerned about the fate of destitute children and infused the *Carol* with many of his own youthful experiences to deal with that issue. He had a miserable childhood; as he himself noted, "I do not exaggerate, unconsciously and unintentionally, the scantiness of my resources and the difficulties of my [boyhood] ... I know that I have lounged about the streets, insufficiently and unsatisfactorily fed. I know that, but for the mercy of God, I might have easily been, for any care that was taken of me, a little robber or a little vagabond" (quoted in Forster 1872: 57). His biographer John Forster's description of Dickens as a child could, with slight modification, apply to Tim as well: "He was a very little and a very sickly boy. He was subject to attacks of violent spasm which disabled him for any active exertion" (26). In addition, the Cratchit family and their humble domicile corresponded closely to Dickens's family and child- hood home at 16 Bayham Street, Camden Town. Willoughby Matchett has suggested that a "reason for identifying the Cratchit home with Dick- ens's recollections of his own is this: the Cratchits are really the Dickenses in disguise" (Matchett 1909: 183). Having essentially lived the life of Tim and painfully aware of the high child-mortality rate (two of his siblings had died in childhood), Dickens developed the *Carol* at least partially as a critique of laissez-faire capitalism and its denial of the basic necessities of life for so many people, particularly children.

His concern is most strongly evident in a scene at the end of the *Carol*'s third chapter (a scene seldom if ever represented in the adaptations). Here Scrooge is shocked to discover two feral children, "Ignorance" and "Want," emerging from the robes of the Ghost of Christmas Present (141–2). Tim is less obviously a metaphor than these appalling and frightening youths, if only because of the autobiographical elements that Dickens had vested in him, but nevertheless he still serves as a powerful reminder of – and plea to do something about – the extreme poverty vis- ited on so many families as a result of unrestrained capitalism. The many *Carol* adaptations usually do make some effort to deal with the squalor represented in Dickens's book but in a qualitatively different way. The wretched conditions are tidied up, sanitized, Hollywoodized. Attributable at least in part to the changing socioeconomic contexts within which the adaptations were produced, the sentimental treatment of the Cratchits' living conditions suggests that the moving-image Tims have a different purpose – a purpose perhaps best explained from a disability studies per- spective.

A disability stereotype

The exaggerations that mark the Tims – the absolute purity, the strong spirituality, the objectification and concomitant lack of a point of view, the return to able-bodiedness – reflect a disability stereotype that has haunted movie and television screens for decades: the so-termed "Sweet

Innocent" (Wolfson and Norden 2000: 295). Akin to the "charity cripple" found in nineteenth-century American literature (Kriegel 1982: 18), the Sweet Innocent follows fairly rigid gender- and age-related parameters. He/she is almost invariably represented as a child or young unmarried woman. Filmmakers and TV producers have usually showed the character as "perfect" in every way except for the impairment; respectful, humble, gentle, passive, cheerful, godly, virginal, pure, and pitiable are adjectives that come readily to mind. The Sweet Innocent is typically far more reactive than proactive and brings out the protectiveness of every good-hearted able-bodied person who comes his or her way. An embodiment of the widespread mainstream belief that Persons With Disabilities must depend on able-bodied society for their every need, the figure is almost always rewarded with a one-way ticket back to able-bodiedness in the form of a miracle cure.

On this issue, it is worth emphasizing the point that movies and TV programs featuring Sweet Innocents have typically gone further than their literary antecedents in resolving the characters' pitiable circumstances. We can see this by comparing the *Carol* with *Les Deux Orphelines*, the 1874 melodrama by Adolphe Philippe d'Ennery and Eugene Cormon. It centers on Henriette and Louise, two young women raised as sisters, and their misadventures in and around Paris while seeking a cure for Louise's blindness. Though not nearly as well known today as the *Carol*, *Les Deux Orphelines* was a resounding theatrical success in its day and served as the basis for at least seven silent film adaptations, the most famous of which was D. W. Griffith's epic *Orphans of the Storm* (1921). (For further analysis of these adaptations see Norden 1994: 35–7, 59–65).

Both Dickens's *Carol* and *Les Deux Orphelines* conclude simply by suggesting that their disabled characters are about to embark on a new life protected from financial worries and/or the machinations of evil able-bodied characters – a new life that may not necessarily include a cure. *Les Deux Orphelines*, for instance, ends with a doctor uttering the somewhat tentative curtain line, "I think I can cure her." For film/TV producers, however, the promise of a harmonious life but with no guarantee of a cure has seldom constituted a sufficient reward for these characters. Rejecting what they believe to be a morally questionable implication – that "good" people might live the rest of their lives with a disability – they are consistent with mainstream society's marked tendency to bestow low social-approval ratings on people with permanent impairments. As social scientist Teresa E. Levitin has suggested, "In a society that values physical health and attractiveness, [Persons With Disabilities] are less than fully acceptable" (1975: 549), even ones who have demonstrated their pro-social qualities. By avoiding the long-term implications of permanent disability in favor of facile cures delivered by God or doctors – figures almost always inscribed as male – the movie/TV industry contributes to the paternalism of the dominant society while simultaneously denying the realities of the disabled experience.

These moving-image representations of Tiny Tim have contributed in a major way to able-bodied society's tendency to view "worthy" Persons With Disabilities as children who need protection and nurturing. In the US they have become contextualized as "Jerry's Kids" (to cite the label for the prominent image promoted by the long-running Jerry Lewis fundraising telethons) even though many of them are adults. As William Stothers points out: "Society idealizes this sentimental image of disability as a pitiful child in desperate need of help...As an enduring symbol of modern Christmas time, Tiny Tim resonates with a deeper, darker meaning for people with disabilities. The problem is that not all people with disabilities are children, but we all tend to be treated as if we are Tiny Tims" (Stothers 1993: B9). By encouraging mainstream society to regard them as children who will "outgrow" their impairments, the movie/TV Tims contribute to keeping Persons With Disabilities dependent and thus "in their place."

This Tiny Tim sentimentality stereotypes people with disabilities and contributes to our oppression. When you think about a person with a disability as someone to feel sorry for, as someone to be taken care of and looked after, it is difficult to think about hiring them as a teacher, an architect or an accountant. That's part of the reason why the jobless rate among working age people with disabilities consistently hovers around 70 percent. (Stothers 1993: B9)

Nancy Weinberg and Carol Sebian have underscored "the biblical tradition of giving alms to the disabled but not accepting disabled persons as equals" (Weinberg and Sebian 1980: 281). This centuries-old practice, expressed in countless cultural artifacts such as films and television programs, chimes with Leonard Kriegel's argument that the chief function of characters such as Tim is "to perpetuate in [their] audience the illusion of its own goodness" (1982: 18). It also has the unfortunate effect of creating a further measure of exclusivity for majority members by allowing them to maintain a sense of superiority and control over Persons With Disabilities. Little wonder, then, that many in the disability community find Tim, the most famous of the film/TV world's Sweet Innocents, a thoroughly repellent figure. Douglas Lathrop sums up this view by bluntly noting that "you could stuff a million Christmas turkeys with the scorn disability activists have heaped on this character" (1997–8: 32). A view echoed by Carolyn Tyjewski, when she complains of "how dehumanizing, condescending and belittling it is for society to continual[ly] beg for us to play Tiny Tim for their amusement, to make them feel good" (Tyjewski 2001: 1).

The moving-image exploitation of Tim shows no signs of abating. But now perhaps we are in a better position to understand why film and television producers continue to recycle Dickens's "God bless us" kid.

REFERENCES

The author wishes to thank William Stothers and David Paroissien for their help.

Anon [Donald Lewis]. 1992. "What Ailed Tiny Tim." *Time* 28 Dec.: 19.
Davis, Paul. 1990. *The Lives and Times of Ebenezer Scrooge*. New Haven, CT: Yale University Press.
Dickens, Charles. 1989. *The Annotated Christmas Carol*. [*A Christmas Carol in Prose*. London: Chapman & Hall, 1843.] With an introduction, notes, and bibliography by Michael Patrick Hearn. New York: Avenel.
Forster, John. 1872. *The Life of Charles Dickens. Vol. I: 1812–1842*. Philadelphia: Lippincott.
Garland-Thomson, Rosemarie. 2001 "The FDR Memorial: Who Speaks From the Wheelchair?" *Chronicle of Higher Education* 26 Jan.: B11.
Guida, Fred. 2000. "Scrooge Lives!" *TV Guide*. 25 Nov.: 30–6.
Kriegel, Leonard. 1982. "The Wolf in the Pit in the Zoo." *Social Policy* 13: 16–23.
Lathrop, Douglas. 1997–8. "Empowering Tiny Tim." *Mainstream: Magazine of the Able-Disabled*. Dec.–Jan. 32: 34–5.
Levitin, Teresa E. 1975. "Deviants as Active Participants in the Labeling Process: The Visibly Handicapped." *Social Problems* 22: 548–57.
Matchett, Willoughby. 1909. "Dickens in Bayham Street." *The Dickensian* 5.7: 180–4.
Norden, Martin F. 1994. *The Cinema of Isolation: A History of Physical Disability in the Movies*. New Brunswick: Rutgers University Press.
Stothers, William G. 1993. "Bah, Humbug: I Hate Tiny Tim." *San Diego Union-Tribune* 23 Dec. B9.
Tyjewski, Carolyn. "Re: Seeking Inspirational Poetry." Online posting. 11 Apr. 2001. Disability Studies in the Humanities (DS-HUM@listproc. georgetown. edu).
Weinberg, Nancy, and Carol Sebian. 1980. "The Bible and Disability." *Rehabilitation Counseling Bulletin* 23.4: 273–81.
Wolfson, Kim, and Martin F. Norden. 2000. "Film Images of People with Disabilities." In *Handbook of Communication and People with Disabilities: Research and Application*. Ed. Dawn Braithwaite and Teresa Thompson. Mahwah: Lawrence Erlbaum. 289–305.
Yamamoto, Kaoru. 1971. "To Be Different." *Rehabilitation Counseling Bulletin* 14: 180–9.

Part V

17 Dickens composed: film and television adaptations 1897–2001

Kate Carnell Watt and Kathleen C. Lonsdale

The works of Charles Dickens have been, it goes without saying, much filmed, beginning in 1897 with *The Death of Nancy Sykes* and followed by nearly one hundred short versions before 1920. There were about fifty in the 1980s alone. It is, therefore, impossible to provide, here or, perhaps, anywhere, a genuinely complete Dickens filmography. We can only lay claim to having listed the adaptations our respondents commented on, supplemented by a number of "major" versions they omitted. We have also included, if only as an indication of Dickens's ubiquity, a small fraction of the earliest film versions and a handful of non-English-language versions.

We have arranged the adaptations by novel, in chronological order by the date of initial publication. Especially for early films, gaps often exist, but we have listed as much information as was available. For each novel, the first adaptation for which we have complete information provides the names of the characters after the actors who played them. For subsequent listings, the character names are omitted but the same order is followed, unless otherwise noted. When interesting casting was used for roles not otherwise listed in our credits, we have included those actors and their characters' names as well. In the case of modernizations, the character names have sometimes been so changed as to obscure their correspondence to the original, and in this case we have listed the most important or interesting actors and their character names.

These listings are not intended as value judgments in any way: some entries have been included because respondents discommended them, while others earned high praise and still others received no comments whatsoever. Respondents' comments tended, for each novel, to center around recent and "classic" adaptations, and we have included selections from their responses.

Our questionnaire was distributed to members of the Victoria Listserv run by Patrick Leary at Indiana University and the Dickens Listserv run by Patrick McCarthy at the University of California, Santa Barbara. In verifying the credits and other details for each film we found Michael

Pointer's *Charles Dickens on the Screen* invaluable. The Internet Movie Database, IMDb.com, and Norrie Epstein's *The Friendly Dickens* were useful secondary sources.

The Pickwick Papers

Mr. Pickwick's Christmas at Wardle's (1901). Dir. W. R. Booth? Film, Black and white, Silent, UK.

Mr. Pickwick's Predicament (1912). Dir. J. Searle Dawley. Starring William Wadsworth (Pickwick), Barry O'Moore (Sam Weller), and Charles Ogle (Buzfuz). Film, Black and white, Silent, USA.

The Pickwick Papers (1913). Dir. and adapted by Laurence Trimble. Starring John Bunny (Pickwick), H. P. Owen (Sam Weller), James Pryor (Tupman). Film, Black and white, Silent, USA. (The three reels were individually entitled "The Honorable Event," "The Westgate Seminary," and "The Shooting Party.")

The Pickwick Papers (1952). Dir. and adapted by Noel Langley. Starring James Hayter (Pickwick), Harry Fowler (Sam Weller), and Hermione Gingold (Miss Tompkins). Film, Black and white, UK.

The Pickwick Papers (1985). Dir. Brian Lighthill. Adapted by Jack Davies. Starring Nigel Stock (Pickwick), Phil Daniels (Sam Weller), and Clive Swift (Tupman). TV, UK.

None of our respondents commented on the existing adaptations of *The Pickwick Papers*, but one did lament, "If only [Orson] Welles had made *Pickwick Papers*, one of the list of possibles when he went to Hollywood." For more on that unattained wish see Marguerite Rippy's account in chapter 13.

Non-English-language versions

Les Aventures de Monsieur Pickwick (The Adventures of Mr. Pickwick) (1964). Dir. René Lucot. Adapted by Michel Subiela. Starring André Gilles (Pickwick), Hubert Deschamps (Tupman), and Georges Audonbert (Snodgrass). TV, France.

Il Circolo Pickwick (Pickwick's Circle) (1967). Dir. Ugo Gregoretti. TV, Italy.

Oliver Twist

Death of Nancy Sykes (1897). Starring Mabel Fenton (Nancy) and Charles Ross (Sykes). Film, Black and white, Silent, USA.

Oliver Twist (1909). Dir. J. Stuart Blackton. Adapted by Eugene Mullin. Starring William Humphrey (Fagin) and Elita Proctor Otis (Nancy). Film, Black and white, Silent, USA.

Oliver Twist (1912). Dir. and adapted by Thomas Bentley. Starring John McMahon (Fagin), Ivy Millais (Oliver), and Harry Royston (Sikes). Film, Black and white, Silent, UK. (First British 4-reel feature film.)

Oliver Twist (1933). Dir. William J. Cowan. Adapted by Elizabeth Meehan. Starring Irvine Pichel, Dickie Moore, and William "Stage" Boyd. Film, Black and white, USA.

Oliver Twist (1948). Dir. David Lean. Adapted by Stanley Haynes and David Lean. Starring Alec Guinness, John Howard Davies, and Robert Newton. Film, Black and white, UK. Called "dark, funny, and cruel," the film is notable for Guinness's Fagin and for its "stunning mise-en-scene," its "filmically inventive raid on the text," and its "evocation of Fagin's lair" in "a fascinating equivalent of Dickens's heightened non-realism."

Oliver Twist (1959). Dir. Daniel Petrie. Adapted by Michael Dyne. Starring Eric Portman, Frederick Clark, and Tom Clancy. Also starring Robert Morley (Mr. Bumble) and Michael Hordern (Mr. Brownlow). TV, Black and white, USA.

Oliver! (1968). Dir. Carol Reed. Lyrics and music by Lionel Bart. Screenplay by Vernon Harris. Musical director John Green. Starring Ron Moody, Mark Lester, and Oliver Reed. Film, Musical, UK. Carol Reed's 1968 musical version has been praised for restoring "a certain playfulness" absent in previous adaptations and for Oliver Reed's intimidating Sikes, but also condemned as "annoying" and even "nightmarish."

Oliver Twist (1982). Dir. Clive Donner. Adapted by James Goldman. Starring George C. Scott, Richard Charles, and Tim Curry. TV, UK.

Oliver Twist (1985). Dir. Gareth Davies. Adapted by Alexander Baron. Starring Eric Porter, Ben Rodska (Oliver), Scott Funnell (young Oliver), and Michael Attwell. Also starring Miriam Margolyes (Mrs. Corney/Bumble). TV, UK.

Oliver & Company (1988). Dir. George Scribner. Adapted by Roger Allers and Jim Cox. Starring Dom DeLuise, Joey Lawrence, and Robert Loggia. Film, Animated, USA.

Oliver Twist (1997). Dir. Tony Bill. Adapted by Monte Merrick. Starring Richard Dreyfuss, Alex Trench, and David O'Hara. TV, USA.

Oliver Twist (1999). Dir. Renny Rye. Adapted by Alan Bleasdale. Starring Robert Lindsay, Sam Smith, and Andy Serkis. TV, UK. Lindsay's Fagin earns high marks, but Bleasdale's provision of a "prequel" – the first episode opens in Rome with Oliver's parents and ends with the "graphic" details of Oliver's birth – generated a range of responses from "witty and daring" and "marvelous" to "patchily brilliant," "overdone," and plain "horrible." Bleasdale's decision to make Fagin a magician "rather than just the usual stage Jew" was singled out for commendation and the production's "heightened comedy" also generally found favor.

Non-English-language versions

Twist Olivèr (1919). Dir. Márton Garas. Adapted by Laszlo Vajda. Starring Jeno Torzs, Tibor Lubinszky (Oliver), and Laszlo Molnar. Film, Black and white, Silent, Hungary.

Nicholas Nickleby

Nicholas Nickleby (1912). Dir. George Nichols. Starring Harry Benham (Nicholas Nickleby), N. S. Wood (Smike), and David Thompson (Schoolmaster Squeers). Film, Black and white, Silent, USA.

Nicholas Nickleby (1947). Dir. Alberto Cavalcanti. Adapted by John Dighton. Starring Derek Bond, Aubrey Woods, and Alfred Drayton. Film, Black and white, UK. Its cinematography, filmed "almost entirely in deep chiaroscuro," found particular favor.

Nicholas Nickleby (1977). Dir. Christopher Barry. Adapted by Hugh Leonard. Starring Nigel Havers, Peter Bourke, and Derek Francis. TV, UK.

The Life and Adventures of Nicholas Nickleby (1982). Dir. John Caird, Jim Goddard, and Trevor Nunn. Adapted by David Edgar. Starring Roger Rees, David Threlfall, and Alun Armstrong. TV, UK. Rees's and Threlfall's performances were extolled, as was the production for being "complete" and "stunning."

Nicholas Nickleby (2000). Dir. Stephen Whittaker. Adapted by Martyn Hesford. Starring James D'Arcy, Lee Ingleby, and Gregor Fisher. TV, UK.

The Old Curiosity Shop

The Old Curiosity Shop (1912). Dir. Frank Powell. Film, Black and white, Silent, UK.

The Old Curiosity Shop (1921). Dir. Thomas Bentley. Adapted by G. A. Atkinson. Starring Mabel Poulton (Nell), Pino Conti (Quilp), and Beatie Olna Travers (Sally Brass). Film, Black and white, Silent, UK.

The Old Curiosity Shop (1934). Dir. Thomas Bentley. Adapted by Margaret Kennedy and Ralph Neale. Starring Elaine Benson, Hay Petrie, and Lily Long. Film, Black and white, UK.

The Old Curiosity Shop (1962). Dir. Joan Craft. Adapted by Constance Cox. Starring Michele Dotrice, Patrick Troughton, and Patricia Jessel. TV, UK.

The Old Curiosity Shop (also released as *Mister Quilp*) (1975). Dir. Michael Tuchner. Adapted by Irene and Louis Kamp. Starring Sarah-Jane Varley, Anthony Newley, and Jill Bennett. Also starring Michael Hordern (Grandfather/Edward Trent) and David Warner (Sampson Brass). Film, Musical, UK. Newley, who wrote the songs, was also praised for his "brilliant" performance.

The Old Curiosity Shop (1979). Dir. Julian Amyes. Adapted by William Trevor. Starring Natalie Ogle, Trevor Peacock, and Freda Dowie. TV, UK.

The Old Curiosity Shop (1994). Dir. Kevin Connor. Adapted by John Goldsmith. Starring Sally Walsh, Tom Courtenay, and Anne White. Also starring Peter Ustinov (Grandfather). TV, USA. Complimented for its performances, particularly Courtenay's, and for its effective use of minimal sets.

Barnaby Rudge

Barnaby Rudge (1911). Dir. Charles Kent. Film, Black and white, Silent, USA.

Dolly Varden (1913). Dir. and adapted by Charles Brabin. Starring Mabel Trunnelle (Dolly), Willis Secord (Joe Willets), and Barry O'Moore (Simon). Film, Black and white, Silent, USA.

Barnaby Rudge (1915). Dir. Thomas Bentley and Cecil M. Hepworth. Adapted by Thomas Bentley. Starring Tom Powers (Barnaby Rudge), Stewart Rome (Maypole Hugh), and Chrissie White (Dolly Varden). Film, Black and white, Silent, UK.

Barnaby Rudge (1960). Directed by Morris Barry. Adapted by Michael Voysey. Starring John Wood, Neil McCarthy, and Jennifer Daniel. TV, UK.

None of our respondents mentioned having seen any of the adaptations listed above. However, a number of people indicated a desire to see *Rudge* done justice in a new production.

Martin Chuzzlewit

Martin Chuzzlewit (1912). Dir. Oscar Apfel. Starring Alan Hale (Martin Chuzzlewit) and Harold Shaw (Tom Pinch). Film, Black and white, Silent, USA.

Martin Chuzzlewit (1994). Dir. Pedr James. Adapted by David Lodge. Starring Ben Walden (young Martin Chuzzlewit), Paul Scofield (old Martin Chuzzlewit), Keith Allen (Jonas Chuzzlewit), Tom Wilkinson (Seth Pecksniff). Also starring John Mills (Mr. Chuffey). TV, UK.

Allen and Wilkinson were lauded, though the production's omission of some of the American scenes left some respondents complaining of a lack of any "sense of moral development."

Greedy (1994). Dir. Jonathan Lynn. Adapted by Lowell Ganz and Babaloo Mandel. Starring Michael J. Fox (Daniel McTeague), Kirk Douglas (Uncle Joe McTeague), and Olivia d'Abo (Molly Richardson). Film, USA.

A Christmas Carol

The Virtue of Rags (1912). Dir. and adapted by Theodore Wharton. Starring Francis X. Bushman, Helen Dunbar, and Bryant Washburn. Film, Black and white, Silent, USA.

The Right to Be Happy (1916). Dir. Rupert Julian. Adapted by Elliott J. Clawson. Starring Rupert Julian (Scrooge), John Cook (Bob Cratchit), and Harry Carter (Jacob Marley). Film, Black and white, Silent, USA.

A Christmas Carol (1938). Dir. Edwin L. Marin. Adapted by Hugo Butler. Starring Reginald Owen, Gene Lockhart, and Leo G. Carroll. Film, Black and white, USA.

A Christmas Carol (also released as *Scrooge*) (1951). Dir. Brian Desmond Hurst. Adapted by Noel Langley. Starring Alastair Sim, Mervyn Johns, and Michael Hordern. Film, Black and white, UK. Sim's performance as Scrooge remains the standard by which all others are judged.

Mr. Magoo's Christmas Carol (1962). Dir. Abe Levitow. Adapted by Barbara Chain. Starring Jim Backus (Mr. Magoo as Scrooge), Jack Cassidy, and Royal Dano. TV, Animated, USA.

Scrooge (1970). Dir. Ronald Neame. Adapted by Leslie Bricusse and Michael Medwin. Music and lyrics by Leslie Bricusse. Starring Albert Finney, David Collings, and Alec Guinness. Film, Musical, UK. Notable for Finney's "euphoric" turn as Scrooge and Guinness's "spooky" Marley.

A Christmas Carol (1972). Dir. Richard Williams. Starring Alistair Sim, Melvyn Hayes, and Michael Hordern. Also starring Michael Redgrave (Narrator). Film, Animated, USA.

An American Christmas Carol (1979). Dir. Eric Till. Starring Henry Winkler (Benedict Slade). TV, USA.

Mickey's Christmas Carol (1983). Dir. and adapted by Burny Mattinson. Starring Alan Young (Scrooge McDuck as Scrooge), Wayne Allwine (Mickey Mouse as Cratchit), and Hal Smith (Goofy as Marley's Ghost). Film, Animated, USA.

A Christmas Carol (1984). Dir. Clive Donner. Adapted by Roger O. Hirson. Starring George C. Scott, David Warner, and Frank Finlay. TV, UK. High marks for Scott's Scrooge.

Blackadder's Christmas Carol (TV) (1988). Dir. Richard Boden. Adapted by Richard Curtis and Ben Elton. Starring Rowan Atkinson (Ebenezer Blackadder), Pauline Melville (Mrs. Scratchit), and Robbie Coltrane (Spirit of Christmas). Also starring Miranda Richardson (Queen Elizabeth) and Miriam Margolyes (Queen Victoria). TV, UK. "Devilishly clever," it reverses Scrooge's progress: here he begins as a philanthropist and becomes selfish after the ghost's visit.

Scrooged (1988). Dir. Richard Donner. Written by Mitch Glazer and Michael O'Donoghue. Starring Bill Murray (Frank Cross), David Johansen (Ghost of Christmas Past), and Carol Kane (Ghost of Christmas Present). Also starring Mary Lou Retton (Tiny Tim). Film, USA. Postmodern in the sense that Murray is a network executive producing *A Christmas Carol* when his late boss's ghost and the spirits arrive. See Chapter 6.

The Muppet Christmas Carol (1992). Dir. Brian Henson. Adapted by Jerry Juhl. Starring Michael Caine, Steve Whitmire (Kermit the Frog as Bob Cratchit), Jerry Nelson (Statler as Jacob Marley). Film, USA. Caine is "menacing and touching by turns" and "the fact that the songs are sung by rats and vegetables is an added bonus."

A Christmas Carol (1997). Dir. Stan Phillips. Adapted by Jymn Magon. Starring Tim Curry, Michael York, and Ed Asner. Also starring Whoopi Goldberg (Ghost of Christmas Present). Film, Animated, USA.

A Christmas Carol (1999). Dir. David Hugh Jones. Adapted by Peter Barnes. Starring Patrick Stewart, Richard E. Grant, and Bernard Lloyd. TV, USA. Stewart's performance was commended for its faithfulness to the text, particularly in the "clever banter" with Marley.

A Diva's Christmas Carol (2000). Dir. Richard Schenkman. Adapted by Richard Schenkman. Starring Vanessa L. Williams (Ebony Scrooge), Bob McNamara (Bob Cratchit), Rozonda "Chilli" Thomas (Marli Jacob). TV, USA.

A Christmas Carol: The Movie (2001). Dir. Jimmy T. Murakami. Adapted by Piet Kroon and Robert Llewellyn. Starring Nicolas Cage (voice of Marley) and Kate Winslet (voice of Belle). Film, partially animated, UK.

Non-English-language versions

Leyenda de Navidad (Legend of Christmas) (1947). Dir. and adapted by Manuel Tamayo. Starring Jesùs Tordesillas, Emilio Santiago, and Ramon Martori. Film, Black and white, Spain.

Non è Mai Troppo Tardi (It's Never Too Late) (1953). Dir. Filippo Walter Ratti. Adapted by Filippo Walter Ratti and Piero Regnoli. Starring Guglielmo Barnabò, Luigi Batzella, and Marcello Mastroianni. Film, Black and white, Italy.

The Chimes

The Chimes (1914). Dir. Herbert Blaché. Starring Tom Terriss (Trotty Veck), Faye Cusick (Meg), Alfred Hemming (Alderman Cute). Film, Black and white, Silent, USA.

The Chimes (1914). Dir. and adapted by Thomas Bentley. Starring Warwick Buckland, Violet Hopson, and Johnny Butt. Film, Black and white, Silent, UK.

The Cricket on the Hearth

The Cricket on the Hearth (1909). Dir. D. W. Griffith. Adapted by Frank E. Woods. Starring Owen Moore, David Miles, and Mack Sennett. Film, Black and white, Silent, USA.

The Cricket on the Hearth (1914). Dir. L. Marston. Starring Alan Hale, Jack Drumier, and William Russell. Film, Black and white, Silent, USA.

The Cricket on the Hearth (1923). Dir. Lorimer Johnston. Adapted by Caroline Frances Cooke. Starring Josef Swickard, Paul Moore, and Lorimer Johnston. Film, Black and white, Silent, USA.

Non-English-language versions

Sverchok na Pechi (1915). Dir. Boris Sushkevich and Aleksandr Uralsky. Adapted by Boris Sushkevich. Starring Mikhail Chekhov, Maria Ouspenskaya, and Grigori Khmara. Film, Black and white, Silent, Russia.

Le Grillon du Foyer (1922). Dir. and adapted by Jean Manoussi. Starring Sabine Landray (Dot Peerybingle), Suzanne Dantes (May Fielding), and Charles Boyer (Edouard). Film, Black and white, Silent, France.

Dombey and Son

Dombey and Son (1917). Dir. Maurice Elvey. Adapted by Eliot Stannard. Starring Norman McKinnel (Paul Dombey), Lillian Braithwaite (Edith Dombey), Odette Grimbault (Florence Dombey). Film, Black and white, Silent, UK.

Rich Man's Folly (1931). Dir. John Cromwell. Adapted by Grover Jones and Edward E. Paramore Jr. Starring George Bancroft (Brock

Trumbull), Frances Dee (Anne Trumbull), and David Durand (Brock Junior). Film, Black and white, USA.

Dombey and Son (1983). Dir. Rodney Bennett. Adapted by James Andrew Hall. Starring Barnaby Buik (Paul Dombey), Julian Glover (Mr. Dombey), and Lysette Anthony (Florence Dombey). TV, UK.

Although none of our respondents mentioned having seen any of the adaptations listed above, several did express an interest in seeing *Dombey* filmed in future.

David Copperfield

The Early Life of David Copperfield (1911). Dir. George O. Nichols. Starring Flora Foster (David Copperfield), Anna Seer (David's mother), and Viola Alberti (Aunt Betsey). Film, Black and white, Silent, USA.

Little Em'ly and David Copperfield (1911). Dir. George O. Nichols. Starring Ed Genung (David Copperfield), Florence LaBadie (Little Em'ly), and William Russell (Ham). Film, Black and white, Silent, USA.

The Loves of David Copperfield (1911). Dir. George O. Nichols. Starring Ed Genung (David Copperfield) and Mignon Anderson (Dora). Film, Black and white, Silent, USA.

David Copperfield (1913). Dir. Cecil Hepworth and Thomas Bentley. Adapted by Thomas Bentley. Starring Kenneth Ware (David Copperfield), Eric Desmond (young David Copperfield), and Alma Taylor (Dora Spenlow). Film, Black and white, Silent, UK.

David Copperfield (1935). Dir. George Cukor. Adapted by Hugh Walpole, Howard Estabrook, and Lenore J. Coffee (uncredited). Starring Frank Lawton (David Copperfield), W. C. Fields (Mr. Micawber), and Edna May Oliver (Aunt Betsey). Also starring Roland Young (Uriah Heep) and Freddie Bartholomew (young David Copperfield). Film, Black and white, USA. Extolled as "high-spirited," "exuberant," and "absurdist," as well as for the performances of Fields and Oliver.

David Copperfield (1969). Dir. Delbert Mann. Adapted by Jack Pulman. Starring Robin Phillips, Ralph Richardson, and Edith Evans. Also starring Laurence Olivier (Mr. Creakle) and Wendy Hiller (Mrs. Micawber). TV, UK. Mann's "deft" direction was particularly noted.

David Copperfield (1974). Dir. Joan Craft. Adapted by Hugh Whitemore. Starring Jonathan Kahn, Arthur Lowe, and Patience Collier. TV, UK.

David Copperfield (1986). Dir. Barry Letts. Adapted by James Andrew Hall. Starring Colin Hurley, Simon Callow, and Brenda Bruce. TV, UK. Respondents hailed this version for Callow's performance and for being "complete."

David Copperfield (1993). Dir. Don Arioli. Starring Julian Lennon, Joseph Marcell, and Andrea Martin. Also starring Michael York

(Mr. Murdstone), Sheena Easton (Agnes), and Howie Mandel (Mealy). TV, Animated, Canada.

David Copperfield (1999). Dir. Simon Curtis. Adapted by Adrian Hodges. Starring Daniel Radcliffe, Maggie Smith, and Bob Hoskins. TV, UK/USA. Maggie Smith's performance was singled out as "brilliant."

David Copperfield (2000). Dir. Peter Medak. Adapted by John Goldsmith. Starring Hugh Dancy, Michael Richards, and Sally Field. TV, USA. This adaptation was condemned as "simplistic" and – for its "horrible" acting, accents, casting, and sets – "appalling." Field and Richards particularly were singled out as "wretched."

Non-English-language versions

David Copperfield (1922). Dir. A. W. Sandberg. Starring Karina Bell, Karen Caspersen, Peter Malberg, Martin Hertzberg, and Poul Reumert. Film, Black and white, Silent, Denmark.

David Copperfield (1965). Dir. Marcelle Cravenne. Adapted by Claude Santelle. Starring Bernard Verley, Michel Galabru (M. Micawber), and Madeleine Clervanne (Tante Betsy). TV, France.

Bleak House

Jo the Crossing Sweeper (1910). Film, Black and white, Silent, UK.

Jo the Crossing Sweeper (1918). Dir. Alexander Butler. Adapted by Irene Miller. Starring Dora de Winton (Lady Dedlock) and Rolf Leslie (Bucket). Film, Black and white, Silent, UK.

Bleak House (1920). Dir. Maurice Elvey. Adapted by William J. Elliott. Starring Bertha Gellardi (Esther Summerson), Constance Collier (Lady Dedlock), and Clifford Heatherley (Bucket). Film, Black and white, Silent, UK.

Bleak House (1922). Dir. H. B. Parkinson. Adapted by Frank Miller. Starring Betty Doyle, Sybil Thorndike, and Harry J. Worth. Film, Black and white, Silent, UK.

Bleak House (1959). Adapted by Constance Cox. Starring Diana Fairfax, Iris Russell, and Richard Pearson. TV, UK.

Bleak House (1985) Dir. Ross Devenish. Adapted by Arthur Hopcraft. Starring Suzanne Burden, Diana Rigg, and Ian Hogg. Also starring Peter Vaughan (Tulkinghorn) and Denholm Elliott (John Jarndyce). TV, UK. Called "a great success," this adaptation was lauded for its "genuine cinematic feel" and for "superb" performances by Rigg and Elliott. The omission of the Jellybys, however, was criticized as "annoying."

Hard Times

Hard Times (1915). Dir. Thomas Bentley. Adapted by Thomas Bentley. Starring Bransby Williams (Mr. Gradgrind), Dorothy Bellew (Louisa), and F. Lymons (Josiah Bounderby). Film, Black and white, Silent, UK.

Hard Times (1977). Dir. John Irvin. Adapted by Arthur Hopcraft. Starring Patrick Allen, Jacqueline Tong, and Timothy West. TV, UK.

Hard Times (1994). Dir. Peter Barnes. Adapted by Peter Barnes. Starring Bob Peck, Beatie Edney, and Alan Bates. TV, UK. Notable for Edney's performance and for its depictions of the factory fire and of the "emptiness" of the workers' lives.

Non-English-language versions

Tempos Difíceis (1988). Dir. and adapted by João Botelho. Starring Ruy Furtado (Tomaz Cremalheira), Júlia Britton (voice Rita Blanco) (Luisa Cremalheira), and Henrique Viana (Jose Grandela). Film, Portugal.

Little Dorrit

Little Dorrit (1913). Dir. James Kirkwood. Adapted by Lloyd F. Lonergan. Starring Maude Fealy (Little Dorrit), William Russell (Arthur Clennam), and James Cruze (William Dorrit). Film, Black and white, Silent, USA.

Little Dorrit (1920). Dir. and adapted by Sydney Morgan. Starring Joan Morgan, Langhorn Burton, and Arthur Lennard. Film, Black and white, Silent, UK.

Little Dorrit (1987). Dir. and adapted by Christine Edzard. Starring Sarah Pickering, Derek Jacobi, and Alec Guinness. Also starring Miriam Margolyes (Flora Finching) and Joan Greenwood (Mrs. Clennam). Film, UK. This version earned high marks for the "breathtaking" performances of Jacobi, Guinness, and the "amazing" Margolyes, but was nonetheless criticized by some for "sentimentality" and for continuity errors.

Non-English-language versions

Klein Doortje (1917). Dir. Friedrich Zelnik. Adapted by Eddy Beuth and Richard Wilde. Starring Lisa Weisse (Little Dorrit). Film, Black and white, Silent, Germany.

Lille Dorrit (1924). Dir. A. W. Sandberg. Adapted by Sam Ask. Starring Karina Bell, Gunnar Tolnaes, and Frederick Jensen. Film, Black and white, Silent, Denmark.

Klein Dorrit (1934). Dir. Karel Lamac. Adapted by Kurt J. Braun. Starring Anny Ondra, Matthias Wieman, and Gustav Waldau. Film, Black and white, Germany.

A Tale of Two Cities

A Tale of Two Cities (1908).

A Tale of Two Cities (1911). Dir. William J. Humphrey and Stuart J. Blackton. Adapted by Eugene Mullin. Starring Maurice Costello (Sydney Carton), Florence Turner (Lucie Manette), and Leo Delaney (Charles Darnay). Film, Black and white, Silent, USA. Starring Florence Turner, the "Vitagraph girl," as Lucie Manette, this three-reel adaptation is "lavish" and a "must-see" silent film with a "large cast" incorporating almost the entire Vitagraph stock company.

A Tale of Two Cities (1917). Dir. and adapted by Frank Lloyd. Starring William Farnum (Sydney Carton/Charles Darnay), Jewel Carmen (Lucie Manette) and Josef Swickard (Dr. Manette). Film, Black and white, Silent, USA. This film version introduced double-exposure shots in order to have one actor play both Carton and Darnay.

A Tale of Two Cities (1922). Dir. and adapted by W. Courtney Rowden. Starring Clive Brook, Ann Trevor, and J. Fisher White. Film, Black and white, Silent, UK.

A Tale of Two Cities (1935). Dir. Jack Conway. Adapted by W. P. Lipscomb and S. N. Behrman. Starring Ronald Colman, Elizabeth Allan, and Henry B. Walthall. Also starring Donald Woods (Charles Darnay), Basil Rathbone (Marquis St. Evremonde), Blanche Yurka (Madame Defarge), and Edna May Oliver (Miss Pross). Film, Black and white, USA. Produced by David O. Selznick, who "spared no expense," this "brilliant" adaptation is acclaimed for its "class, wit, and affection" as well as for Colman's "canonical" turn as Sydney Carton.

The Only Way (1948). Starring Andrew Osborn, Jeanette Tregarthen, and Harold Scott. TV, Black and white, UK.

A Tale of Two Cities (1953). Dir. Dik Darley. Adapted by John Blahos. Starring Wendell Corey, Wandra Hendrix, and Murray Mattheson. TV, USA.

A Tale of Two Cities (1958). Dir. Ralph Thomas. Adapted by T. E. B. Clarke. Starring Dirk Bogarde, Dorothy Tutin, and Stephen Murray. Also starring Christopher Lee (Marquis St. Evrémonde) and Donald Pleasance (Barsad). Film, Black and white, UK. Bogarde's performance found favor, but the script's compression of the historical time-line and its revelation of Darnay's ancestry at the outset were criticized by some respondents.

A Tale of Two Cities (1958). Dir. Robert Mulligan. Adapted by Michael Dyne. Starring James Donald, Rosemary Harris, and Eric Portman. Also starring Agnes Moorehead (Mme. Defarge), Denholm Elliott (Charles Darnay), and George C. Scott (Jacques). TV, Black and white, USA.

A Tale of Two Cities (1958). Produced by Rudolph Cartier. Adapted by Cedric Cliffe. Music by Arthur Benjamin. Starring John Cameron, Heather Harper, and Heddle Nash. TV, Opera, UK.

A Tale of Two Cities (1965). Dir. Joan Craft. Written by Constance Cox. Starring John Wood, Kika Markham, and Patrick Troughton. TV, UK.

A Tale of Two Cities (1980). Dir. Jim Goddard. Adapted by John Gay. Starring Chris Sarandon (Sydney Carton/Charles Darnay), Alice Krige, and Peter Cushing. TV, USA. Sarandon's performance was appreciated for its nuance but the production as a whole was criticized for providing "little sense of the mob or of an overall social sweep."

A Tale of Two Cities (1980). Dir. Michael E. Briant. Adapted by Pieter Harding. Starring Paul Shelley (Sydney Carton/Charles Darnay), Sally Osborn, and Ralph Michael. TV, UK.

A Tale of Two Cities (1989). Dir. Philippe Mounier. Adapted by Arthur Hopcraft. Starring James Wilby, Serena Gordon and Jean-Pierre Aumont. Also starring John Mills (Jarvis Lorry), Anna Massey (Miss Pross), and Xavier Deluc (Charles Darnay). TV, UK/France. Filmed in celebration of the bicentennial of the French Revolution, this "marvelous" version's use of French and British actors adds a "unique verisimilitude." Gordon and Deluc, in difficult roles, were particularly praised.

Great Expectations

The Boy and the Convict (1909). Dir. Dave Aylott. Film, Black and white, Silent, UK.

Great Expectations (1917). Dir. Robert G. Vignola and Joseph Kaufman. Adapted by Paul West and Doty Hobart. Starring Jack Pickford (Pip), Louise Huff (Estella), and Grace Barton (Miss Havisham). Film, Black and white, Silent, USA.

Great Expectations (1934). Dir. Stuart Walker. Adapted by Gladys Unger. Starring Phillips Holmes, Jane Wyatt, and Florence Reed. Film, Black and white, USA.
In this "mediocre" production the "stiff and hammy" performances of Holmes and Wyatt are singled out for particular criticism.

Great Expectations (1946). Dir. David Lean. Adapted by Anthony Havelock-Allan, David Lean et al. Starring John Mills, Valerie Hobson,

and Martita Hunt. Also starring Jean Simmons (young Estella), Finlay
Currie (Magwitch), and Alec Guinness (Herbert Pocket). Film, Black
and white, UK. This "brilliant" version, considered "*the* great adaptation," has "perfect casting" and "beautiful camerawork" that conveys a
"dark and depressing tone." Currie's and Hunt's performances earned
particular commendation. See also Chapter 3.

Great Expectations (1954). Dir. Norman Felton. Adapted by Dora
Folliott. Starring Roddy McDowall (Pip) and Estelle Winwood (Miss
Havisham). TV, USA.

Great Expectations (1959). Produced by Dorothea Brooking. Adapted
by P. D. Cummings. Starring Dinsdale Landen, Helen Lindsay, and
Marjory Hawtrey. TV, UK.

Great Expectations (1967). Dir. Alan Bridges. Adapted by Hugh Leonard.
Starring Gary Bond, Francesca Annis, and Maxine Audley. TV, UK.

Great Expectations (1974). Dir. Joseph Hardy. Adapted by Sherman
Yellen. Starring Michael York, Sarah Miles, and Margaret Leighton.
Also starring James Mason (Magwitch) and Robert Morley (Uncle
Pumblechook). TV, USA/UK. Although York was found "occasionally
dull" and both Miles and Leighton were played as "pathetic hysterics,"
the production as a whole was considered effective.

Great Expectations (1981). Dir. Julian Amyes. Adapted by James Andrew
Hall. Starring Gerry Sundquist, Sarah-Jane Varley, and Joan Hickson.
TV, UK.

Great Expectations – The Untold Story (1987). Dir. and adapted by Tim
Burstall. Starring Todd Boyce, Anne Louise Lambert, and Jill Forster.
TV, Australia. See Chapter 4.

Great Expectations (1989). Dir. Kevin Connor. Adapted by John
Goldsmith. Starring Anthony Calf, Kim Thomson, and Jean Simmons.
Also starring Anthony Hopkins (Magwitch) and John Rhys Davies (Joe
Gargery). TV, UK. Simmons, who played Estella in 1946, here plays
Miss Havisham as "agoraphobic" and "more complex than cruel."
Hopkins also gives a "stand out performance."

Great Expectations (1998). Dir. Alfonso Cuaron. Adapted by Mitch
Glazer. Starring Ethan Hawke (Finn), Gwyneth Paltrow (Estella),
and Anne Bancroft (Nora Dinsmoor). Also starring Robert De Niro
(Arthur Lustig), Film, USA. Despite "strong cinematography," this
adaptation's focus on "sexual tension" and its omission of many secondary characters and plotlines placed it low in our respondents' esti-
mation. See Chapter 9.

Great Expectations (1999). Dir. Julian Jarrold. Adapted by Tony Marchant.
Starring Ioan Gruffudd, Justine Waddell, and Charlotte Rampling.
Also starring Bernard Hill (Magwitch) and Ian McDiarmid

(Jaggers). TV, UK. Rampling's performance was lauded and the production as a whole was praised for being "well acted and beautifully photographed."

South Park "Pip" (2000). Dir. and adapted by Trey Parker and Matt Stone. TV, Animated, USA. This "sort of reverential" parody of Masterpiece Theatre is a "totally frivolous, though wholly amusing, adaptation of *Great Expectations*." See chapter 15.

Non-English-language versions

Stor Forventninger (1920). Dir. A. W. Sandberg. Adapted by Laurids Skands. Starring Martin Herzberg (Pip), Olga d'Org (Estella), and Marie Dinesen (Miss Havisham). Film, Black and white, Silent, Denmark.

Les Grandes Esperances (1968). Dir. Marcel Cravenne. Starring Madeleine Renaud (Miss Havisham), Charles Vanel (Magwitch), and Jean-Roger Caussimon (Jaggers). TV, France.

Our Mutual Friend

How Bella Was Won (1911). Film, Black and white, Silent, USA.

Eugene Wrayburn (1911). Starring Darwin Karr (Eugene Wrayburn), Richard Ridgeley (Mortimer Lightwood), and Bliss Milford (Lizzie Hexam). Film, Black and white, Silent, USA.

Our Mutual Friend (1958). Dir. Eric Taylor. Adapted by Freda Lingstrom. Starring Paul Daneman (John Harman), Zena Walker (Bella Wilfer), and Richard Pearson (Mr. Boffin). TV, UK.

Our Mutual Friend (1976). Dir. Peter Hammond. Adapted by Donald Churchill and Julia Jones. Starring John McEnery, Jane Seymour, and Leo McKern. TV, UK.

Our Mutual Friend (1998). Dir. Julian Farino. Adapted by Sandy Welch. Starring Steven Mackintosh, Anna Friel, and Peter Vaughan. Also starring Keeley Hawes (Lizzie Hexam) and David Morrissey (Bradley Headstone). TV, UK. Commended for its "complexity" and its balance of the comic and grotesque, as well as for being "visually stunning" and for fine performances by Friel and Morrissey, the production was nonetheless criticized for omitting key plot elements.

Non-English-language versions

Vor Faelles Ven (1919). Dir. A. W. Sandberg and Peter Malberg. Adapted by Laurids Skands. Starring Ange Fonss, Kate Riise, and Jonna Neiiendam. Film, Black and white, Silent, Denmark.

The Mystery of Edwin Drood

The Mystery of Edwin Drood (1909). Dir. Arthur Gilbert. Starring Cooper
    Willis (Edwin Drood), Nancy Bevington (Rosa Budd), and James
    Annard (Neville Landless). Film, Black and white, Silent, UK.
The Mystery of Edwin Drood (1914). Dir. Herbert Blaché and Tom Ter-
    riss. Adapted by Tom Terriss. Starring Rodney Hickok (Edwin Drood),
    Tom Terriss (John Jasper), and Vinnie Burns (Rosa Budd). Black and
    white, Silent, USA. This adaptation is notable largely for Terriss's
    "jumpy" performance as the opium addict/choirmaster.
The Mystery of Edwin Drood (1934). Dir. Stuart Walker. Adapted by
    Leopold Atlas, John L. Balderston, and Gladys Unger. Starring David
    Manners, Claude Rains, and Heather Angel. Film, Black and white,
    USA. This "gothic" but "surprisingly funny" adaptation is overflow-
    ing with "moody" and "shadowy" atmosphere. Rains is "superb" and
    "creepy."
The Mystery of Edwin Drood (1952). Dir. Robert Stevens. Adapted
    by Halstead Welles. Starring John Baragrey (John Jasper) and Susan
    Douglas (Rosa Budd). TV, UK.
The Mystery of Edwin Drood (1960). Dir. Mark Lawton. Adapted by John
    Keir. Starring Tim Seely, Donald Sinden, and Barbara Brown. TV,
    UK.
The Mystery of Edwin Drood (1993). Dir. and adapted by Timothy Forder.
    Starring Jonathan Phillips, Robert Powell, and Finty Williams. Also
    starring Nanette Newman (Mrs. Crisparkle). Film, UK. The pacing
    of this adaptation was considered "gradual," even "boring," and some
    felt that the acting and production values were also poor.

Index

Only Way, The, 117, 120
orphans, 21
Orphans of the Storm (1921), 196
Orson Welles and Charles Dickens
    1938–41, 145–54
    the allure of Hollywood, 148–54
    "First Person Singular," 145–8
Ortman, Marguerite, 177
Orwell, George, 94
Our Movie Made Children (book), 156
Our Mutual Friend, 18
    film and television adaptations of, 215
    Jewish character in, 18
    ordinary characters in, 91
Ovosodo, 53

Pagetti, Carlo, 53
Paltrow, Bruce, 91
Paltrow, Gwyneth, 99
Paradise Lost, 43
parallel editing, 124
parallel plotting, 123
Parish, Mitchell, 77
Payne Fund Studies, 156, 168
Peggotty, Dan (*David Copperfield*), 178
people with disabilities, 189
Petrie, Graham, 35
phantasmagoria, 65
photography, invention of, 65
physiognomy, 18
Pickwick Papers, The
    film and television adaptations of, 145,
        153, 202
picturesque theatre, 65
Pip (*Great Expectations*), 14
    actors' portrayals of, 39
    as contemporary character in Cuaron's
        film adaptation, 97
    in the opening scene of *Great
        Expectations* (1946), 113–14
    portrayal in Australian television
        adaptations, 47, 48
    portrayal in theatrical films, 20
    relationship with Estella, 41, 74–5
    in scenes at Satis House, 42
    in *Southpark* version of *Great
        Expectations*, 172, 181, 185
Plummer, Bertha (*The Cricket on the
    Hearth*), 188
point of view (POV), 133
Polhemus, Robert M., 6–7, 12–24
Pollard, Elizabeth Watson, 158
Postman, Neil, 186
Potemkin, 130
prestige productions, 171–2, 174

Previn, Soon-Yi, 79
Priestley, J. B., 171
progressivism, 173
projectors, 158
psychoanalysis, 11
psychology, 11
Public Broadcasting System (PBS), 181
Purification of the Virgin, 67

racial representation, 18
radio plays, 145
railroad in cinema, 125–6
Ramis, Harold, 63
Rampling, Charlotte, 78
rapid montage, 130
rationalism, 13
reading, 25
Reed, Oliver, 13
Rippy, Marguerite, 7
RKO, 149–51
Robson, May, 171
Romano, John, 7, 12–26
Romantic literature, 64
Rubin, Danny, 63
Rubini, Sergio, 6, 53
Rules of the Game, The, 4
Russell, Ken, 19
Ryan, Meg, 100

sadism, 29
sadomasochism, 35
Salvatores, Gabriele, 54
Satis House, 41, 42
Schaefer, George, 150, 151
Sconce, Jeffrey, 7
Scorsese, Martin, 106
Scott, Walter, 2
screen, 72
screen memories, 72
"Screen memories in Dickens and Woody
    Allen," 72–85
    the big picture on Dickens's screen, 82–5
    the biographical imperative, 73
    seeing stars and stardust
        Great Expectations, 74–7
        lyrics of *Stardust*, 77
        Manhattan, 79–81
        Stardust Memories, 77–9
        Woody Allen's relationship with
            women, 81–2
scripts, 89
Scrooge (1935), 188
Scrooge (1970), 188
Scrooge, Ebenezer (*A Christmas Carol*), 29,
    147, 190